The publisher gratefully acknowledges the generous support of the Fletcher Jones Foundation Humanities Endowment Fund of the University of California Press Foundation.

Beyond the Walled City

Beyond the Walled City

Colonial Exclusion in Havana

Guadalupe García

UNIVERSITY OF CALIFORNIA PRESS

University of California Press, one of the most
distinguished university presses in the United States,
enriches lives around the world by advancing scholarship
in the humanities, social sciences, and natural sciences. Its
activities are supported by the UC Press Foundation and
by philanthropic contributions from individuals and
institutions. For more information, visit www.ucpress.edu.

University of California Press
Oakland, California

Library of Congress Cataloging-in-Publication Data

García, Guadalupe, 1975–.
  Beyond the walled city : colonial exclusion in
Havana / Guadalupe García.
    p. cm.
  Includes bibliographical references and index.
  ISBN 978-0-520-28603-0 (cloth : alk. paper)
  ISBN 978-0-520-28604-7 (pbk. : alk. paper)
  ISBN 978-0-520-96137-1 (ebook)
    1. Havana (Cuba)—History.   2. City planning—
Cuba—Havana.   3. Urban policy—Cuba—Havana.
4. Racism—Cuba—Havana.   5. Havana (Cuba)—Race
relations.   6. Spain—Colonies—America—History.
7. United States—Territories and possessions—History.
I. Title.
  F1799.H357G38   2016
  305.80097291'23—dc23
                                        2015015815

Manufactured in the United States of America

25 24 23 22 21 20 19 18 17 16
10 9 8 7 6 5 4 3 2 1

In keeping with a commitment to support
environmentally responsible and sustainable printing
practices, UC Press has printed this book on Natures
Natural, a fiber that contains 30% post-consumer waste
and meets the minimum requirements of ANSI/NISO
Z39.48–1992 (R 1997) (Permanence of Paper).

Contents

Illustrations

TABLE

Acknowledgments

I was sitting in my graduate advisor's office at the University of North Carolina at Chapel Hill many years ago when he asked me if I knew who collected and disposed of garbage in colonial Havana. And, he pressed on, what did the colonial authorities *do* with it? His questions, coming after I had already begun my research into the growth and expansion of the city, disarmed me, provoking the inquiries that would eventually become the focus of this book. What expectations came with living in a colonial city, and how did the various components of that city affect the empire and subjects that surrounded it? I have searched for answers to these questions throughout various time periods and places, and in archival and other sources describing the importance of African, Spanish, Cuban, and North American influences; this book is the result.

The intellectual debts I accrued on the road to completing this book are many. I am first and foremost indebted to Louis A. Pérez Jr., who not only posed the questions above all those years ago, but also taught me about Cuban history and the fine art of historical inquiry. Perhaps even more importantly, he taught me what it means to belong to a scholarly and intellectual community across borders and divides. His support has been a constant presence throughout this long process. Professors at the University of North Carolina at Chapel Hill and Duke University, namely Kathryn J. Burns, John Charles Chasteen, Lars Schoultz, and Jocelyn H. Olcott, provided invaluable feedback and support along the way. Years after leaving graduate school I continue to see their influence in my work in numerous and often unexpected ways.

I would never have gotten to Chapel Hill had it not first been for the time I spent in the Latin American Studies Department at California State University, Los Angeles. It was at Cal State L.A. that I first found an intellectual community among a politically active student body and faculty who believed in community and community activism. Those underfunded classrooms were the first place where I felt the thrill of critical inquiry and the multiple possibilities embedded within any single question. My experiences there have since become the model for my own graduate teaching, and I strive to provoke in my graduate students what those professors and students inspired in me. Enrique C. Ochoa drew me to history and taught me about what it meant to be a critically engaged scholar. Pete Sigal's brilliance continues to move me, and though he told me once that we as historians are limited by the questions that the documents can answer, his work continues to stretch the limits of this statement. He remains the main reason why I gravitate toward questions that I often think I cannot answer. Among my fellow students, Marlene Medrano, Mary Portillo, Celia Sanchez, and Juanita del Toro, among others, were the friends with whom I first traveled to Latin America. Ironically, though none continued to work on Cuba, they taught me what it meant to be a *cubanist* long before I arrived at UNC. José Najar continues to be a close confidant and friend who reminds me that in fact, *sí se puede*. For their continued friendship, I'd like to thank Martha Estrella and Spencer Downing.

In Cuba, I was lucky to have the support of colleagues, friends, and institutions. The University of Havana, the Instituto de Historia, and the Centro Juan Marinello sponsored my research over the course of many years. I am especially grateful to Belkis Quesada, Henry Heredia, Milagros Martínez, Carmita Castillo, and Raúl Hernández for their continued support. At the Archivo Nacional de Cuba, the team of archivists and researchers answered my questions and made my work possible, and I wish to extend my heartfelt thanks especially to Jorge Macle Cruz. Friends and colleagues at the Castillo de San Salvador de la Punta, in particular José Ignacio Pagés Alba and "Echeverria," provided invaluable guidance and conversations, many of which took place, appropriately, in the cramped inner quarters of the city's forts. I'd also like to thank Alfredo Prieto, Mágia López, and Alexey, who came into my life late in the research and writing process, but who remind me each time that I'm in Cuba that some conversations are best had over food and drink and among friends.

This project has also benefited from friends and colleagues who over the years have generously provided their time, support, and feedback. At UNC Chapel Hill, David Sartorius, Josh Nadel, Joy Jackson, and Devyn Spence Benson were especially helpful through the various stages of the dissertation that became this book. I learned a lot from the intellectual journeys that they shared with me, first as colleagues and later as friends. At the University of Central Florida, Luis Martínez-Fernández was a crucial part of this project, as were Amelia H. Lyons and Spencer Downing. Robert Cassanello, Connie L. Lester, and Rosalind Beiler were generous with their support and kind with their patience. In the Department of History at Tulane University, I wish to thank Jim Boyden, as well as my colleagues Elisabeth McMahon, Randy J. Sparks, Kris Lane, and Justin Wolfe, for their continued help in navigating Tulane's institutional channels. Marilyn Miller and Marc Perry, fellow cubanists, also proved to be valuable resources throughout this process. I especially wish to thank my friend and colleague L. Rosanne Adderley, without whom completing this book while at Tulane would have been a markedly different experience. Her work and support continue to inspire hope in the profession. Various people read portions of the book in progress and helped me revise its chapters. My graduate students at Tulane provided insightful critiques through spirited conversations around this work and topic. My research assistants, Elena Llinas and Alyssa M. García, also provided invaluable help in moving the book along, especially in its early stages. Elizabeth Manley, Thomas J. Adams, and the changing members of our junior faculty writing group, especially Jana K. Lipman, were key in helping me formulate various aspects of my work. While at Tulane I have benefited from the generous financial support of the Roger B. Thayer Stone Center for Latin American Studies and Cuban and Caribbean Studies Center. Hortensia Calvo and the staff at the Latin American Library of Tulane University have also been sources of information and support.

I have often been surprised at the generosity and kindness of scholars whose work I have long admired. David Sartorius, Matt Childs, Ada Ferrer, among others, all extended kindness and considerations when I least expected them to, and I'm thankful for the example that they continue to set. Devyn Spence Benson is not only a friend and colleague, but also someone with whom I walked the final steps of this process, and I'm thankful for the company and encouragement. Lisa B. Y. Calvente read, reread, and commented on every chapter of the manuscript, often more than once, and pushed me to consider arguments I could not have come up with on my own. Sherwin K. Bryant arrived midway through the process of research and writing, and saw it—and me—through its final completion. The early modern era especially would not have seemed nearly as exciting, nor the process of examining it as open to possibilities. This book would not have been possible without everyone's generous support, and I hope I have made each person's investment in this project a worthwhile one. Finally, without the extravagant patience and work of my editor, Kate Marshall, and the editorial and production team at UC Press, this book would not have come to fruition at all.

My small and close-knit family has been instrumental throughout this long process. I want to thank especially Lien Calvente, who welcomed me into her home. Every year I look forward to those visits and the hospitality and stories she provides. Lisa Calvente has traveled with me to many of the places I've done research in and has heard most of my archive stories, including those that never made it into this book. I'm especially thankful for having long forgotten how to mark the distinction between family, friend, and colleague as a result of knowing her. My bothers, Javier and Luis, were perhaps the first and most enthusiastic supporters of this book, though they will likely be surprised to read this. Their support came in the form of airport rides (including on Thanksgiving day), gas money, and drinks during my multiple visits home each year. They, like my parents, snuck dollar bills and food into my bags before I left Los Angeles for yet another destination, and their love often gave me the push to continue. My parents, Esperanza and Anastacio García, have never yielded in their fierce support of their children. For very different reasons, they are my example of enduring and palpable strength. My niece, Alyssa M. García, is my constant and tangible reminder of what that can look like.

As I was finishing this book, news of the death of Mario Coyula Cowley marked a great loss to the intellectual community. Mario understood Havana the way only one who lives and loves a city can. From his apartment window above the skyline he made me *see* the presence of history through urban design when I was still a graduate student. But for his quiet kindness it would not have been possible for me to pursue my research in the direction that I eventually did. Before he passed I promised him a complete draft of the manuscript, and it is my great regret that I did not finish it in time to repay his kindness with this book. In honor of his memory, I'd like to dedicate this book to a new life. Luna Manye Williams was born to my closest friend when the book was still a full three years from completion. If she remembers anything at all about it, I hope it will be that it was finished in time for her to enjoy this, and the many other cities, I want her to see.

New Orleans, June 2015

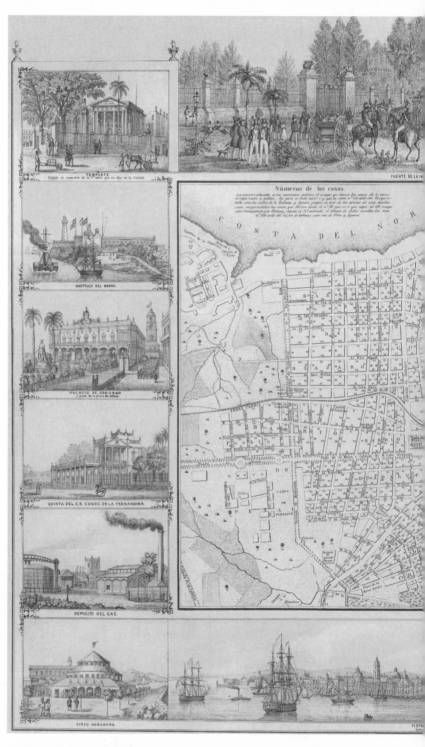

FIGURE 1. B. May y Ca., *Plano pintoresco de La Habana con los números de las casas*, 1853. Mapoteca M-521, Archivo Nacional de Cuba (ANC), Havana.

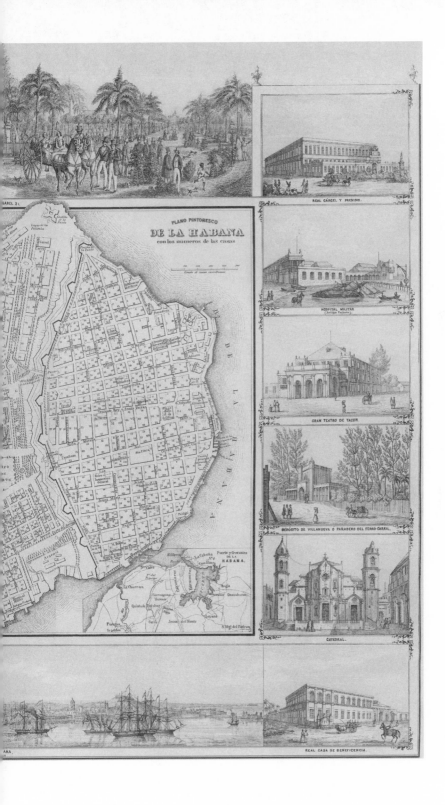

PLANO PINTORESCO
DE LA HABANA
con los números de las casas

REAL CÁRCEL Y PRESIDIO.

HOSPITAL MILITAR
(Antigua Factoría.)

GRAN TEATRO DE TACON.

DEPOSITO DE VILLANUEVA O PARADERO DEL FERRO-CARRIL.

CATEDRAL.

REAL CASA DE BENEFICENCIA.

Puerto y Ensenada
DE LA
HABANA.

Introduction

The Walled City

Before anything may be built, the city must be imagined.
—Angel Rama, *The Lettered City*

On August 8, 1863, just five years before the first war of independence erupted in Cuba and the crown turned its attention to the more pressing matter of the war, a groundbreaking event was—quite literally—taking place in Havana.[1] Earlier in the year, the crown had approved a proposal to demolish the ancient city walls, and the August 8 groundbreaking effectively ended the debate of whether or not *la muralla* (the city wall) was a hindrance to the city's development. Havana residents had been debating the merits of the wall for centuries. Those who championed *amurallamiento* had long argued that the city's geographic vulnerability on the Gulf of Mexico and its strategic importance in Atlantic trade networks were reasons enough for enclosure. Detractors, on the other hand, pointed to the practical reasons in favor of demolition. They argued that by the middle of the nineteenth century, the walls had outlived their military usefulness. The city's ever-increasing population and the well-planned neighborhoods immediately west of the walls were evidence that the structures were an encumbrance to urban planning efforts. The muralla partitioned the city in two, restricted the practical movement of residents, and interfered with the expansion and modernization of the capital. Traffic blockages occurred every morning and evening as merchants entered and left the city, and *vecinos*[2] complained of illicit activities in the dark and cramped inner quarters of Havana. The narrow, winding streets of the *intramuros* (inside the walls) were a contrast to the wide-open spaces outside the walls and made colonial oversight especially difficult. Demolition would at long last allow the colonial administration to unite extramural growth with the colonial core while at the same time extending the reach of the Spanish government to areas outside the intramural city.

Political developments made demolition an attractive move by the middle of the nineteenth century. This was a prosperous but uncertain time in Cuba. Decades earlier, the region's wars of independence had resulted in the loss of the Spanish mainland and made the administration especially vigilant of its colonial subjects in Cuba.[3] The island was one of the last remnants of the crown's once expansive overseas empire, and Havana was a key component of the administration's ability to legitimize its rule. Not only was the city the port through which colonial wealth flowed, but it was also the space in which wealth and power were concentrated. The categories of individuals were many and overlapping. *Criollos* (American born), *peninsulares* (Iberian born), colonial officials, merchants, laborers, blacks (of various socioeconomic classes and legal distinctions), wealthy landowners and their families who made Havana their home for parts of the year, servicemen stationed in Havana, workers who came and went according to fluctuations in the seasonal economy of the port (or who found themselves in the city between sugar *zafras* [harvests]), and enslaved individuals all resided within the same circumscribed area.[4] By the mid-nineteenth century sugar, coffee, and tobacco may have generated much of Cuba's wealth, but by 1863 one out of every five Cubans lived in the capital city. This was a fact not lost on the monarchy: for Cuba to remain a Spanish colony, Havana had to contain the myriad and often competing interests of its residents and project the continued presence and power of the Spanish crown. Since the middle of the sixteenth century, the monarchy had made significant efforts and expended significant funds to build a city befitting the economic position that Havana had achieved.[5] Instead of cosmopolitan prosperity and urban security, however, the nineteenth-century city magnified the competing interests and urban divisions that colonial administrators had been grappling with since they first introduced enclosure centuries earlier.

Amurallamiento was the crown's early seventeenth-century answer to Havana's geographic vulnerability and evidence of the need to protect colonial holdings.[6] In Europe, the high cost of construction and the maintenance that city walls required signaled the importance and wealth of a town or city. But in the Americas, walls had proven an expensive and impractical encumbrance for mainland cities with existing populations. In these areas, governing councils reappropriated spaces or favored religious tools to keep native populations at bay, but even these strategies met with limited success.[7] Only in cases in which the crown's financial returns were threatened could the expenditure of walls be justified. In Havana, the 1555 invasion by French corsair Jacques de Sores had underscored that the high cost of construction would pale in comparison to the cost that the crown would sustain if the city were left unprotected. Sores not only overtook the town but also captured and ransomed the Spanish commander before he set the city on fire and ended his siege.[8] In the decades that followed the disastrous attack, the *cabildo* (town council) used Havana's strategic position and the growing economic functions of the port to convince the crown to fortify the city, noting that the success of Spain's transatlantic commerce depended on the future existence of the town. With Havana's significance in trade and political networks well established by the end of the sixteenth century, royal officials went on to design the city to "exclude and protect."[9] Royal urban design in Havana was thus introduced to neutralize threats to the king's legal urban body while communicating ideas of order, hierarchy, and difference. *What* the city should exclude and protect, and *who* would benefit from its protection, were questions that spanned the length of Spanish colonial rule in Cuba.

By the time of the August 8, 1863, groundbreaking, many in Havana eagerly awaited the extension of the public works projects that would cross intramuros and *extramuros* (outside the walls) and unify the two areas of the city.[10] Local officials in particular held this view. Antonio Mantilla, Havana's *gobernador civil* under the government of Captain General Francisco Serrano Domínguez (1859–1862), favored an urban plan that included an uninterrupted urban landscape: "The renovation of the geometric plan that will soon be under way," he stated, "will link *la ciudad antigua* [the old city] with *la ciudad nueva* [the new city]."[11] Not only could demolition physically link the two cities of intramuros and extramuros, but it would also free readily available and much-needed land for new construction, thus promising a new phase of modern renewal. But in 1868, as the *ayuntamiento* (municipal council) continued to approve the parceling and sale of the land where the walls still stood, demolition continued but development came to a standstill. The outbreak of the Ten Years' War in 1868 in the Cuban countryside was the reason for the delay in demolition. By the time the final struggle for independence began in 1895, local faith in the administration had been irrevocably shaken. The interruption that the war caused highlighted the colonial administration's failure to complete the urban reforms proposed decades earlier, underscored mounting tensions between disparate interest groups in the city, and called into question the viability of the colonial government. The breakdown of colonial legitimacy in the urban space foreshadowed the end of Spanish hegemony in Cuba. That Havana would be a key factor in the loss of Spanish control over the island should be unsurprising, since the administrative basis of Spanish colonialism was itself urban based. But that it remained true through the end of the nineteenth century, when Havana was still relatively unscathed from the physical destruction of war and when the source of Spanish wealth came from the island's role as an export colony, reveals the enduring correlation between Spanish colonialism and urban governance. Urban development as a legitimating force of empire was an ideology that remained constant through the wars of independence and that would continue to organize urban space beyond the end of colonial rule and well into the twentieth and twenty-first centuries. In fact, it was not until after the end of Spanish colonial rule that the final bricks of the wall would come down and the remaining spaces of the city fill with the public parks and gardens characteristic of the architectural design of early twentieth-century Havana.

ACROSS SPACE AND TIME IN THE COLONIAL CITY

By the inauguration of the first Cuban republic in 1902, only a few remnants of the almost six thousand feet of brick and mud remained as physical evidence of the once imposing structures around the city's *recinto colonial* (colonial enclosure). Yet despite the eventual demolition of the walls and the radically different political administrations that went on to govern the island, las murallas continue to live in the public imagination of the city. Their affective presence was among the first things that I noticed when I arrived in Havana, eager to begin my research. The Cuban National Archives are located near the southernmost corner of the old city, the intramuros, and are almost adjacent to where the walls once stood. The railroad station, the old shipyard location, and the last remnants of the brick wall (the only substantive remains in the city) are a ten-minute walk from the narrow streets that lead to the stately building housing the island's *patrimonio* (cultural heritage) on the "other" side of the ancient city walls. Although (with the exception of the few feet on the western and southern edges of the city) the walls no longer remain, they nonetheless delineate a clear perimeter between

La Habana Vieja and Centro Habana, marked by the wide *calzadas* (roadways) and the almost immediate change in the city's physical topography. The difference is clear if you pay attention to the landscape. Still, on that first trip I was at a loss to explain casual references to "intramuro" and "extramuro" areas of the city. I understood the terms to be allusions that marked the decidedly "blacker" spaces of Havana at the same time that they referred to areas of the city altered by centuries of construction but where physical space still had a powerful ability to mobilize multiple, historically specific meanings and reorganize understanding of Cuban history. In Havana, race carries its own nuance, and the ways in which intramuros/extramuros designations have the power to continue to organize areas of the city are evidence of the spatial dimensions of the terms.

To paraphrase architectural historian Mario Coyula, Havana is a place "that has always imagined itself as white." This had little to do with the racial markers born out of nineteenth-century processes. In the Caribbean, cities organized exclusions based on where they stood in relation to the seat of colonial power, even as the literal location of those spaces changed through the course of time. The walls marked these relationships spatially as they excluded sectors of the Havana population from a legal urban body.[12] It was these exclusions that allowed the city to constitute its own whiteness and to simultaneously produce blackness, and references to the "intramuro" and "extramuro" spaces of the twenty-first-century city are rooted in an understanding of these historical processes.

That Havana can be conceptualized as two cities encapsulated by intra/extramuros contained within the same liminal geography will come as no surprise to readers familiar with the city. The two square miles of space that define Old Havana were accorded global recognition by the 1982 UNESCO designation of the city as a World Heritage Site.[13] The colonial core that encompasses the entirety of the ancient walled city (but only a select few of the structures outside it, even though some of those settled areas are as old as, if not older than, areas of the intramuros) was in large part created by the UNESCO designation. Not coincidentally, the designation by UNESCO, taken in tandem with the discourse of Cuban government officials, also emphasizes the tourist-generating spaces of the city. The intramuro section, with its narrow and at times winding or angular streets, stands in stark juxtaposition to the modern, twentieth-century construction that lies outside it. The colonial architecture and neoclassical facades, as well as the fact that the built environment remained largely intact (thus making restoration and preservation the focus of the media coverage that gained the city UNESCO's attention), are results of the historical processes that embroiled the country. Every major historical and political period of the island is intimately inscribed onto Havana's topography. The city emerged from the final war of Cuban independence in 1898 with little damage to its built environment. The U.S. government then occupied the country from 1898 to 1902 and made urban works projects the focus of its administration in an effort to divorce the city from its Spanish origins and to bring Havana into the orbit of U.S.-style (instead of European) modernity. By the inauguration of the first republic in 1902, the city was once more a model of Latin American sophistication.[14] It remained that way well into the twentieth century. With the inauguration of the Cuban Revolution in 1959, the economic and human resources of the new government were channeled away from the capital city and into economically depressed areas of the countryside in order to level the radical differences that existed between urban and rural Cubans. When financial stagnation and economic crisis forced Fidel Castro's attention back to the deterioration of Havana decades later, the administration left the old city intact and developed instead new suburbs to improve living conditions for Cuban workers.[15] The Special Period (Special Period in Time of Peace) that the country entered into after the 1989 disintegration of the Soviet bloc then launched the island into a moment of economic austerity. The era brought global attention to Cuba as the last socialist bastion of both the Old and New Worlds, and this placed Havana and its physical environment—as the prime destination of would-be spectators—at the center of Cuba's historical narratives. These distinct periods have coalesced around the city. The result is an urban topography in which one can read the island's historical and political periods etched into the city's physical spaces.

With its 1982 UNESCO World Heritage Site designation, Havana became the focus of collective restoration efforts to rescue its colonial heritage from the ongoing disrepair caused by the tropical climate and the government's lack of material and financial resources. Along the way, the political periods that produced the urban landscape—marked by the growth of tobacco, slaveholding, and sugar, as well as by the economic presence of the United States—came to define contemporary understandings of urban growth in troubling ways. When walking from the northernmost point of the city at the fort of La Punta and across the length of some twenty city blocks to its southern tip, one moves away from the port, plazas, and cathedrals that constituted the colonial state. Thereafter, the poor condition of city blocks that remain untouched by the restoration efforts corresponds to the long-standing socioeconomic and racial divisions that still organize the walled city. Where once the walls produced visible divisions between physical space and residents, in a twenty-first-century context intramuros and extramuros now describe invisible markers with clear racial and class connotations exacerbated by the presence of UNESCO and the growth of the tourist economy—which are the new forces shaping the face of urban development in familiar (and colonial) ways.[16] UNESCO's reach, unsurprisingly, is carving new spaces and patterns of exclusion as it emphasizes areas of the city to restore. The ways in which restoration occurs is defined—still—by the invisible walls that surround the recinto colonial.[17] Las murallas' ability to delineate city space continues to reinforce colonial patterns of inclusion and exclusion. What's more, their shifting and multiple meanings facilitate the official and legal process of excising peoples and spaces from an urban body politic.[18] Their ability to demarcate city space now depends on their ability to mobilize still-powerful symbols of colonial exclusion—symbols, I argue, that were introduced centuries ago with the construction of the walls.

The continued importance and ongoing significance of intramuros and extramuros in the contemporary city suggests that the walls designated something much more powerful than the beginning and end of the colonial core. It suggests that colonial rule in the Caribbean was predicated on multiple exclusions that facilitated Havana's position as the center of Spain's Atlantic empire. While the terms of exclusion changed with the course of colonial rule, exclusion nonetheless remained a constant element of the city. The walls can thus be understood as a metaphor for the ways in which Spanish dominion unfolded in the region; their multiple and changing functions reveal the intricacies and transformations of colonial rule over centuries of Spanish government. The imperial continuities evident across physical and temporal spaces are thus central to this study. Rather than explore centuries of urbanization, I examine here the expansion of Havana in order to elucidate patterns of empire. The history of the walled city also reveals the local, contested nature of colonialism in residents' attempts to understand, define, and control the course of urban change. This book takes as a starting point the multiple exclusions that organized Havana and its *barrios* (neighborhoods) in an attempt to understand the transformation of the intramuros from a secure space of Spanish colonialism, protected and defined by walls, into the precarious environ that centuries later would contain the populations that administrators correctly guessed would deal the final blow to colonial rule. It argues that while imperial responses to the potential of violent intrusion organized space in the early city, local responses to Atlantic, imperial, and colonial tensions determined the course of urban expansion—and, by extension, the future of a Spanish colonial administration that looked to Havana to legitimate its rule in Cuba.

APPROACHING THE CITY

Located at the cross sections of the Straits of Florida (to the north), the Caribbean Sea (to the south), the Windward Passage (to the east), and the Gulf of Mexico (to the west), Havana is centrally located between the main waterways that facilitated Spanish access to its colonial settlements. Havana's coordinates at the 23°08′N 082°20′W parallels coincide with the Gulf Stream current that originates off the coast of Florida. This warm-water stream accelerates northward from the east coast of the United States to cross the Atlantic Ocean. There, at the 40°0′N 30°0′W parallels, the Gulf Stream splits into two currents, with the northern stream reaching northern Europe and the southern stream recirculating into West Africa. The coordinates are important because the European discovery of the Gulf Stream in the early sixteenth century, together with a sailor's close attention to trade winds, facilitated Spanish contact with the Indies after first contact.[19] The island's connection to the physical geography of the Greater Caribbean, however, predates this contact, as does its importance in the trade and other networks of native inhabitants in the region.[20] Early Spanish mastery over the art of sailing and the 1519 relocation of Havana next to the natural deepwater bay of Havana Harbor gained the city colonial prominence and brought it into the nexus of the various networks that crisscrossed the Atlantic, Gulf, and Caribbean regions.

Just decades after its founding, Havana had emerged as a natural stopping ground for the *galeones* (galleons) and the *flotas* (fleet system) and was critical in the process of protecting the crown's American investments in gold, silver, and other treasures from the Indies. Its location also facilitated the extralegal networks that flourished in and around the region. The city enjoyed a privileged position through the apogee of seventeenth-century commercial trade that connected Havana, Mexico City, and Manila and reached as far away as China.[21] Havana's geographic location made it an indispensable part of the monarchy's Atlantic economy, connecting as it did the transatlantic shipping empire that allowed Spain to emerge as a sixteenth-century global power.[22]

Havana's propitious location and the importance of the port to economic development have been well documented in the abundant studies that exist on the role of fortification, sugar, slaves, coffee, and tobacco in Cuban history.[23] The Cuban monopoly on tobacco in 1717, the creation of the Havana Company in 1740, and the expansion of Cuba's agricultural and export economy all increased the investment and circulation of capital within the city, resulting in a visible impact on the built environment and organization of city space. The importance of these economies has meant several things for scholarly approaches to Havana. Economic approaches to urban history treating these processes necessarily look outward toward the metropole and confine their study to a specific time period. As tropes for the study of urban history, for example, tobacco, sugar, coffee, and slavery are tied to geopolitical and other transformations, in which chronology conceals patterns of imperial rule that might otherwise go on to inform and organize understandings of urban change.

The Caribbean is a perfect example of the possibilities of new approaches in Latin American urban history. Many of Latin America's major (and not-so-major) cities share colonial origins and held complementary positions within imperial, economic, or political networks. The field of Latin American urban history might draw connections across the region in ways that cut across imperial borders and highlight similarities born of colonial processes. Different empires once divided the area, but it was nonetheless bound by a geography that defined colonial settlement patterns and resulted in similar legacies of colonialism. Indeed, the fact that two or more governments shared or simultaneously claimed control over the same spaces is an indicator of the need to probe further into the ways in which Caribbean geographies contained spatially overlapping sovereignties and the ways in which geography and space facilitated colonial urban rule and affected built environments. The processes that I discuss here are rooted in the geography of the Caribbean and are defined by the discomfort and tensions that the greater Atlantic produced. My approach to Havana as a locale is informed by an understanding of space according to which, as Patricia L. Price notes (in part quoting Richard Thompson Ford), "'spatial organization has always been a mode of [racialized] social control and differentiation' . . . at different scales of territorial organization."[24] Studies of contemporary urban spaces often use this as a common point of departure, but it has yet to inform analyses of early colonial cities.[25] The hesitancy around this approach is in part the result of the complexities embedded in discussing racial difference in the early modern period, but it is equally the result of the underlying belief that the early modern Caribbean was an outpost of empire instead of a central component within it.

Instead, Latin American urban history has tended to overemphasize the importance of the region's major cities. These were the viceregal capitals that Europeans rebuilt from the ruins of indigenous cities into their own symbols of colonial power and that the Caribbean decidedly lacked.[26] This is not to imply an absence of literature on the Caribbean. Rather, it is to argue that the region is discussed with an almost exclusive focus on the economic functions of the port and trade between Spain, Cuba, and the mainland. These are tales told from the vantage point of the metropole that not only exclude the many forms (legal and otherwise) in which colonial wealth was constituted but also reinscribe the history of Europe onto American spaces.[27]

The arrival of Atlantic history has brought important strides away from this line of inquiry. As Alejandro de la Fuente noted in his seminal study of sixteenth-century Havana, this field has been predicated on the near exclusion of the Spanish Atlantic and its African influences, overshadowed by the history of European and late colonial trade.[28] Furthermore, when Africa does appear, it is as an appendage to existing networks, important for its role in providing slaves. Though the approach may acknowledge the economic significance of slavery it nonetheless orients the continent through its coast toward Europe while framing Africa's contribution to trade as secondary in a European economic project, much in the same way that studies of the economic and military functions of Spanish American ports retell the history of "other places."

The implications of this extend far outside the field of Latin American history. Discussions of western European urbanization, for example, fail to acknowledge the central role of Spanish American cities and colonialism in shaping global, urban sensibilities and empires. The focus on industrialization and industrial capitalism, despite an acknowledgment of the importance of expanding overseas markets, highlights forces that unsurprisingly locate the origins of urbanization in London, with little discussion of how contact, conquest (of peoples and spaces), and colonialism were processes that came together to produce American and European urban spaces.[29] The governing of peoples and places informed continental ideas of Europe by producing the sovereign territories and colonial subjects necessary for urban imperial powers. In discussions of early Spanish governance, for example, the exercise of empire turned on the crown's ability to legitimate conquest and assert rights over space and territories through the bodies of black and enslaved subjects.[30] I suggest here that the legitimation of conquest and the colonial practice of Spanish governance similarly hinged on claiming territories through urban rule.

In this study of Havana, I argue that colonialism in the Spanish Caribbean was not simply a project concentrated in the institutions, disciplines, and discourses of the empire. Colonialism also entailed a distinctly physical component in which spatial relationships were central to the exercise and proliferation of colonial power. Havana is key to this understanding because the city was unique in its ability to sustain an empire constituted through place and ratified by law. Santo Domingo, the first permanent urban settlement in the Americas, failed to produce a city able to sustain the interests of the empire, and Spain's tenuous hold on the island and eventual loss of the western side of Hispaniola only served to underscore this fact. The waning importance of Santo Domingo did not occur as a result of the crown's focus on the mainland, as much of the scholarship on the early modern Caribbean assumes. Rather, the shift away from Santo Domingo, which catapulted Havana into prominence, was the result of Havana's ability to "exclude and protect" but simultaneously allow for the flow of goods and capital through the city's port. The tension between the need to protect and enclose and the desire for colonial wealth and material expansion is thus one of the central themes that this book explores. I focus on the ways in which the maritime functions of the city influenced its spatial and social evolution beyond its economic development. The port, for example, did not just regulate the flow of commerce and people. It also functioned as the "gateway[s] through which European dominance . . . and power" seeped in, in ways both literal and symbolic.[31] The port was the point of entry for the pirates, corsairs, privateers, slaves, foreigners, and all others whose presence grew to challenge the hegemony of Spain's power.

One of the challenges of approaching Havana has been the long-held understanding of the city as a "Latin American" exception in an otherwise Caribbean and Atlantic region. The scholarly literature has narrated the city as a space that is simultaneously colonial and modern, urbane and provincial, Spanish and criollo, but rarely, if ever, African.[32] This narrative of exceptionality stands in opposition to the black, eastern, and "Caribbean" city of Santiago. While studies on slaves and slavery in western Cuba foreground the fact that people of African descent lived and worked both within and outside the tobacco-, coffee-, and sugar-producing regions of the island, the *absence* of studies on black urban spaces (especially prior to the nineteenth century) reinforces the idea that the city was effectively a European space.[33] Colonial logic, however, turned on the city's ability to index difference and produce a normative and legitimate space from which to expand. This means that racial difference in cities like Havana emerged as a concept from colonial governing practices in which physical landscapes and territories (and not just early modern scientific ideas of bodies, blood, and biology) were critical in the production of Europe and non-Europe. In these spaces, colonialism produced places that were always and already imbued with racial difference, even before there were bodies to be governed.

The erasure of early modern practices in the Caribbean and the systematic and field-wide emphasis on Europe has disregarded an urban evolution that might have otherwise gone on to challenge the epistemologies and theoretical margins of urban studies as a field.[34] Instead, urban studies has matured with an almost complete absence of the Gulf and Caribbean from its body of literature and without a discussion of how diverging local experiences changed the face of Europe's empire in the Americas. The almost complete lack of Caribbean urban histories is thus the result of Latin American urban history's position within the Western and Eurocentric tradition of urban studies. The field, influenced in its inception by the Chicago School and dominated largely by social scientists who emphasized scientific analysis, group behavior, and the processual structures of living urban laboratories, responded primarily to the rampant pace of urban and industrial growth in the United States. Theories were driven largely by a desire to explain both the nature of a city and "urbanism as a way of life" in ways that included explanations for the breakdown of traditional communal structures in communities of color.[35] In its body of theory, the field privileged a Western and racist understanding of urban development and went on to evolve into other, equally questionable U.S. and Eurocentric approaches.[36] The fact that the Chicago School and the Los Angeles School after it went on to influence studies on Latin America to the extent that they did has meant that the same variables extrapolated from studies of North American cities by urban sociologists—such as Louis Wirth's emphasis on population numbers, density, and social heterogeneity—have long shaped the questions that scholars have asked about Latin American urban development and the approaches to Latin American urban spaces.

The view of port cities as economic appendages or as irrelevant to the larger questions of concern to urban studies has caused the Caribbean to occupy a limited space in the literature.[37] To illustrate, most studies of urban Latin America begin by tracing the origins of all cities to Greek and Roman practices.[38] Ibero-American urban traditions (or, better put, urban desires) stemmed from the Greek notion of *polis,* Roman ideas of *civitas,* and the Augustinian "city of God" model.[39] These traditions came together for Iberians around the Greek and Aristotelian notion of *policía.* Where civitas emphasized the civilizing force of local urban governance and polis underlined the importance of a political contract among disparate groups, policía collapsed urban living into an equation that precludes anyone living outside a city from partaking in the experience of European civilization. This Iberian emphasis on policía reveals one of the ideological tenets at work in Hispanic urban spaces, including Caribbean ones. The city stood as a legal and political entity in sharp contrast to those who roamed *al árabe,* a concept that excluded nomads, gypsies, Jews, and North Africans from the scope of European civilization and rendered them incapable of ever attaining it, since policía could be achieved only within restricted (and in the Americas, gridded) European spaces.

Immediately after first contact, the religious orders that made their way across the Atlantic viewed the Americas as a blank and utopic slate on which a spiritual empire might be built. The notion of an urban, Christian civilization in the Americas stems from Saint Thomas Aquinas's take on Saint Augustine's "city of God" and is one of the most powerful taxonomies in studies of early cities.[40] The Dominican, Franciscan, Mercedarian, and other religious orders that arrived shortly after the conquest are evidence enough of the urgency that unsaved souls in the Indies had for the imagination of Europeans. According to Richard Kagan, financial realities in Europe, compounded by the sustained hope for a spiritual haven in the Americas, explain the general lack of walls in urban spaces. How else to explain why American cities became "world[s] without walls" when their European counterparts were pointedly walled and the Spanish laws of the *Siete Partidas* called for towns to be walled in order to distinguish between civilized men and "infidels"?[41] Walls in the Americas would have been superfluous to the spiritual endeavors of the religious orders and an economic inconvenience, not to mention wholly impractical in existing urban areas with large indigenous populations. Neither the crown nor its colonial administrators were at all interested in razing intricately built cities only to build them anew. Other, practical reason for the lack of walls also abounded. On the mainland, walls would have done little to alleviate the fear of the indigenous raids that worried colonial administrators throughout the sixteenth century. In these already dense urban centers where cities predated European colonization, Europeans complained about an indigenous and black population that refused to stay within their assigned place outside the city center, making any further attempts to divide the populations futile.[42]

In Havana, European urban desire took a different form. In this brave new world "without walls," port cities stand out as a glaring exception, especially those established in the first half of the sixteenth century, before the Laws of the Indies stipulated a regular urban pattern. The question that urban historians of these early American spaces should be asking is what early Caribbean cities can tell us about the contours of conquest and colonialism in the Americas. The study of early Caribbean cities is of pressing importance in colonial studies and urban history because these cities reveal the local fears that colonialism and empire produced. Like Havana, most port cities were founded without the fear of indigenous raids (for lack of a stable urban population) or the direction of the regular colonial grid or the Laws of the Indies (because their founding predates the regulations). Much like mining towns, early port cities experienced spontaneous growth, captured in their irregular grids. Here, the mounting fear of European invasions drove urbanization and amurallamiento forward. French, Dutch, and English inroads into the Atlantic coincided with the rising prominence of ports and the development of transatlantic commerce, especially after the 1680s. In Havana, Cartagena, Lima, and San Juan, ports eventually magnified the importance of each city and made them increasingly susceptible to European attack, thus justifying initial royal expenditures—much as they had in European cities—to enclose them with walls.[43]

The established taxonomies of Latin American cities work only without the existence of early port and Caribbean cities.[44] Far from being a regional or even historical anomaly, in its system of defense, structure, and organization Havana was similar to port cities around the globe. Ottoman and Mediterranean cities, for example, underwent processes similar to the ones discussed here, especially in terms of colonialism's effect on urban geography and human practices.[45] Walled places like Batavia, where imperial presence conflicted with local initiatives, are a reminder of the frameworks for Latin American urban history that have yet to be explored. The similarities between regionally different cities have given rise to a literature specifically devoted to the study of ports and their hemispheric, regional, and global significances as well as their economic and political impact. This book owes much to the concepts that emerged from pioneering studies on Asian ports, which approach these as "prism[s] through which the general history of Asia is uniquely refracted to reveal new elements, dynamic forces, and relationships . . . these, moreover, lend themselves to comparisons with the evolution of other world regions."[46]

ORGANIZATION AND TERMINOLOGY

The book consists of two parts and six chapters. Part 1 establishes the chronology of conquest, inter-imperial competition and conflict, militarization, and the diverse agro-export economy forged and developed alongside slavery that created the sociopolitical milieu in which Havana achieved its urban form. Chapter 1 provides a discussion of the categories of inclusion and exclusion used throughout the book. It traces the ways in which the crown defined and implemented its early governing practices in relation to Havana's geographic position and its role in the system of early modern conquest, trade, and commerce. Local administrators began to look inward at the internal organization and structure of the city as a complement to royal concern with the Atlantic, thus establishing the preoccupations that would guide its future development. Chapter 2 discusses eighteenth-century land developments in Havana. It focuses on the period immediately before and after the British assault of 1762, when the first large-scale expansion of the extramural city occurred. Because of the established importance of the port, land scarcity, land tenure, and population control became central concerns of the colonial administration that spanned the military reorganizations of the late eighteenth century. The chapter illustrates that while land use changed as a result of new construction, colonial urban practices coalesced around exclusion as a historical concern, becoming inscribed upon and entangled within the topography of Havana. Chapter 3 explores the human dimensions of colonial urban policies as it foregrounds the ways in which the administration implemented modernization measures across the extramuros. By the middle of the nineteenth century, new roads, *paseos* (promenades), and other urban structures allowed prominent residents to reimagine the once undesirable area as a space of Spanish advancement. These spatial and infrastructural changes are framed within a discussion of how blackness was visibly expunged from extramural spaces while remaining a central component of the city's topography and intimately connected to the process of urban change. The chapter focuses on the ways in which individuals moved through the resulting city spaces, which were multiple, layered, and simultaneously occurring within the contained geography of colonial Havana.

Chapter 4 describes the colonial administration's campaign to organize, reorder, and unify the city at the apogee of colonial rule. The chapter explores the political tensions of late nineteenth-century Cuba through changes in Havana's landscape, which included the demolition of the city walls. The existing racial and political heterogeneity of the city, increasing immigration numbers, and urban poverty converged in the organization of city space and became the driving forces behind administrators' approach to developing the central districts and emerging neighborhoods of Havana. Part 2 turns the vantage point away from the city as subject to focus on the urban population and its impact on a well-established nineteenth-century colonial urban plan. Chapter 5 explores the impact of war and its effects on colonial urban policies. Demographic shifts associated with emigration and exile, as well the Spanish policy of *reconcentración* (military relocation of individuals), radically altered the demographics of Havana and encouraged residents to associate the perception of bodily threat with blackness, as well as correlate hygiene with race. Concern over the mounting independence struggles also caused the administration to suspend urban services, which residents interpreted as a failure to guarantee the safety of the city in the face of an *internal* Cuban threat. Chapter 6 is framed around a discussion of the North American occupation of the city. Scholars have often attributed the explosion of public works projects during this period to the United States government of occupation. The chapter, however, argues that the terms of urban development were established during colonial rule through the practices and processes discussed in the earlier chapters. Chapter 6 thus establishes the centrality of urban development in the capital city to Cuba's transition from "ever-faithful" colony to neocolonial enclave in the early decades of the twentieth century. By moving past the urbanization impetus of the U.S. occupation and into the early decades of the twentieth century, when Cubans once again recommenced urban works projects, the final chapter illustrates how urban rule and empire remained intricately connected processes.

The majority of the visual sources in the book are maps I collected from various archival holdings and through the generosity of Cuban colleagues. Some are well known to scholars in the field and I chose those for their ability to represent an urban colonial vision. Other illustrations depict lesser-known aspects of urbanization that I included for their ability, along with the text, to problematize any one single vision of Havana. Many of the images can be found in more than one repository, and whenever possible I consulted the original. I also chose to reproduce the original document intact instead of cropping portions of the map to record physical locations, and if the outcome was at times cumbersome, the fault is entirely my own. I did this because I wanted to illustrate and interrogate spatial relationships through the textual (re) productions of Havana found in period maps and accompanying documents. I was less interested here in reproducing for readers a picture of Havana's physical geography. Because some readers may also be interested in the particularities and changes in the city layout, and because these are important changes to document, I have made these more detailed maps available through my author's page on the University of California Press website.

As a research site, Havana is bound by the epistemologies and organization of various fields. Without rehashing their debates, I want to point to some of the more self-conscious choices I made with regard to terminology. I refer to Havana "in the Atlantic" when I discuss the transoceanic exchanges that began with colonialism. It is a conscious mobilization of the geopolitical processes that occurred in the region from the early modern period onward.[47] By contrast, I use the terms "Caribbean" and "Gulf" to position the island within a specific geographic space. Also, the definition of the early "town" or "city" in early Latin America—as in Europe— had little to do with an expectation of services (urbanism), though this is something that would change over the course of colonial rule.[48] I use the terms "town" and "city" depending on the year; after the 1592 royal designation I use "city" exclusively, since the title was not only evidence of Havana's status but also a legal designation. Lastly, colleagues on the island as well as off have devoted several hours of their time to engaging me in discussions of the racial designations that I use. I refrain from using "Afro-Cuban" in the book even when my discussion shifts to the post-1898 period. I do this in part to avoid anachronisms and for consistency in the text, but also because the historical processes that have long excluded blackness from a normative idea of what it means to be Cuban seem to converge in the very creation of this twentieth-century term.

It is fitting that the fate of the walled city was decided in the twilight of the colonial empire and demolition of the walls completed on the brink of multiple Cuban transformations. Historically, the success of Havana depended on the crown's ability to limit access to city space. By the end of the nineteenth century, however, the fear that pirates, corsairs, privateers, and foreign armies once exacted had been long displaced by new threats facing the island. The threat that administrators imagined by 1898 emanated from within the walled city itself as well as from the provinces in the east. Criollos, immigrants, and the African-descended (both enslaved and free) threatened to expose the contradictions of colonial rule through competing claims to the city and its resources. When the Cuban Liberation Army (CLA) marched west, for example, the act signaled more than the possibility of the end of colonial rule in Cuba. When the civilized exclusivity of the city was put in question by the potential of the "savage hordes of murderous blacks with rings in their noses" that western Cubans thought a plausible outcome of the liberation campaign, it foreshadowed, among other things, the end of a three-hundred-year secure colonial project.[49] The potential success or failure of the CLA had of course little to do with the physical vulnerability of the city. Still, this fact did not prevent cabildo leaders from considering plans to refortify Havana and extend the walls once more, and this only a few years before the demolition ordinance became a reality.

In 1840, 1844, 1855, and again in 1861, the city council considered new proposals to reinforce and expand the walls. The ancient structures had long outlived their purpose of safeguarding city residents from maritime or other attacks. In fact, the British sacking of Havana in 1762 had exposed the military failure of the walls; instead of attempting to enter Havana through the port, British vessels sailed past the city and marched west in a land invasion that rendered the walls obsolete.[50] Their weaknesses as structures of military defense were well known to colonial engineers, who on more than one occasion advocated updating or eliminating the structures. And yet, for almost a century after the event, the walls remained intact as the city council continued to consider proposals for expansion. This is a curious development, and one I interpret as evidence of the increasingly porous nature of Havana and its ability to threaten the longevity of colonial rule. Construction of the walls was inextricably linked to the practice of colonialism in Cuba, just as their demolition was intimately connected to the demise of the Spanish empire in the Atlantic.

CHAPTER I

Producing Place

Colonialism and Governance in the Early
Modern Caribbean

And the Admiral [Christopher Columbus] went ashore in the
armed launch, and Martín Alonso Pinzón and his brother
Vicente Anes, who was captain of the *Niña*. The Admiral
brought out the royal banner and the captains *[sic]* two flags
with the green cross, which the Admiral carried on all the
ships as a standard, with an F and a Y [Ferdinand and
Ysabela], and over each letter a crown. . . . The Admiral
called to the two captains and to the others who had jumped
ashore . . . and he said that they should be witnesses that, in
the presence of all, he would take, as in fact he did take,
possession of the said island for the king and for the queen
his lords, making the declarations that were required, and
which at more length are contained in the testimonials made
there in writing.

—Christopher Columbus, *The* Diario *of Christopher Columbus's*
First Voyage to America, 1492–1493

But such cities as lie to the west, and which are sheltered
from winds blowing from the east, and which the hot winds
and the cold winds of the north scarcely touch, must
necessarily be in a very unhealthy situation.

—Hippocrates, *On Air, Waters, and Places*, 400 B.C.E.

The first recorded drawing of Cuba appears in the navigational map that Juan de la Cosa reputedly drew ca. 1500. The navigational map is drawn on a roughly three-by-six-foot parchment, where Cuba forms the largest island in an archipelago that is distinctly separated from the rest of the world by the vast expanse of the Atlantic ocean.[1] The most prominent features of the Antilles are the nuances of the coast, a royal flag superimposed over one of the islands, and their exaggerated position within the lines of latitude that seamen used to navigate west. The islands are bereft of the symbols that the Spanish cartographer used to mark the presence of sovereignty and rule in Europe, Asia, and Africa. Instead, the emphasis on exploration, trade, and conquest that La Cosa drew onto the portolan map organized European understandings of physical environment. It would go on to produce the early modern geography of Cuba. The island emerged as a space excluded from the rest of the world but capable of inclusion through the extension of commerce, trade, and urban government. Establishment of the latter would become one of the focal points of Spain's early trans-oceanic voyages and settlement claims in the Caribbean.[2]

In late fifteenth- and early sixteenth-century Europe, the economic importance of trade and commerce gave mariners and seamen privileged access to scientific and geographic knowledge. At sea, mariners relied heavily on navigation instruments to plot the direction of their voyage, but they had limited experience sailing as far west as they were now venturing. On these new voyages they would have noticed the inexplicable jump of the compass needle as they made the journey west, but they would not have known that the pull of the earth's magnetic core was distorting their compass readings and causing them to record the coordinates of new lands incorrectly.[3] While magnetic declination was thus the cause of the physical distortions of American spaces visible in the early modern work of mapmakers, mariners and their patrons were also influenced by the scientific ideas of the period. Some of these ideas asserted that sailing west would ensure trade with India just as surely as navigating south, as Nicolás Wey Gómez argues, would offer the greatest possibility of encountering a place where geographical position and climate had converged to produce lands and peoples that were "bound to possess a nature . . . that seemed to justify rendering them Europe's subjects or slaves."[4] Early modern ideas converged with the science of geography to organize European understandings of the Antilles as a landscape already excluded from the early modern world familiar to Europeans. This was the case even as men like La Cosa underscored the rich potential of the island to serve the purposes of empire and ensure Spain's political position by securing trade routes for the Spanish crown.

The founding of Havana occurred over a decade after Juan de la Cosa first depicted the island of Cuba but it was nonetheless marked by the scientific and legal discourse of the period. In 1508, Hispaniola governor Nicolás de Ovando dispatched Sebastián de Ocampo and a reserve of men to explore Cuba. The island was familiar to the men as a source of indigenous labor for the *encomienda,* the system of forced labor that Ovando expanded during his tenure[5] in Hispaniola, where the decline of the indigenous population was already under way. Ocampo, however, was sent not on a military expedition but to explore the island for reserves of gold. As they circumvented the island, the men noted the extensive harbor on the northwest coast of Cuba and named it the Puerto de Carenas. They had just "discovered" Havana's port, though the extent of its importance would not become fully clear until the town of Havana was established and moved to the northern coast in 1519.[6] In these early years, however, the crown's attention, like that of the officials who arrived with Columbus on his second voyage, was fixed on maintaining a stable presence in the Americas. The first *audiencia* (court) was established in Santo Domingo in 1511 and incorporated Cuba.

Political conflict in Hispaniola, however, continued to delay further exploration of Cuba until Diego de Velázquez, a soldier and conquistador and the future governor of Cuba, was chosen to launch a military expedition from Baracoa in 1511. Velázquez made his way from the easternmost areas of Cuba and traveled west along various routes with a contingency of men, engaging and subduing the indigenous population and establishing Cuba's *villas* along the way.[7] Velázquez had witnessed the Spanish campaigns against Amerindian populations in Hispaniola, as had the Taino peoples, who moved between Hispaniola and Cuba in an attempt to elude officials bent on enslaving them for the encomienda. Velázquez was prepared for war. He enlisted the help of Pánfilo de Narvaez, who arrived from Jamaica and waged a brutal campaign that along with disease resulted in the dwindling numbers of Amerindian people. By 1514, some five hundred Spaniards had traveled west and established Cuba's first six villas. Those Amerindian people who survived fled inland or into the hills, away from Spanish towns and cities, to establish the first palenques, which centuries later would become associated with *cimarrones* (runaway slaves). The processes of conquest, settlement, and urban rule were inextricably linked; unlike exploration, the military expedition to establish a Spanish presence on the island required that Velázquez subdue the population and mark the territory with towns by way of the legal and military rites that extended Spanish governance across the island and incorporated Amerindian people as forced laborers. In the process, the town became the principal instrument through which the expedition claimed the entirety of Cuba as a Spanish possession.

Much like La Cosa, Velázquez recognized the constitution of place as a separate process from the production of space that European cartographers were actively engaged in. The focus on place as an outcome "of interactions and interrelations" marks its distinction from the regions represented in maps, plans, and documents and the physical, built environment that materialized as a result.[8] Europeans founded over one hundred towns and cities in the early modern Caribbean during the first half of the sixteenth century. Between 1580 and 1620, that number almost doubled. A total of 150,000 Europeans resided in these early American spaces.[9] The legal rites that Columbus exercised on the shores of Hispaniola were likely repeated in expeditions that mirrored those of Velázquez and legally claimed the region for the Spanish crown. Yet despite the presence of colonists and the extension of laws, none of these early towns and cities achieved and maintained the prominence of Havana. In fact, unless they were port cities, most were relocated or abandoned altogether as residents either moved the physical location of towns to ensure survival or moved on themselves in search of the economic opportunities that encomienda and mining provided settlers on the mainland. Havana's endurance and its early success—it had developed into a transatlantic shipping hub by the end of the sixteenth century—was both the product of the town's emergence as a site advantageous to residents' needs and a *place* able to spatially reflect and produce imperial goals, even before a classic urban model based on the principles of mercantilism had emerged.

While Havana's original founding by Diego de Velázquez had established the town on the southern shores of Cuba and off of the navigable waters of the Mayabeque (western Cuba's largest river system), residents eventually abandoned this original site and moved the town to the north coast at the mouth of the Almendares River some seven kilometers west of the city's present location. In 1519 they migrated the town again toward the Puerto de Carenas, where the present city of Havana still stands.[10] This final relocation would later bring Havana into compliance with King Philip II's as-yet-unissued 1573 *Ordenanzas de descubrimiento, nueva población y pacificación de las Indias,* which would mandate that all coastal towns have access to a port to facilitate Spanish trade.[11] The purpose was to ensure the circulation of colonial goods in accordance with mercantilism. In the decades that followed its legal founding, the town gave material form to the royal directives that embodied the geographic, scientific, and mercantile knowledge of early modern Europe. Its physical location accounted for the discrepancy between a region that geography and modern science dictated was servile and inhospitable to Europeans, and the laudatory comments that Bartolomé de las Casas and Columbus bestowed upon the environment of Cuba. Both men noted its "temperate" climate and las Casas even found the island to have a cooler and more agreeable climate than did Hispaniola, thus rendering it a healthier place for Europeans by comparison.[12]

However strong the correlation between place and empire, however, the internal organization of Havana and its built environment did not simply reflect imperial design. As Alejandro De la Fuente notes, to only think of early modern Havana as a protected outpost of the crown "conflates lived experience with design."[13] Instead, the city emerged a colonial urban place shaped by its distinctly Caribbean location but attuned to the needs of town residents. In its physical environment as in its social organization, Havana responded to local concerns even as vecinos leveraged the royal desires and the economic and other uncertainties of the European Atlantic world.

The crown's economic future in the region was inextricably connected to its ability to safeguard its key colonial possessions, much as the survival of Cuban towns was linked to residents' ability to force the crown's attention. As early as 1515, Velázquez and other royal officials composed the first petition for enslaved Africans to Cuba. They asked for *"doce negros"* who had labored in public works to help outfit the eastern towns. In 1518, residents and officials petitioned for the importation of slaves from Africa, and the crown authorized Pánfilo de Narváez, Bernardino Velázquez (a relation of the conquistador-turned-governor), Bernardino Quesada, and Gonzalo de Guzman to traffic in slaves.[14] Slavery was understood as an integral component of the conquest, claiming, and protection of new lands.[15] The slave trade (legal and illicit) brought an increasing number of enslaved people to Cuba as laborers to replace the declining Amerindian population. At this early juncture of Cuba's history, the indigenous population and enslaved Africans were understood by both vecinos and the crown as necessary components of the town's survival (encomienda) and the island's safety (labor, fortification, and legitimation). The title of vassal, however, was not conferred on Amerindians until 1542 as an extension of an earlier, 1503, decree. Their position as royal subjects along with that of enslaved Africans allowed the crown to further claim the island as its own.

In order to neutralize the threat of piracy and European competition, "fortification" emerged as the central concern behind the survival and success of Havana, and this was especially the case following the 1555 attack by Jacques de Sores.[16] Local officials and residents, however, already understood the importance of living in a protected city. In 1544, almost ten years before Sores sacked the town, Governor Juan de Ávila arrived in Cuba to find Havana *"mal trazada y ordenada"* (poorly drawn and disorganized).[17] Disorder in the built environment was a concern for the safety of the town that also implicated sovereign authority. A poorly built town that lacked an urban defense plan increased its susceptibility to attack. It would also jeopardize the safety of residents should an invasion occur, as these would be unable to repel an invasion in a poorly planned environment. In order to protect Havana, the governor ordered the roads leading to and from the Cuban countryside blocked. The dense forest to the west of the town provided some protection, but it also allowed access to Havana from land, a concern over location that worried town administrators as early as the sixteenth century and foreshadowed the reason behind the disastrous English attack of 1762.[18] The Sores attack elicited a response from the crown in line with local concerns over the need to outfit the town, although the concerns of officials, unlike those of town residents, were focused decidedly on the Atlantic. The crown had lost relatively little in terms of the devastation that Havana suffered in 1555 (in part because it had invested little), and thus its concern stemmed only from the belief that the location of Havana was one worth protecting. Residents, on the other hand, had witnessed almost every home go up in flames. The hospital, jail, and barracks—symbols of urban and civilized living—were also destroyed.[19] To rebuild the town and ensure both the livelihood of residents and the location of the port, the crown needed to fortify Havana.

Before the Sores invasion, protection of Havana had been left to the fort of La Fuerza (built 1539–1540), the first military structure located on the western entrance to the bay. After it proved unable to repel the 1555 attack, residents let it fall into such a state of disrepair that by 1565, when Governor Francisco García Osorio arrived in Havana, he found it overrun by vegetation and the grazing area of livestock. In 1575, in anticipation of the construction of a new fort, Governor Gabriel Montalvo asked for and received royal orders approving demolition of the old structures.[20] The crown-commissioned work on the new Castillo de la Real Fuerza (built 1558–1577) began under the direction of Bartolomé Sánchez and culminated under the direction of Francisco de Calona with a fort placed well inside the mouth of the bay.[21] Havana's Plaza de Armas, up until this moment the center of political and military life in Havana and adjacent to the south side of the fort, was cleared and incorporated into the grounds of the new structure. The marriage between government, fortification, and militarization was also evident in the prominence that this ideology took over areas of civil life. The fort's *alcalde* (commander), Diego Fernandez de Quiñones, would write the crown asking permission to demolish the church and hospital next to the fort in order to clear more land and provide ever more strategic protection (the crown turned down the petition, though the next time Havana faced imminent danger it would willingly plunder church lands).[22]

In 1589, construction on two more forts was begun, this time under Juan Bautista Antonelli, who first studied Havana's topography before deciding on the locations of the Castillo de los Tres Reyes del Morro (El Morro Castle, built 1589–1630) and the Castillo de San Salvador de la Punta (built 1589–1600) on either side of the bay, allowing its entrance to be closed with a heavy chain of cedarwood beams and iron links and making the city virtually impregnable by sea.[23] Other constructions followed to counter the threat that Dutch, French, and British forces posed. *Torreones* (towers), for example, shaped the uninterrupted northwest coast of Cuba.[24] The Castillo de San Salvador de la Punta, the Fortaleza de San Carlos de la Cabaña (built 1763–1774), and the city walls (built 1674–1797, approval of which came under the government of Governor Francisco Rodríguez de Ledesma) were similarly planned to prevent penetration of the town.

The fortification effort was meant to protect Havana's location from European competitors as well as safeguard Spain's transatlantic shipping empire. Political developments between Spain, England, and the Netherlands under the Hapsburg dynasty had already inaugurated Spain's era of political decline. The British siege of Cádiz in 1596, which momentarily stopped transatlantic commerce to Havana, did not simply jeopardize the economic importance of the Caribbean town; it was also a poignant reminder that European threats spanned the Atlantic and threatened Spain on its own shores. Between 1561 and 1725, Dutch, British, and French forces occupied no fewer than thirty-two

Spanish possessions in the circum-Caribbean.[25] A stagnating population on the peninsula compounded geopolitical troubles and further contributed to its imperial decline. By the end of the seventeenth century, Spain's hegemony over the Caribbean would be unquestionably broken, but even at this earlier juncture of Havana's history, English commercial inroads into the Caribbean (in 1604) and Dutch expansion (through the 1648 Treaty of Münster and the 1621 creation of the Dutch West India Company) eroded the Spanish monopoly and signaled the growing threat to Spanish shipping and commercial power.[26]

Spain's geopolitical position, as well as the growing economy of the port and the town's role in both transatlantic and interregional trade during the last decades of the sixteenth century, accounted for the reasons behind administrators' continual orientation toward the Atlantic. As early as 1543, the Spanish fleet system came together from Trinidad, La Guaira, Maracaibo, Cartagena, Portobelo, San Juan, Santo Domingo, and Veracruz. The galeones from the flota, loaded with goods and people, were welcomed for the trade and commerce (as well as employment) opportunities that they provided when they arrived in Havana for the yearly return trip to Seville and Cádiz.[27] The city's ability to redistribute export goods among regional ports as well as to import regional products bound for Seville made it particularly successful. When it did not have the population to absorb the goods flowing through the port, Havana's success depended on trade relationships and the flow of information (to facilitate the exchanges) between itself and regionally accessible colonial ports and cities. It was these relationships, as Alejandro De la Fuente suggests, that allowed Havana to grow and prosper to the extent that it did through the latter decades of the sixteenth century.[28] The combined impact of imperial and regional trade, however, also meant that the city was an entryway for multiple global interests and needed the patronage of the crown. Indeed, fortified ports and plazas dotted the links in Caribbean trade. From San Juan to Santo Domingo, on to Santiago de Cuba and Havana, and from Cartagena to Veracruz, the coastal towns and cities that connected one another economically developed intricate systems of security to combat the inherent porousness and vulnerability that all port cities faced.

While officials looked outward toward the Atlantic to neutralize existing threats, a local pattern of town organization and residential living that looked *inward* and toward the hinterland emerged alongside royal efforts to address the vulnerability of the town. In 1576, Captain Francisco Calvillo, who had produced the first plan of Havana, drafted a proposal to wall the city with a *muro* (wall) "two tapas wide and four tall." The plan included safeguarding the city, Calvillo noted, whether by walls, canals, *fosos* (moats), or *trincheras* (ditches).[29] In the 1580s, an attempt to protect the city by Governor Gabriel de Luján consisted of barricading access to all major streets in Havana. The governor informed the crown only after he had begun constructing stone walls complete with turrets for firing arms.[30] The makeshift wall caused transport blockages into Havana, and subsequently the roads had to be reopened. Another attempt followed in 1582, though this time the governor allowed for the flow of goods and transport by installing doors that could be regularly opened, closed, and locked.[31] The first map of Havana, made in 1567 and attributed to Captain Francisco Calvillo, offers an indication of both the importance and insecurity that the Atlantic inspired. The plan pictures a small cluster of homes on the northwest peninsula where the city is located and an imposing image of the Castillo de la Real Fuerza, with an inscription noting that "this port is deep and might accommodate many ships." This was a message about the town's potential economic importance and its need for military fortification.[32]

Military maps produced in the early seventeenth century acquired a vantage point that moved away from the Atlantic and toward the built environment of Havana. These illustrate an understanding of the precarious demographic position and the porousness of the town's structure. Residents continued to re-send petitions for slaves to replace the dwindling Amerindian labor force to the crown, though during the first half of the sixteenth century only 1,500 slave licenses were authorized for the entirety of the island (the official number was undoubtedly augmented by the intercolonial and contraband trade). Their importance became apparent after Jacques de Sores burned the town, when the crown's royal slaves rebuilt Havana. Slaves arrived in Havana from the eastern areas of the island, where, having exhausted reserves of gold, they were set to work mining copper. Their arrival in the city underscored colonial concerns over the safety of Havana, for even as the Atlantic remained important, local officials and residents already understood the panoply of threats to include African and criollo slaves living and laboring within the town limits.

The number of slaves in Havana increased after 1590, when larger numbers than in previous decades arrived. This coincided with an upsurge in demographics as trade also grew around Havana. De la Fuente notes that between 1580 and 1610, the population of the city quadrupled. By 1610, between 500 and 800 vecinos made their legal residence in Havana,

FIGURE 2. Francisco Calvillo, *Plano de La Habana en perspectiva*, 1567. Mapoteca Santo Domingo, 4. Courtesy of Ministerio de Educación, Cultura y Deporte, Archivo General de Indias (AGI), Seville.

with their households at an average size of 5.25 members. These numbers would place the permanent free and white population of Havana between 2,600 to 4,000 people. By 1610, between 7,000 and 10,000 people were living in the city and its hinterland. The enslaved population of African descent grew more rapidly than did white vecinos, establishing one of the tensions that would concern administrators for the duration of colonial rule. The enslaved population constituted roughly one-half of the city's residents by 1610, between 1,300 and 2,000 individuals.[33] The rise in numbers accounts for a petition that the white and European residents of Havana presented to the governor in 1606, in which they alarmingly placed the number of slaves on the island at 20,000.[34] The fear of white residents was located not just within the possibility of a slave revolt, but also within the possibility that enslaved individuals would conspire with the pirates and corsairs that frequented the island and thus deal a disastrous blow to Spanish colonial rule.

Amidst the external political instability that the region faced and the internal instability of Havana, Santiago de Cuba, on the eastern end of the island, remained the place of residence for the island's governor and the capital city until 1589. Havana's growing prominence was nonetheless widely acknowledged among royal administrators. Governor Gonzalo Pérez de Angulo (1550–1556) actually petitioned to live in Havana as the town gained importance, and the governor that came before him, Antonio de Chavez (1546–1548) had similarly made his residence in both Santiago and Havana.[35] The cabildo met Pérez de Angulo's interest with resistance, and the governor was forced to take his case to the audiencia in Santo Domingo, where but he was unsuccessful in his claim for residency until July 26, 1553.[36] It is unsurprising that the town council opposed the sudden presence of the governor. The cabildo had managed to create a local economy that by the time of the governor's petition could sustain the population without economic dependence on the hinterland, and the cabildo had itself become an important ruling body. On the Iberian peninsula the cabildo was organized around three *regidores* and two alcaldes and represented the city in regional and other affairs.[37] In the Indies, the structure of city government was first and foremost legal; the audiencia in Santo Domingo was the principal unit of government below the Council of the Indies. The three *oidores* (judges) in the audiencia and a *fiscal* (prosecutor), along with the *alcalde* (magistrate), *escribano* (notary), and *procurador* (defender), were instructed to follow Spanish practices in all criminal and civil matters. In Cuba, the cabildo was organized around three regidores and two alcaldes and wielded power over land distribution until 1729, far longer than in other areas of the mainland.[38] The significance of this was far-reaching, indicating the importance of early Caribbean city government. It ensured that in Havana, local authorities residing in the city were in a unique position vis-à-vis their American counterparts to determine how the city developed.[39] No audiencia or viceregal government here dictated a sovereign plan for colonial development. Not until 1640 would the audiencia even challenge the cabildo's right in its capacity to grant land, and by then most of the sought-after areas around the city had already been distributed.[40]

When the town council approved Pérez de Angulo's request, it did so in recognition of Havana's importance in transatlantic commerce and its susceptibility to pirate and foreign attack. The cabildo actively tried to convince the monarchy that the survival of the city was linked to the success of Spain's transatlantic shipping empire. It argued that the city was a site of singular importance on the island, warranting the residence of the governor. While the two positions might appear contradictory, they provide evidence of administrators' and residents' abilities to place local needs before royal policies but to invoke royal policy when it was strategically useful to do so. When the city was set ablaze by Jacques de Sores in 1555, for example, the cabildo's records disappeared in the ashes. While the fire destroyed the city's early documentation, what it left behind was a record of the residents' and cabildo members' ability to dispense with and selectively choose and implement the directives that would guide urban life. Residents took advantage of the 1555 catastrophe and the disappearance of official royal correspondence to continue the sale of previously regulated goods such as wine, soap, and candles. One can only guess that the limited availability of these goods and the perception of a sudden lack of regulation allowed residents to disregard those economic directives that only benefited royal coffers.[41]

The cabildo's and residents' abilities to govern as well as determine the expansion of the city came under scrutiny once Havana experienced the economic growth that made it, and not just its location, worth protecting. In this regard, Atlantic notions of security evolved from Iberians' experiences in the Reconquista, the Iberian reconquest of territory lost to Muslim rule centuries earlier. The crown's experience with *moriscos, judíos,* and *conversos* (Muslims, Jews, and converts) made urban centers key in the conquest and colonization of peoples considered culturally unassimilable but nonetheless capable of furthering the monarchy's economic interests. Centuries of Reconquista, itself a process that revolved around concerns over land more than Iberian preoccupations with religion, also made territories important in the crown's ability to mark sovereign rule.[42] Between 1492 and 1610, the crown issued a series of measures on the peninsula that first compelled conversion and then expelled members of the non-Christian community. While feudal lords maintained that moriscos might serve labor needs and provide fiscal revenues, they also held that the population posed a danger to the internal security and survival of the burgeoning kingdom. The growth of municipal census records on the peninsula coincides neatly with the years of morisco and converso persecution and illustrates that the crown was most vigilant of *how* the population of Spain was growing precisely as it attempted to secure land for Iberian residents.[43] Not surprisingly, after the 1610 expulsion orders, municipal records declined significantly.

The concern with who populated the kingdom extended to the Indies, although the extent to which the crown was interested in policing this movement is a matter of debate.[44] Immigration from the peninsula was restricted to naturales of Castile, León, Aragon, Valencia, Catalonia, and Navarra, although the restriction was frequently violated. Portuguese travelers in 1531, for example, were allowed to immigrate for a period of up to six years in order to stabilize the white population of Cuba. Through various other means, too, such as the legally sanctioned mobility of black Iberians who could either claim religious exemptions as Old Christians by tracing their lineage to one Christian parent or, via participation in civic and religious life, *earn* the religious title, individuals mediated the ban on Portuguese, Muslim, and Afro-Iberian movement within the empire, particularly during the sixteenth century.[45] Despite the royal exception to Portuguese immigration, and perhaps in part because of tightening legal restrictions coming from the crown after 1608, some members of Havana society were forcibly expelled. Expulsion of individuals would become a theme of the administration throughout the course of colonial rule, used especially in times of political danger.[46] At this early juncture of the city's history, as De la Fuente notes, Governor Gaspar Ruiz de Pereda in 1608 had orders "to expel all Portuguese that you find in the city, single and married . . . and leave only those who have been vecinos and married for more than ten years."[47] By 1611, the governor had expelled or attempted to expel ninety-two Portuguese and "other foreigners" from the city. It was not just economic interests that were at stake for local administrators. While the crown continued to look outward toward the Atlantic, officials also understood that they could not ignore the internal security of Havana.

Cabildo records from 1555 through the end of the sixteenth century reveal the primary concerns of colonial administrators. After ensuring the arrival of foodstuff from the mainland, regulating the infrastructure and built environment of the city was the issue that most occupied administrators. Their attention was directed toward the church, the waterway, forts, and the Zanja Real (the aqueduct under construction from 1566 to 1592, designed to pipe water into the city; its course was planned to run from the La Chorrera River west of the city to the Plaza Mayor, though by 1600 it had only reached to the edge of the city). The council's attention was also focused on the construction of new vecino homes. Land grants were awarded to vecinos specifically so that the city could continue to produce sufficient food should the fleet system be delayed. Construction on lots, too, was required to ensure a stable population, and thus food, population numbers, and land development all formed part of an interconnected web of internal concerns that organized sixteenth-century Havana.

The inward gaze of residents and administrators reflected in the execution of military maps did not come at the expense of attention directed toward external forces. The port and the barrios adjacent to it were the spaces where the global, Atlantic, and Caribbean processes that conditioned royal attention and the internal, local concerns of city residents converged. The demographic increase in immigrants and enslaved Africans and their movement through the port were acutely felt in the latter decades of the sixteenth century. The numbers of those enslaved increased from a few hundred in 1540 to almost two thousand by 1600; this number had more than doubled by 1610.[48] The numbers also coincided with a rise in the population of *negros horros* (free blacks) and a slew of new legal restrictions that goverened the public aspects of urban life of slaves and free black residents.[49] In August 1550, for example, decrees were issued for the city meant to bring public drinking under control, and these targeted black residents specifically. Free black women also prospered from the sale of wine to other blacks, thus leading to the prohibition of 1565. By 1568, at least forty black slaves had purchased their freedom and, having petitioned the cabildo for land, had acquired property that in subsequent years would come under attack *"a causa de sus materiales [que] se queman fácilmente"* (as a result of the flammable materials).[50] By the 1570s, the free and mobile black population of the town had achieved an economic success that allowed them to acquire land and slaves, and to leave behind wills and property as "vecinos" of Havana.[51] The term defined one as a legal head of household, subject to taxes and tribute but also presumably entitled to the privileges that came with being a subject of the king. Unlike on the peninsula, and despite the fact that the structure of city government and land ownership had transferred to the Indies, in Havana the demographic needs of the city allowed women (widows) and free blacks to occupy a place in this legal category. Once the white and enslaved population of the city had increased, only the indigenous population would be included in demographic accounts without distinction, something that can be attributed to the decline in numbers that would have made any distinction superfluous.[52] This extension of "vecino" to free black residents suggests that space, as well as bodies, marked distinctions among the crown's subjects.[53] Whereas the designation implies inclusion, black residents inherited the restrictions that had been reserved for Amerindians under encomienda; even negros horros were required to account for their movements through the city. Tellingly, however, the vecino designation is a sign that at this early juncture, colonial legal statutes were more specifically targeted at policing the crown's *realengo* (land belonging to the king) territories and town spaces.

A pattern of organization had thus emerged by the middle of the sixteenth century that divided Havana in two and accounted for the emerging distinctions between colonial subjects and space. The division established the early colonial basis for the trope of "two Havanas" that has so often guided discussions of the colonial city, especially its built environment.[54] In its inception, however, the division was one closely attuned to the emerging distinctions that subsumed racial difference into landscapes and environment. The early residential expansion of the city serves as an illustration of this.[55] The first Havana barrio consisted of the northern waterfront triangle of the city bordered by the bay, the Calles Obispo and Habana,[56] and the entrance of the port. Barrio La Punta was named after the Castillo de San Salvador de la Punta and housed government, military, and religious structures, including the Plaza de Armas, the Real Fundación de Artillería, the Iglesia Parroquial Mayor, the Convento de Santo Domingo, and the Hospital de San Felipe y Santiago (renamed later the Hospital de San Juan de Dios). The neighborhood was the commercial and manufacturing center of the city, a distinction earned in part by its proximity to the port. The population of the neighborhood grew north of La Punta at Calle Habana, but in the area adjacent to the banks of the bay and between the four main plazas—Plaza de la Catedral, Plaza de Armas (built 1559–1586), Plaza de San Francisco (originally the Plaza del Cuerpo de Guardia), and Plaza

Nueva (later the Plaza Vieja)—there emerged as early as the seventeenth century a centrally located and powerful residential barrio composed of vecinos who had been able to secure land grants from the crown or otherwise purchase plots.[57] By contrast, bordering these town-square-adjacent barrios were largely black and African spaces also used for African and African-derived social and religious practices. The proliferation of elite residences (and the circle of marginal ones) illustrates the importance of the port, trade, commerce, and the Atlantic economy in the life of Havana society. The need to protect it was also visible in the emergence of the *cuartel de milicias* (militia barracks) on the Plaza de San Francisco, the plaza closest to the port. The military garrison of royal troops, composed by 1681 of some eight hundred men (having experienced a large increase of some three hundred men in a few years), remained at an average of six hundred men and adjacent to the port.[58] The area by the plaza had been a long stretch of coast, and although it had been included in city plans since 1603, it would not be built until 1628, when the cabildo invested the initial one hundred ducats to provide the flota and the Spanish armada with a space to disembark. By 1633, the jail and the *casa capitular*[59] also stood at the edge of the Plaza de San Francisco. The *cuerpo de guardia* (police house), the customs house, and the convent for which the plaza had been named made up the remaining seventeenth-century structures around it.

The barrio of Campeche, located in the southeast end of the city, developed differently from the northern area of La Punta. The cabildo often redirected land petitions to Campeche instead of granting land in La Punta, and fishermen, workmen, and others who made their living from port activities (legal and extralegal) were directed there. The Amerindian town of Campeche also existed in the southernmost area of the city between the Calles Merced, Cuba, and Desamparados before its residents were expelled from the city. A series of laws reinforced the trend toward segregation, beginning with the 1557 failed proposal to expel free blacks.[60] By 1610, the free black population in Havana owned 21 percent of plots of land, though De la Fuente notes that such ownership was concentrated in Campeche.[61] By 1611, free blacks residing in Havana were forced to register with the city magistrate, and by the early seventeenth century, economics and militarization, while still the most significant factors affecting urban growth, were certainly not the only forces shaping the colonial city. Venerable *"barrios sin cuarteles"* would also spring up from the mid-sixteenth century onward, decidedly black and African spaces, to enclose and encroach upon the elite areas of Havana.

Land patterns not only divided Havana into two distinct barrios but also forced sectors of the population to outlying areas completely. The separate town of Guanabacoa, across the bay from Havana, quite literally created a second space in which individuals could reside. By 1555, surviving cabildo records describe the remaining Amerindian population of the area as dispersed throughout the hinterland and made up of vagabonds without legal residence. Their impoverished existence and the colonial administration's inability to track individuals led to the creation of the "Indian" town of Guanabacoa safely on the other side of the bay. The order was given at the suggestion of the governor, and although the original cabildo record with his stipulation has been lost (or burned), after 1555 there are recorded references to the *"pueblo indio de Guanabacoa"* (Indian town of Guanabacoa) where at least one hundred people were said to reside.[62]

The creation of Guanabacoa allowed the extension of order, policía, and fiscal responsibilities (after 1542) to native peoples at the same time that it positioned them outside of Havana.[63] Their removal was the first in a series of steps that allowed the city to be configured around specific ideas of Spanish civilization that were based on demographic and legal exclusion. In 1557, another proposal emerged, this time to expel all free black residents from Havana, which would have effectively segregated the town.[64] The proposal was defeated in part because of its timing; it contradicted both royal directives and local needs to increase the demographics of the town by whatever means necessary. In the Americas as on the Iberian peninsula, residents of towns and cities were required to bear arms for the king, and thus the increase of vecinos also maximized Havana's ability to survive an attack. The 1555 invasion by Sores had illustrated the military purpose that free and enslaved black residents might provide. Colonial officials had rounded up black residents and these contributed to the front lines of the counterattack, injuring or killing the French corsairs. When nine of the black combatants were captured, Spanish colonial officials refused to pay the ransom and the French corsair hanged the men in retribution. After the attack, enslaved Africans were brought in to rebuild the town; vecinos also contributed to the defense effort by offering slaves in the rebuilding process.

The development of Havana foreshadowed the colonial ideologies that the royal ordinances of 1573 mandated all Spanish American towns and cities follow. The ordinances stipulated a regular grid pattern, streets that radiated outward in the four cardinal directions and that could accommodate a growing population, churches and monasteries, marketplaces, and hospitals for the poor.[65] They communicated Spanish ideas of order and hierarchy, but, being issued in 1573, they arrived too late to affect Havana's footprint.[66] The city, like many port towns founded before the ordinances were issued, never radiated outward as the regulations stipulated. Instead, Havana expanded from north to south along Calle Habana and then west, not to mention the segregated town southeast of the initial core. To counter the disorder, the Cáceres ordinances, issued in 1574, just one year after the royal directives, set forth the first set of guidelines governing municipal life in Cuba. Alonso de Cáceres y Ovando arrived from the neighboring audiencia of Santo Domingo specifically to investigate land dispute issues arising from the lack of boundaries in land granted to residents.[67] The eighty stipulations in the ordinances emphasize that in order to expand the town, *solares* (plots of land) should be awarded *"a las personas que los pidieren, en cualquier parte"* (to those persons who asked in any area) and that "que cuando se concediere algún solar, se le de con condición que lo pueble dentro de seis meses" (when a plot of land is granted, the condition to take up residence in it within six months is issued with it). The cabildo made solares available not just to those in agricultural production, which would help sustain the city, but also to potential vecinos of the town, as petitions from the mid-1550s onward illustrate.[68] Its urgency, expressed by providing vecinos only six months to assume ownership and build once they were awarded existing plots of land based on this right of first entry, was a means to maintain a stable population and ensure the safety of the city.[69] When the cabildo awarded land, it reminded vecinos that their award was contingent upon their ability to maintain the safety of the town. Construction taking place on solares should take care not to jeopardize safety. At the cabildo meeting of January 11, 1566, Gonzalo Llanes asked for and was granted a solar, and the cabildo's only stipulation was that the grant should be awarded *"sin prejuicio de tercero con que no habra camino que salga a la playa"* (without prejudice so long as no pathway to the shore is opened), a stipulation that was repeated time and again.[70]

The cabildo also made other strategic decisions when it came to awarding land through *mercedes*. These were circular grants typically three leagues in radius, though measurements were not always taken until after the passage of the Cáceres ordinances. In popular accounts of how (or how little) land was measured, including Irene A. Wright's and Duvon Corbitts's seminal studies on the topic, the process was rumored to be so ad hoc that boundaries were designated based on how far one could hear a cock's crow.[71] The land grants typically housed farms and ranches and were held by residents in usufruct, which meant that the king retained sovereignty over all land in the Indies, and vecinos held legal title only to the improvements made to solares that they were granted, and only as long as they continued to pay taxes.

Realengo land was the land that remained between the boundaries of mercedes, in the less desirable areas of the city, and belonged specifically to the crown. It was land that, as Mariano Peset and Margarita Menegus assert, did not belong to Castile or the empire but rather to the king himself.[72] Realengo lands, almost two centuries after the crown had established a claim over Cuba, evidenced that sovereignty born from a claim to land and space remained largely unchanged. In fact, the word itself was the product of the Reconquista and referred to land taken "back" from Muslim proprietors. By the early seventeenth century, realengos were found largely in what would become the extramuros, the area outside the city walls, which, before the walls were ever built, was a little-desired area since it came without many of the privileges that urban life entailed. When awarding mercedes and solares, the cabildo held the right to send land petitioners to the extramuros. In case of complaint, the cabildo could resort to official directives to uphold its decisions. Before it made land awards, it was compelled to poll potential neighbors and hear any objections that they might have to their new vecinos. And it was not just vecinos but also colonial officials who could decide the fate of new residents. The procurador could also decide if the residence of a new vecino was in the public's interest, and the alcalde, too, was obligated to check the location of each merced.[73] So long as its land-granting ability persisted—and it persisted until 1640—the cabildo, like the crown, leveraged a special power over the town and its residents.

SPACE, PLACE, AND COLONIAL BODIES

Concern with the physical environment of the city was an extension of learned men's concerns with the physical body in late medieval and early modern Europe. The universally accepted science of humoralism dictated that bodies (health and temperament) were naturally the result of diet and climate. Accepted ideas on the Iberian peninsula held that *ayres* (airs) had the ability to affect one's character, physical appearance, and health. Exposure to too hot or too cold a region might result in bodily and physical changes that could alter the constitution not just of the indigenous and African laborers in the Antilles but also of

Europeans.[74] Early administrators were already concerned with their ability to create and maintain a civilized space for Iberians within the geography of the Caribbean, which seemed to lack obvious places where permanent settlements would thrive and which was vulnerable to military and political threats of various sorts. Havana's multiple relocations provide evidence of the necessity to secure not only a location that would maximize the ability of the town to survive but also one that would secure settlers' interests. The constant instability they faced as a result of external and internal threats was compounded by the natural geography of the region, where the warm and moist air and swamp-like conditions in the archipelago not only were a constant threat to the health of Iberians but also, because of their belief in the mutability of the physical body, held the potential to introduce attributes of Africans and indigenous inhabitants into Iberian bodies.[75]

This concern with environment, climate, and the mutability of the physical body underscores the importance of place. The American landscape was thought to cause illness and malaise, and bodies might only be protected by a change in physical environment. Thus, once settler colonialism became a reality, beyond the trade focus of the crown's initial expeditions, space emerged as an important consideration in the process of imperial expansion. The 1513 royal orders issued to Pedrarias D'ávila (Pedro Arias Dávila) on his expedition to the Darien community on the Castilla del Oro coast of the Caribbean mainland illustrate that sovereign claims in the New World consisted of geopolitical and territorial claims that would produce places fit for Iberian living.[76] The orders are the first to communicate the importance of urban living, decades before these ideas would be codified in the Laws of the Indies. Dávila was asked to focus on the town's built environment so that "in places newly established proper order can be given from the start."[77] The crown's expenditure of funds and manpower facilitated the excursion of over 1,500 men, among whom were the future administrators, governors, and conquistadores of American towns.[78] Settlers arrived to the region as vassals of the crown, and as such they were an extension of the sovereign's reach. The importance of constructing an environment where they might thrive was lost on no one; the fact that within a few months half the settlers perished as a result of sickness and disease further illustrates that the early exercise of building a colonial empire that included subjects was first and foremost about the crown and settlers' abilities to produce landscapes in accordance with imperial and Spanish needs, and this rested largely on the ability to produce urban life. Already, natural science tied environment and geography to Iberian civilization, and early settlers' own experiences in the region with death and disease that they attributed to climate and geography would continue to reinforce this correlation.

Ironically, the first outbreak of disease in Havana went almost undetected by Europeans. Disease arrived with Diego de Velázquez in 1519 in the form of smallpox and measles and was described as a "grievous pestilence" that brought death and destruction to the Amerindian population.[79] The first outbreak of *vomito negro* (yellow fever) to affect Havana's colonial residents first occurred in 1648, after which the city continuously suffered outbreaks of both *viruela* (pox) and yellow fever.[80] The rate of death during these outbreaks reached as high as 129 per 1,000 inhabitants.[81] Yellow fever was not yet endemic in Cuba, and thus these early outbreaks in Havana would have reinforced the connection between a physical environment poorly constructed and the illness of individuals. The marshlands in the northeast area of Havana next to the bay (which the Plaza de la Catedral would later occupy), commonly referred to as La Cienega, were breeding grounds for the disease, as mosquitoes—the unknown culprits behind the outbreaks—could be found around the stagnant water. The Zanja Real had been transporting water to the city since 1566, but it did not meet the needs of residents, and it was therefore commonplace for individual households to keep cisterns that would collect rainwater; when not properly maintained, the cisterns would turn into breeding grounds for larvae transmitting the disease.[82]

Trade and commerce—the colonial raison d'être for the royal directives that sought to organize city space—were also implicated in the spread of disease. In the cabildo of October 7, 1648, for example, the sole topic of discussion consisted of the infections of *"peste"* (plague) on the Mexican mainland in the Caribbean region of Campeche and how to deal with the possibility of infectious goods and people en route to Havana through the Caribbean port of San Juan, Puerto Rico.[83] In 1648, despite Governor Diego Villalba y Toledo's best efforts, an epidemic broke out during the summer months (believed to have originated in Veracruz), during which officials estimated that in less than two months, one thousand deaths occurred, among them perishing *"la mejor y más lucida gente"* (the best and most distinguished people). Not only did disease run rampant among military men, but it also affected doctors, priests, and notaries, since these were often called to the bedsides of those infected and then contracted the disease through exposure.[84] The tangible and material repercussions of the outbreaks were swift: the high number of dead and dying in the military garrisons as well as the toll that the infections took on population numbers left the city vulnerable to attack, since a diminished or weak population could pose little defense in case of invasion. Deaths among the city's population of priests, notaries, and doctors were also concerning, since these were especially valued members of early Havana society, and the proportionally high number of deaths among the city's white inhabitants, versus the city's black and African-descended residents, reinforced the idea among colonial society that they were living in a climate not suited for European civilization. The earlier, laudatory comments of Columbus and las Casas and the fulfillment of the city as a prosperous entrepot of trade had successfully tied Havana's fate to the future of the Spanish empire and extended royal governance over people through the spaces of the town. This had not, however, quelled local fears over the unstable condition in which residents lived, but rather reinforced the notion that survival and civilization depended upon the exclusion of black bodies and spaces from the precarious but civilized spaces of urban life.

Juan López de Velasco, the crown's first geographer, whose physical and scientific knowledge of the Indies was instrumental in drafting the 1573 ordenanzas, was also a key figure in producing colonial hierarchies that relied on the natural space of the Antilles to categorize and define included or excluded spaces and individuals. López de Velasco introduced the *Relaciones geográficas* for the more than five hundred communities that stretched from the Antilles to the Andes.[85] His work, based on parish reports and administrative questionnaires, was an attempt to introduce a scientific mode of categorization that would allow men on the peninsula to make sense of and organize the emerging world to the west.[86] The mechanism of control was based on physical geography and spatial differentiation. In Havana, local officials had envisioned the town as a place separated from the natural environment of the area and its non-European inhabitants. The indigenous population and the growing presence of Africans, both enslaved and free, compounded the destabilizing effect of conversos, Jews, Moors, and Portuguese entrants. This was part of the life cycle of the port; the flota system brought goods and men as well as the threats that emanated from the Atlantic in the form of foreign armies, pirates, corsairs, immigrants, and enslaved Africans. In later centuries, the port would also become the point of entry for the ideological currents that threatened to destabilize

Spanish colonial rule with the tides of revolution that flowed freely along the Atlantic.[87]

Amid external threats and the internal instability that physical environment and demography produced, Cristóbal de Roda's 1603 plan emerged as the first to materially visualize a city enclosed by walls. That the plan was drawn at the start of the seventeenth century, after the demographic changes of the city, illustrates the ways in which social and political tensions were subsumed into the built-environmental features of early modern Havana. The walls that Roda envisioned were no exception. The military architect designed the structures to encircle the first barrios of La Punta and Campeche. The plan contains two lines; the outer line delineates the *cerca nueva* (new enclosure) and a perimeter of 150 hectares.[88] By contrast, the faint outline of the *cerca vieja* (old perimeter) included in the sketch is made in reference to an earlier and failed proposal to wall the city that was put forth by Governor Juan Maldonado. By the time Roda began his work in 1603, the demographic increases that the city had experienced during the last decades of the sixteenth century made this earlier plan obsolete. To account for future projected growth, Roda's plan encompassed an area three times that of the actual city.

The grid plan of 1603, like others that followed, was an attempt to superimpose order on a distinctly Caribbean space. More than a decade earlier, in 1592, Havana had been conferred the title of city in an acknowledgment of its importance and an indication of the crown's need to protect it from external (those emanating from the sea) and internal (from the island's hinterland and its own population) threats. The 1603 need to define a city limit and reinforce its perimeter with walls was in many ways a practical one. Vecinos had a tendency to expand into rural areas, opening pathways to the sea and pilfering timber, thus quite literally leaving the city open to invasion. Planners took care that the projected walls did not excise the port from the main plaza, since it was from this area that colonial wealth flowed. In fact, the walls oriented the entire city toward the Atlantic in ways that reinforced the economic importance of the port and underscored the longtime concerns of royal administrators.[89] These concerns, however, were most certainly not the only guiding factors behind construction of la muralla. In Santiago de Cuba, for example, the crown's early seventeenth-century fortification of the city was similarly planned in response to French and Dutch inroads into the Caribbean. The production of copper made securing the port necessary and was the reason behind construction of the Castillo de San Pedro de la Roca in 1633 and the garrison of two

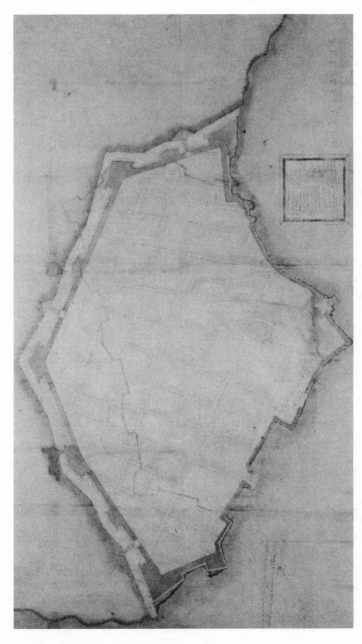

FIGURE 3. Cristóbal de Roda, *Descripción y planta de la ciudad de La Habana*, 1603. Mapoteca Santo Domingo, 20. Courtesy of Ministerio de Educación, Cultura y Deporte, Archivo General de Indias (AGI), Seville.

hundred men who were housed in that city. Fortification, however, was still considered inadequate to shield the city from invasion, but amurallamiento, according to Francisco Pérez Guzmán, was not an option, in part because of the geography of the area but also because of the strong opposition of residents to the idea of being enclosed by walls.[90]

In Havana, the wall served to superimpose a beginning and end to the city. In doing so it secured an exclusive space and created the intramuro/extramuro distinction that would endure for the length of colonial rule. With construction of the wall, the extramuro would become neither the rural hinterland associated with the cultivation of sugar and tobacco (and thus with the future economic prosperity of the island) nor the civilized space of the city that functioned as the administrative center of Hispanic Caribbean civilization. The city walls reinforced the notion that those who lived outside the city lived within a marginal space in relation to the colonial public sphere, when and if their existence was acknowledged at all. To live within the city was to live not only within the relative safety of the empire but also within the axis of colonial civilization itself. The 1603 plan made a self-conscious attempt to create an ordered and organized space out of the irregular grid that the city's earliest residents had created. Havana's foundational arteries—the calles of Habana, Mercaderes, and Obispo—emerged as the prinicipal *caminos* and emanated outward from the elite city center, with the military construction of the Castillo de la Real Fuerza becoming the center from which streets were traced.

The blank spaces outside the cartographic representations of Roda's plan reflect the differences between social space and natural space. This is a distinction premised on the idea that natural space encompasses a geographic area where social relations (in contrast to social space) have yet to be defined and where the markers and signifiers of civilized living are absent.[91] Patricia L. Price notes that "critical geographers have long worked with concepts of inclusion and exclusion to contend that what, and who, is socially valued enjoys a presence in the landscape, while that and those who are devalued are kept out of sight. . . . People *and places* that are racialized or otherwise stigmatized are literally and figuratively erased from the official landscape."[92] "Race" in this case was a multifaceted project forged out of the colonial governing practices that included environment and organized urban space. The cabildos' interpretation of royal directives adapted Iberian sensibilities to the particularities of living in the Caribbean. Price notes, in part quoting Richard Thompson Ford, that "spatial organization has always been a mode of [racialized] social control and differentiation' . . . at different scales of territorial organization."[93] The organization of the city was one of the central ways in which early colonial taxonomies were tested. Already, Havana had evolved from the few clustered dwellings that Calvillo had depicted into a city where the divisions that administrators and residents imagined materialized by way of the physical structure of the walls.

Once construction of la muralla began in earnest, only the official spaces mapped inside the carefully planned grid existed in the European imagination, as evidenced by the maps and plans of the period. In contrast, the extramuro spaces associated with indigenous and black vassals and vecinos were represented as a vast emptiness with few of the signifiers that mapmakers often used to mark human settlements, despite the population that the area contained.[94] That imperial administrators expunged extramuro space and subjects from the large majority of colonial plans suggests a violent process of erasure tantamount to representational death for many of Havana's residents affected by the crown's legal directives. This lack of representation further served to create a normative space within the walls, where the town's system of security rested upon the administration's ability to establish measurable differences (through space) between subjects of the crown that would subsequently justify exclusion.[95] The processes of erasure, Price notes, are "most if not all . . . legally facilitated, justified, and normalized."[96] Thus the legal urban body was constituted by the inclusion of only certain groups of the crown's subjects, and distinctions were marked spatially. This physical, territorial marking explains at least one of the reasons why black and indigenous subjects could be both figuratively and literally excluded from areas of the city while at the same time allowed to live with relative ease in peripheral areas outside the grid. Unlike areas of the mainland where slave, indigenous (until the demographic decline), and black populations filled urban spaces, early modern Havana experienced little contradiction between colonial mechanisms of security at work within walled, European spaces and the all-important vecino designations that black residents enjoyed in the extramuros.

Importantly, however, while geography allowed royal officials to excise subjects from the colonial grid, the crown nonetheless extended its power over the extramuros through legal and other directives. The area fell *outside* the city but *within* the empire and was a constitutive component of the colonial city. Early seventeenth-century representations of the extramuros are often bereft of individuals but do contain the symbols of colonial economic wealth. The wharf, the port, the channel and entrance of the bay, the wooded areas that provided timber for Cuba's nascent shipbuilding industry, and the fallow lands used for tobacco and sugar cultivation all symbolically announced Cuba's prosperity. Cartographers "marked, noted, [and] named" these areas in an act of representation that produced them as an extension of the city and brought them into the fold of colonial governance.[97] The incorporation of the extramuros into the city grid thus came through the presence of colonial economic structures. These extended to the extramuros the forces of civilization that Spanish administrators and imperial cartographers assigned to all cities and that had been so visibly absent in La Cosa's 1500 depiction. Importantly, however, incorporation extended to space but not people, except in Guanabacoa—an altogether different legal space separate from Havana. In Havana, the city ended long before the private *huertas* (agricultural land) of rural landholders, and maps ignored the *caserios* that made up the city *arrabales* (suburbs), magnifying instead the internal population with its order and policía, which the walls were charged with safeguarding.[98]

The process of simultaneously excising individuals from the idea of the city while appropriating their space had Iberian origins and was a process also practiced in areas of the intramuros. The 1610 expulsion of Granada's moriscos served the unification of Spain by allowing the land once occupied by this population to be fully integrated into a legal urban body.[99] By the mid-sixteenth century, free black vecinos resided outside Havana's city center in the barrios of Plaza del Cristo, La Anoria, and Quisiguaba. Julio Le Riverend reminds us that before the city walls were built, Havana was *"un muestrario de fecundación interracial"* (a cauldron of racial mixture) that came to a segregated head as the walls were being constructed.[100] The introduction of the walls thus did not mark a new colonial trajectory. Rather, they visibly displayed the purpose of the city in the Spanish Atlantic.

The title of "city" in this early period of Havana's history has been considered by scholars more "a legal fiction, not a physical reality" and a designation almost always arbitrarily made by the crown, which thus held little significance through the first decades of the sixteenth century.[101] Iberian concepts of law and sovereignty, as well as scientific knowledge of geography and environment, however, illustrate through Havana's experience of conquest, settlement, and colonization that the landscape of city wasn't easily constituted. Once produced, Caribbean cities would have a lasting effect on the body of laws that organized the landscapes of the early modern Caribbean and the American mainland.[102] The 1524 *Ordenanzas de buen gobierno* issued by Hernán Cortés, for example, while they address the concerns of conquistadores in mainland cities, guided the founding of settlements in New Spain based on the lessons and experiences learned in the circum-Caribbean region.[103]

The emphatic shift, where matters of colonialism were concerned, away from the Caribbean and toward the mainlanddid not mean that the crown had lost interest in its Caribbean possession or that European interest in Cuba's physical environment had waned. On the contrary, both grew in accordance with Havana's emergence as a prominent urban port. The town and its residents had succeeded in establishing it as a bustling entrepôt in its own right, having capitalized on its position as a nodal point within the nexus of circum-Caribbean trade. Unlike other shipping points, its relationship to the viceregal centers did not limit its activity or place it in a service position vis-à-vis the commodities of mainland cities.[104] Instead, Havana was able to remain a central point in the web of Spanish commerce while establishing a relationship with the hinterland, thus transcending the single-use value of many other colonial towns and cities.[105] Its ability to accomplish this solidified its future economic success but would also become the source of its social instability. Royal officials had long looked to the Atlantic to pinpoint threats to the hegemony of Spain, while local administrators were already beginning to look inward at the spaces of the city to redress colonial insecurities. In the decades that followed, these insecurities would be attached directly to the rightful claim to land and the organization of urban space. Residents and administrators alike, it seemed, would not be easily divested of the legal fiction that defined the city of Havana.

PART ONE

Intramuros and Extramuros

CHAPTER 2

Place

Not only Castile . . . should be obligated or interested [in
these matters], but also the other Kingdoms and Provinces of
this Crown and Monarchy, which . . . it is only just that they
offer [help], and indeed some form of aid shall be asked of
them . . . if a prompt and effective remedy cannot be found,
it shall be found in land . . . for houses fall, and none are
rebuilt: Places grow wild: vecinos flee and scare, and leave
fields deserted. . . . And as such it will be convenient to look
for the means through which His Majesty may alleviate his
Real Hacienda.

—Gil González Dávila on King Philip III, *Monarquía de España*, 1771

They [the colonies] were conceived of as the personal
possession of the crown, attached to Spain through the
person of the reigning prince. This conception of Castile's
colonial acquisitions, once it is grasped, makes clear the
broader meaning of the term *"real hacienda"* (royal estate),
as including the colonies in their totality.

—Arthur Scott Aiton, "Real Hacienda in New Spain under the
First Viceroy," 1926

Just five years after Crístobal de Roda's plan, Governor Gaspar Ruiz de
Pereda sent a letter to the crown inquiring about future plans for the construction of la muralla. Already, a stretch of the wall had been completed
at La Punta at the northern edge of the city, and the governor was eager
for news on how the project should progress.[1] The crown's response was
swift: the governor was informed that construction should cease at
once and that he should account for the slaves employed on the project.

Concerns over cost, funding, labor, and need would subsequently define the crown's approach to the project and account for the numerous delays, inquiries, and false starts. For the better part of almost two centuries, this pattern would persist. Construction of the wall would be completed much like it had begun: with a maximum of disturbance for city residents, especially those who lived or labored in the brick-and-mortar path of the imposing stone walls. The case of Magdalena de Cobrera illustrates the concerns that city residents faced well past the initial construction.

In 1691, as construction was at its height, Magdalena de Cobrera brought a petition to the *fiscal* over the amount of funds that the administration had promised in compensation for the land that had been taken from her *huerta* (farm) for construction. Her husband, Gaspar de Arteaga, was now deceased, and Magdalena had a young child to provide for. Her claim was settled in an uncertain and likely unfavorable conclusion in 1695.[2] Thirty years later, her now-adult daughter, a woman by the name of Petronila Medrano y Cobrera, also brought a claim against the administration, this time for the crown's failure to compensate *her* with new lands that were promised when those of her mother were confiscated for construction of the wall.[3] Petronila would see a slew of legislation in her lifetime; three years earlier, Sebastián Calvo de la Puerta, a vecino from her barrio, had brought a suit against her over the uncertain ownership of land that had resulted when the crown had promised them both new lands in compensation for earlier confiscations. This was the origin of Petronila's 1722 complaint to the fiscal asking for just compensation for her (or rather, her mother's) property.[4] By 1864, over a century after Magdalena de Cobrera first brought her petition to the fiscal, the Ministerio de Ultramar was still dealing with the remnants of the same case.[5] Archival records of this sort involving litigation over land disputes are strewn across various collections in the Archivo General de Indias in Seville and the Archivo Nacional de Cuba in Havana. The evidence suggests that these were multifaceted struggles involving various branches of the colonial administration that embroiled residents (both enslaved and free) of the city of Havana in the largest construction effort to take place in the city.

Between the dates that frame the initial construction of the wall and the land disputes that drove Petronila Medrano y Cobrera to the fiscal, Havana underwent various changes that were tied to the economic transformations of eighteenth-century Cuba. This is when sugar, tobacco, and trade emerged as familiar tropes in accounts of the eighteenth- and nineteenth-century island. The noted historian Francisco Pérez Guzmán, however, notes the historiographical tendency to overemphasize these factors in the development of Havana; militarization was also an important aspect of the city's development.[6] Militarization and sugar, however, present two opposing poles from which to approach the history of eighteenth-century Havana. While the first continues to look out toward the Atlantic, the latter is focused inward on the changes that were the result of the hinterland's importance. Both approaches, however, limit their scope to the latter half of the eighteenth century, because this is when sugar cultivation reached island-wide significance and because 1762 marked the fall of Havana to a competing empire. The dates also underplay the single largest construction effort undertaken in the entirety of Havana's history: the building of the walls. The enormity of this undertaking was the result of the colossal amount of land, funds, and manpower that the project took to complete from the latter decades of the seventeenth century through the middle of the eighteenth century.[7] The effort and funds expended were on par with the gravity of concerns that residents expressed over land rights and land-use patterns, although it was not simply land that was at stake for either residents or colonial administrators. Rather, the question remained over *who* had the right to decide the city's trajectory and under what terms the city would expand. The questions revealed the larger entanglements of eighteenth-century colonial sovereignty, and they were the same outgrowths of colonial governing practices that constituted race through the inscription and organization of the urban landscape. The social reorganization of the city was further complicated by the social transformation of eighteenth-century Cuba, in which sugar and militarization were integral components. Late seventeenth- and eighteenth-century uncertainties were subsumed into the debates over land rights. Ironically, the 1762 British attack on Havana revealed that while the defense of the city might yet turn on the threat of the Atlantic, the focus of the colonial administration was decidedly concerned with the strategic development of land in and around the city.

CONSTRUCTION

The walls that would eventually materialize from Roda's plan would stand 8 feet tall and 1.4 meters wide. Their projected length was 5,770 Cuban *varas* (approximately 16,050 feet), enough to roughly enclose the perimeter of the existing built area of the city.[8] When the Council of the Indies' Junta de Guerra finally reapproved the plan in 1640, the project was estimated to last three years. When the necessary funds failed to materialize, however, construction once again quickly came to a halt, only to be restarted again in 1655 under Governor Juan Montaño Blázquez. Shortly after construction began this third time, the governor died, and with him so did the construction project that he had been supporting. A royal decree in 1656 officially suspended further efforts, and the project would not see any serious movement again until 1674, when Governor Francisco de Ledesma, working with engineer and native *habanero* Juan de Siscara, finally restarted the plan.[9] True to Roda's corrective plan, the structures would enclose the city behind a protective curtain of stone and mortar.[10] The northernmost point of the city, at La Punta, where the initial effort had taken place, was again the site of construction. The initial wall was completed in 1680 and extended from La Fuerza to La Punta; eight years later it would include the aptly named Puerta de Tierra (literally, the "land door").[11]

Construction unfolded amid concern over funds to finance the project. Mexican coffers had long financed the fortifications effort in Havana, and officials in New Spain resented the use of mining funds for the fortification of Havana, particularly since the crown had already committed 20,000 pesos annually (over 200,000 in total) from coffers in New Spain to help finance its cost.[12] Funds, however, were slow to make their way to Havana from Mexico.[13] To solve the issue, the crown looked to tax anything that might bring a contribution. It levied a tax of twenty-five pesos on each *barruca de aguardiente* (barrel of liquor) and twenty pesos on each barruca of wine, thus passing on at least part of the cost to residents and passersby.[14] The *sisa* (tax) was not without its detractors. *Comisarios de barrio* (neighborhood deputies) were each in charge of implementing the *real cédula* (royal decree) issued in 1674 when construction began in earnest under Governor Ledesma.[15]

Emerging alongside colonial concerns with funding was the question of who would actually construct the wall. Already, the crown had shifted resources away from the mining regions of the island and toward the renewed project, and residents who were eager that construction continue added their own resources—often in the form of enslaved men—to the effort.[16] But even this was insufficient. By 1693, it was painfully obvious to all that there was simply not enough manpower to accomplish the task. Governor Severino de Manzaneda wrote to the crown asking for reinforcements and suggesting that hiring paid workers might be the way to go. Manzaneda soon found, however, that conscripting *vagos* (vagrants) and emptying the city jail in search of workers provided a more efficient alternative.

In 1673, the king ordered that the slaves employed in the mines of El Cobre in eastern Cuba should be brought to Havana to labor instead on construction of la muralla.[17] The journey to Havana from the copper mines at El Cobre spanned over seven hundred kilometers and crossed the length of the island.[18] This was the second time in Cuba's history that the crown had mobilized its slave labor force and shifted resources away from areas of economic production to help Havana. The first time, of course, was when Jacques de Sores set the city on fire. And now, in the middle of a construction crisis, slaves arrived once again to build and fortify the city. Their arrival would have only served to underscore colonial concerns over the city's safety, for even as the focus of the crown remained fixed on the Atlantic, officials and residents understood the panoply of threats that the city faced. With the bay sufficiently protected, they were concerned about the possibility of a land invasion, and the arrival of slaves from the eastern areas of the island fully illustrated the city's permeability. The fact that slave labor was a necessary component of the material core of Havana's socioeconomic and political infrastructure illustrates the ways in which construction of the walls revealed the colonial anxieties behind late seventeenth- and eighteenth-century urban policy.

By the end of the seventeenth century, especially, after three years had stretched to over half a century of construction, court cases protesting taxes illustrated resident discontent. The large population of men associated with the functions of the port (only some of them vecinos) in particular felt that the crown's edict should not apply to them. José Pardio, Nicolás Antonio de Ponte, Francisco Fernández de Leon, and Felipe Lezcano, for example, who made their living as *cargadores* (porters) of the *navio* (ship) *La Santísima Trinidad,* petitioned the fiscal to be exempted from the tax of one real that the crown levied on each *cuartillo* (half-liter) of aguardiente.[19] Their association with the maritime functions of Havana made them an indispensable part of the city's economy, and they were thus extended rights not afforded to those who merely toiled on the construction projects. By 1688, Havana's governor, Diego Antonio de Viana, would write the crown justifying the high cost and delay in the walls' construction even as opposition to the project grew.[20] In 1680, Roda's walled city model had to be modified to encompass all of Havana, and even Roda was now among the dissenting voices who critiqued amurallamiento, citing the high cost of construction and population increase as the primary reasons behind his opposition to the project.[21] Between 1701 and 1710, Havana became the primary destination of *situados,* or annual funds transferred from the mineral-enriched coffers of Mexico City, Lima, Quito, and Santa Fe de Bogotá to cover the costs of outfitting and defending the monarchy's strategic ports. By 1750, funds destined for Havana were four times those for Santo Domingo, the second Caribbean destination for situados.[22] In terms of economics, at least, the funds that the crown was willing to spend were evidence of the importance that Havana had acquired as a result of shifting economies and the royal need to protect the city.

Havana was the primary port from which Spain's silver fleet sailed and the organizing site for the Armada de Barlovento, which ensured the flota's safe crossing of the Atlantic. The fleet would gather in the safety of Havana's harbor and await the rest of the convoy while stockpiling provisions for the return trip to Spain. This was a service that other ports were unable to provide. The port at Veracruz, though able to ensure the safety of its own city, was virtually powerless to defend the treasures of the flota for lack of a natural harbor; Cartagena, too, was of little use in this regard, since British Jamaica lay between it and the trade winds and currents necessary to make the voyage back to Spain.[23] Its prosperity as a result of trade and its strategic location were the reasons why Havana had surpassed the royal outfitting of other Caribbean cities.[24] Its importance meant that between 1742 and 1744 the crown committed some fifty-eight thousand pesos to protection of the fleet.[25]

The military implications of Havana's success also affected its infrastructure. Already, the town council in 1550 had prohibited black residents from cutting mahogany and cedar within two leagues of the city. It issued a more far-reaching ruling in 1552, when it included "forasteros" in the prohibition and created a protected area adjacent to the town. These prohibitions against deforestation would continue to be repeated throughout the seventeenth century. Once trade became a lucrative enterprise, the concern that the felling of trees would leave vecinos and the church without construction materials was displaced by the concern that the decimation of the forest woods would leave the city exposed on its western border. More pressing than its immediate security, however, was the abundance of timber necessary for the nascent shipbuilding industry.

Havana became the center of shipbuilding in the latter half of the sixteenth century and into the seventeenth century. The industry received a major revival in 1713, when by royal decree the crown mandated the *arsenal* (shipyard) built outside of the walls. Construction took place inside of the bay on the southern edge of the city, where between 1748 and 1761 alone fifteen vessels were built. The relocation of the arsenal coincided with the Bourbon reforms and the recommitment by the monarchy to Spanish naval power.[26] The royal shipyard, tasked with building galeones in 1551, grew to be one of the most important yards in the Americas. The royal preoccupation with trade and the need to secure commerce converged in the Havana arsenal; the arsenal was one of the earliest symbols of how the two concerns would reorganize city resources (timber) and spatial practices.

Roda's opposition to construction of the walls, like that of his contemporaries, was rooted in the ways in which residents experienced locally the effects of Cuba's late seventeenth-century and early eighteenth-century economic and political transformations. The increase in and importance of trade swelled Havana's population. Population density in the city (only the intramuros composed the legal urban body) expanded from 108 residents per hectare to an urbanized area of 151 hectares and a density of 330 inhabitants per hectare on the eve of 1762.[27] Previous, early sixteenth-century concerns with stable population numbers and demographic stability had been all but left behind, as had any concern with the importance of Havana within the matrix of cities that made up the crown's colonial empire. And while disease still periodically ravaged the city, residents and *forasteros*[28] viewed this as an extension of the natural world on which Havana had been built, insisting instead that the merits of the city lay elsewhere; by the early eighteenth century, Havana could boast three parishes organizing the intramuros, ten convents, two hospitals that vecinos regularly frequented, and two schools for children, with one of them dedicated explicitly to the education of young girls.[29]

The importance of a growing population was not simply in the increase in numbers but also the radically altered social interactions that emerged as a result. The arrival of the slave ship *Luanda* in Havana in 1600 added 195 enslaved Africans to the existing population and caused an unprecedented shift in demographics.[30] The non-European and black population of the city, once excised from the body politic, was now a visible presence in all aspects of urban life. Artisans took advantage of the unique opportunities that port cities afforded, and *coartación,* or the right of slaves to purchase their own freedom, also contributed to the growth of both the free population of African descent as well as the enslaved population; the practice of coartación also prompted authorities into a hypervigilance where demographic trends, new mobilities, and visibility were concerned.

Changes in the Cuban hinterland similarly affected Havana's local topography. Innovations in sugar and tobacco significantly decreased the availability of land once the crops overtook the small-scale ranching enterprises that vecinos had previously engaged in. The social changes wrought by the success of sugar and tobacco in early eighteenth-century Cuba were several. The establishment of the Havana Company in 1739 was among the most visibly important. The company was commissioned to regulate agricultural exports and increase slave imports, something that placed it in competition with the Dutch West India Company, which over a century earlier had secured the slave-trading monopoly in the Caribbean. It never reached the success of the Dutch West India Company, but by midcentury, sugar and tobacco were nonetheless the driving forces of the internal Cuban economy and complemented the importance of transatlantic and interregional trade.[31] While shipbuilding had previously organized city infrastructure and resources, sugar was now emerging as a major contender. Reinaldo Funes Monzote notes that competition for land and timber was at the heart of struggles over much of Cuba's natural resources. The location of the shipping industry in Havana, though it competed for land, also facilitated the expansion of sugar by expanding trade abroad. The Bourbon monarchy in Spain, too, from 1713 on authorized several of the changes affecting the landscape, including securing contracts with the English South Sea Company for slaves and a state monopoly on tobacco, and the end of levies against Cuban sugar in Spain.[32]

With trade and sugar thriving in Cuba, by 1740 Havana faced serious issues of land scarcity. Scholars have argued that this was in part the result of the sugar boom of the mid-eighteenth century, which enlarged the *cinturón azucarero* (sugar boundary) around Havana, marking the end of the use of the Cuban hinterland for agricultural production and the beginning of the extramural city.[33] As sugar expanded, sugar mills took up an average of twenty to thirty caballerias of available land. Guanabacoa, across the bay, became one of the central locations where owners petitioned the crown for land for sugar plantations, though the area south of Havana at the source of the Almendares River (then known as La Chorrera), as well as the area west-southwest of the city in Jesús del Monte, were also important sites.[34] These were once traditional woodlands that sugar displaced (located within eight leagues of the city port). Most notably in Guanabacoa, sugar had displaced Amerinadian communal lands when vecinos petitioned the crown to cultivate the area; its location closer to the port than some of the more outlying areas made it attractive for settlement. In 1659, Guanabacoa created its own cabildo, amid royal protests that Amerindian lands were being decimated at the hands of habaneros. In 1733, however, with the rise in sugar's importance, the crown declared Guanabaco a villa.

By the early eighteenth century, the population of Havana had also expanded outside the existing (and projected) walls, and the hinterland was expanding inward, toward the city. Sherry Johnson describes this process as the collision of two forces, one emanating outward from the city and the other emanating inward from the countryside, thus creating a "pincer effect" on the area of land immediately next to the city walls.[35] Exacerbating this growth was the early eighteenth-century expansion of sugar *ingenios* (mills) that Manuel Moreno Fraginals describes as part of the cinturón azucarero's encroachment upon the city of Havana.[36] Land scarcity, however, was not simply the result of a growing sugar industry or of internal population pressures, though both of these were significant components of the collision of forces in eighteenth-century Cuba.

The crown tackled the resulting diminishing availability of land in eighteenth-century Havana by revoking the land-granting rights of the cabildo on November 23, 1729, and passing accumulated construction costs on to Havana residents. In 1728 and again in 1749, the administration reiterated the importance of the sisa in terms of completing construction of the walls.[37] Because mercedes were made by the cabildo in usufruct and not in perpetual title, and the king retained sovereignty over land in the Indies, the crown could exercise that sovereignty over land rights. It confiscated land from vecinos in one of two ways. Land adjacent to the area under construction was taken away with the promise of compensation, or else vecinos were promised a solar of similar value elsewhere.[38] The resulting litigation went on for years and sometimes decades, though there is evidence that in some cases at least the crown responded with compensation, particularly when women and widows were involved—though women, when they petitioned the crown to be compensated or awarded tracts of land, asked for significantly fewer hectares than did men. In realengo lands especially, women claimed land for subsistence while men asked to plant, harvest, and make changes to the land in ways that would increase its eventual value. The cabildo had enjoyed unprecedented (and unparalleled across Spanish America) formal land-granting powers since the 1574 Caceres Ordinances, which established how concessions for large estates were made (for livestock, one of the primary industries in Cuba, and sugar and other crops). It distributed land in the unit form of *hatos* of two cuban leagues, *corrales* of one Cuban league, and later, smaller farms known as *estancias*, along with the haciendas. Mercedes, however, did not confer title over land and obligated vecinos with responsibilities such as supplying Havana with food.

To deal with the skyrocketing number of court cases over land issues in 1729, the crown rebuked the cabildo's ability to award land. By extension it also took away its ability to define the structure of the city. That ability would be centralized in a *"junta de venta y composición de tierra"* (governing board of sales and land composition) that, much like the ayuntamiento of the sixteenth century, would create a royal representative in the Indies. By 1755, the subdelegate of the junta was to be chosen in the Americas, though the power to choose this person now lay with the viceroy and hence with the legal body that served as the embodiment and representative of the king in the rest of the Americas already.[39] The audiencia would adjudicate any litigation resulting from a land dispute in which the subdelegate was involved, thereby ensuring that all future claims to land would rest within the legal body that was responsible only to the crown.[40] In coastal and port cities, however, this process could be passed on to the governor, maintaining at least one local channel through which the matter could be settled.[41]

Marking territories and claiming sovereignty through land thus continued to be one of the key ways in which the monarchy, the cabildo, and local residents exercised power. The 1729 decision curtailing local power was further reinforced in 1735 with another royal decree affecting the extramuros. In 1735, despite the expansion of the cinturón azucarero in the hinterland and an increasing intramuro population, there still existed realengos in between the circular land grants (often much larger than the solares of the intramuros) that had been awarded to vecinos by the cabildo. The growth and expansion of solares in the intramuros meant that these once faraway realengos were now located in the land adjacent to the walls and in the extramuro barrios that had been originally envisioned as outside the civilized area of the city. The 1735 royal decree ordered that persons entering into realengo territories had to register themselves and their land, under penalty of losing said territory. Twenty years later, the monarchy issued another royal decree attempting to counteract the loss of land.

While the entirety of the Indies was thus the monarchy's *"real hacienda,"* as Arthur Scott Aiton suggests, Havana made the administration especially attentive to continuing to mark and display royal sovereignty.[42] The 1755 decree meticulously stipulated the process of land grants, land sale, and realengo composition *(las mercedes, ventas, y composiciones de realengos, sitios, y valdios [baldios])* and left virtually no land-granting process unaddressed in centralizing dominion over the city and the ad hoc process of land tenure.[43] Those in possession of a realengo prior to 1700 could retain their land, whether they had made the required "improvements" or not. Those people who could not prove possession before 1700 had to provide proof of title or else "be dispossessed and removed from said land and said land will be awarded anew" *(seran desposados, y lanzados de la tales tierras, y se harád merced de ellas)*. Any improvements made to the land would be summarily lost in the process. While this alone would have been cause for grave concern among vecinos of the extramuros, the final clauses of the decree were even more devastating. In order to ensure the efficacy of the process, residents were encouraged to "denounce" their neighbors for a variety of reasons, including lack of title or failed improvements to their land grant. After a denouncement, royal authorities would issue "just reward" *(les dara recompensa correspondiente)* in the form of the right to purchase the land denounced.[44]

No legal measure since the sixteenth-century *Ordenanzas de descubrimiento* and the Cáceres ordinances had organized Havana's landscape to the extent that the decrees between 1729 and 1755 did. The royal ordinances regulated the ad hoc way of awarding land that had previously existed, though in their wake they also litigated and tied up land in the court for years, precisely because the previous system had not required the formalities that now existed. And litigation was not all directed toward the crown; vecinos frequently brought each other to court to settle boundary disputes and adjudicate land ownership.[45] Whether these lawsuits were directed at the crown or at each other, the sites over which both vecinos and the crown were most concerned were the realengos of the extramuros. The barrio of Guadalupe—the name given to the growing extramural barrios until the latter half of the eighteenth century—was rife with tensions that, for vecinos at least, revolved around the rightful ownership of land. The extramuros experienced the majority of its growth after 1750, while the intramuro barrios of Campeche and La Punta (which grew to surround the early villa) filled out prior to the combined reorganizations of shipbuilding, sugar, and construction of the muralla.[46]

Colonial focus on the barrio of Guadalupe and the land confiscations taking place therein ensured that existing realengos could be subdivided into solares, thus enriching the *real hacienda*, or the crown's royal holdings.[47] The new legislation also ensured the removal of the residents who had freely peopled the area after 1700; this was a conglomeration of individuals largely composed of those originally denied encomiendas

or "good" land in close proximity to the developing plazas and structures of defense in the intramuros. It was also a population distinct from
the sugar-producing vecinos of Guanabacoa, Jesús del Monte, and La
Chorrera. Instead, these were the same class of vecinos whom the cabildo
had a century earlier encouraged to settle outside the colonial grid, now
being displaced by the combined forces of royal decrees, the denouncements made by others who wanted their land, the growth of the agricultural sector, and the demographic growth occurring in the intramuros.

Even though construction of the wall was considered first and foremost a military endeavor and its presence through 1762 a military instal-
lation, militarization could not have been the sole or even the primary
force responsible for the expansion and displacement of people from the
extramuros, as the patterns of extramural growth were already well
established by the time that Britain declared war on Spain in 1739 and
subsequently brought military action to the Caribbean theater. This is
not to suggest that the militarization efforts that the 1762 British occupation of the city set in motion did not exacerbate processes already in
place; in fact, after the 1739 declaration, a proposal was made to demolish *all* of the living structures in the barrios of the extramuros in order
to facilitate the defense of the city. Had it been approved, the sugar-
producing areas of the hinterland would have remained unaffected. But
had the motion passed, it would have meant that those already pushed
to the southern areas of the extramuros would have been erased completely from the emerging grid, which now included the land adjacent to
the walls.[48] Land conflict in the extramuros introduced by construction
of the wall and exacerbated by the economic infrastructure of the city
foreshadowed colonial inroads into the area; even as the administration
built a wall to ensure the safety of the city, the population had already
expanded outside of the designated area. What's more, the pattern of
development by which La Punta and Campeche surrounded the elite
spaces of the early villa was only reinforced by construction. Amid these
sociopolitical and economic changes taking place, the 1762 British occupation of Havana would provide the narrative with which colonial officials pushed to expand the colonial city into the existing extramuros.

MILITARY REORIENTATIONS

European conflict in the eighteenth century led to the disastrous military
events that took place on June 6, 1762.[49] Problems on the continent
had long manifested as decidedly Atlantic affairs for colonial territories.

Prior to the attack, colonial officials received warning that a British attack was imminent. The warning came from Spanish subjects who resided across the Caribbean islands, illustrating the interconnected nature of the eighteenth-century Caribbean not only for the European powers that laid claim to its territories but also for the subjects of the various crowns who held on to complicated political allegiances, if not always economic or social ones. *Desertores* (deserters) and corsairs also chimed in to warn Cuba's governor, Juan de Prado, of the British plot, but Prado reportedly dismissed the warnings.[50] Days before British ships were sighted, the governor lost at least two more opportunities to go on alert. A French colonial subject, described only as a "desertor," and a British corsair with presumably economic or perhaps personal ties to Havana, also related news of the impending attack. The confluence of interests that united this early and disparate human warning system is evidence of the permeability of the city and its port and the mobility of city residents. Ironically, this was the very thing that colonial officials had been trying to prevent in fear that it would lead to a loss of Spanish power.

Colonial officials soon had a much more serious situation to contend with. At dawn on the morning of June 6, they sighted 145 to 200 ships sailing off the western coast of Havana. Officials dismissed the expedition as a call to port and only became concerned when, at high noon, the ships continued on their route and bypassed the entrance of the port, heading toward the nearby town of Cojímar, some fourteen kilometers east of Havana.[51] George Keppel (Conde de Albemarle), under the direction of Admiral George Pocock, led the British expedition. Their men disembarked at Cojímar, where the British engineer Patrick Mackellar, who was aboard one of ships, noted that a "considerable number of peasants and negroes in arms" met the crew to defend the largely unfortified town against the attack.[52] Prado had already given the order that all available troops and the *milicias de blancos, pardos, y morenos* (white, mixed-race, and black militias), as well as the *lanceros de campo* (soldiers tasked with defending the hinterland), go out and meet the attack, but none arrived in time to stop the British forces.

The governor's mobilization of manpower underscored several issues. The crown did not hesitate when it came to sending its own Spanish subjects to defend the city, but it concentrated resources and fortified the city mostly to guard against a naval invasion.[53] To supplement this naval power, it housed two peninsular battalions of infantry regiments in Havana (Aragón and España) that augmented the existing forces of the Fixed Infantry Battalion and the Cuban militias. All together, about eleven thousand people should have been at the governor's disposal, but these consisted heavily of the naval squadrons and sea-based lines of defense. Ten ships of the line, frigates, and support vessels made up a large portion of Havana's system of defense.[54] The expense to the crown was substantial, although many of the young men assigned to the task were themselves poorly compensated.

The day following the British landing, Cuban notices of the attack arrived in the eastern area of the island, along with letters in the surrounding islands asking for reinforcements to protect Havana's plaza.[55] By June 8, British forces had marched toward Guanabacoa with little impediment save for the initial defense that the "peasants and negroes in arms" had launched. To protect the city, the chain between the Castillo de San Salvador de la Punta and El Morro Castle was drawn across the well-fortified entrance of the bay, effectively closing the port as officials scrambled to minimize losses. Nonetheless, losses were numerous in the early days following the attack; the coastline was attacked with only the *baluartes* (military towers) to defend it, and cannons, ships, and men were lost in the effort by sea.[56]

If the effort to defend the city by sea was ineffective, by land the response was disastrous. The forts had been built anticipating an attack by sea, and protection of the city similarly revolved around safeguarding the port and bay. Even after the attack by land commenced, colonial efforts remained focused around the city's plaza and El Morro Castle, ignoring the fact that it was the surrounding barrios that were most vulnerable. The inability of officials to think outside the maritime functions of the city illustrates the centrality of the intramuros in colonial minds, something that would be a decisive factor in how events unfolded. The intramuros became the site where the city's defenses were concentrated. The city doors, now evenly spaced along the muralla, were carefully guarded even when reinforcements for the city were coming from outside the walls. It was an advantage that the English troops would exploit. Once they reached the outskirts of Havana, they set up camp in Guanabacoa and from the vantage point on high ground and across the bay proceeded to coordinate the attack. The lack of a well-orchestrated Spanish response left the defense of Havana to its forty thousand inhabitants, most of whom had fled the city almost as soon as the attack began. The governor had ordered all residents who remained in Havana but who could not contribute to its defense to leave immediately. The order caused long lines to extend from the city gates all the way to the rural hinterland. The "limited contribution of native Americans [criollos] to defense," Allan Kuethe notes, was one of the primary reasons behind the relative ease with which the city fell to British forces.[57]

The lack of an intramuro defense meant that extramuro forces, as well as those of Guanabacoa, were especially visible in the coordinated attacks. The most celebrated of these was the regiment led by Guanabacoa's alcalde, José Antonio Gómez, known colloquially as Pepe Antonio.[58] When colonial administrators failed to respond to British vessels on June 6, Pepe Antonio reputedly organized several dozen men into military groups and made his way toward Cojímar to meet the British.[59] Six days later and amid heavy losses, the Spanish *partidarios* captured a regiment of surprised British soldiers and proceeded to march the group into the middle of Havana's plaza in a performance that not only mocked the British but also highlighted the inefficiency of the Spanish administration.[60]

The defense of Havana thus fell to the extramuro and African-descended men who fought as part of the Cuban militias that had been mobilized almost as soon as the attack began, as well as to the guerrilla partidario forces, lanceros, and enslaved squadrons. Black *milicianos* (militiamen) formed part of a colonial tradition in which military service served as a means to increase status and achieve colonial inclusion.[61] For colonial administrators, the moreno and pardo regiments were an important if uneasy component of incorporating the interests of black elite families into colonial structures. Black militias went on to receive commendations for their loyalty and service during the 1762 struggle. Enslaved black men, too, formed an integral part of the defense of the city.

Complex factors compelled both groups of men to defend Spanish colonial rule: service afforded opportunities for upward social mobility and allowed the men and their families to claim certain rights. David Sartorius also asserts that for free black subjects as well as enslaved men, support for the Spanish crown was a multifaceted project that constituted an alternative community outside of the nascent nation-state. Within the bounds and framework of imperial exclusion, black subjects formed political communities that calculated ideas of liberal citizenship—the same ideas that would figure prominently in the early republic.[62] While territories did not necessarily define or organize the loyalties of colonial subjects, the political claims and "narratives of loyalty" from enslaved and conquered subjects served to further the empire's territorial claims.[63] This framework helps us to better understand the events that unfolded in the different environs of the city when the British attack on Havana began. Men were called in from the labors that they had been performing and were put to work reinforcing the plazas, walls, and doors to the city.

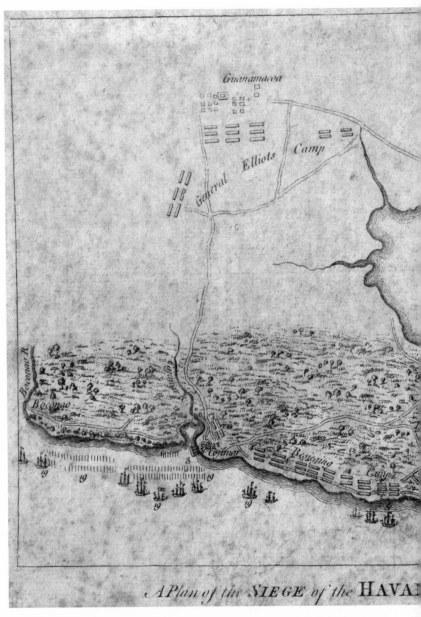

FIGURE 4. *A Plan of the Siege of the Havana,* 1762. Courtesy of the John Carter Brown Library at Brown University.

Guessapoa

HAVANA.

Governors Fort

Puntal Lazaro

Morro

Col House Lane

Choren

Chorera R.

FIGURE 5. *Toma de La Habana por los ingleses*, 1762. Courtesy of the Archivo Histórico de la Oficina del Historiador de la Ciudad de La Habana (OHCH), Havana.

Vecinos offered the crown the services of their slaves, and those who remained were enticed with promises of freedom, though vecinos would later claim that enslaved blacks participated of their own "free" will, without any such expectations. Of course, the claims would later be used to withhold freedom as often as they were used to bestow titles of heroism and reward enslaved blacks with manumission.

In one of these noble tales, a squadron of the royal slaves was said to have armed the city in five days. They worked diligently to dig trenches, repair infrastructure, and fortify the city—once again occupying a central role in the physical construction of Havana. In another tale, twenty enslaved men volunteered to defend La Cabaña under Colonel Luis Vicente Velasco. Some of the men were owned by Velasco himself and had been promised freedom in exchange for military service. But so many more enslaved men volunteered of their own free will that Velasco later claimed that he lost count of their identities or how many there were.[64] With only machetes to defend themselves, they captured seven of the thirty-man British contingent and managed to injure or kill several others.[65] When vecinos told these tales after the assault, the stories reinforced the leadership of white criollos, as many of the enslaved men were loans from white vecino owners, who also received the glory of the men's service.

The abundant stories of white criollo leadership assuaged the fear of these same men and women. If free black and enslaved men, for example, could launch a better defense of Havana than could the Spanish colonial administration, then the transformations of eighteenth-century Cuba were grave indeed. The eighteenth-century shift from tobacco to sugar had already made slavery singularly important to Cuba's economy. Any disruption to racial hierarchies that would have reaffirmed the historical role of free black vecinos as independent vassals of the crown would also have put the future economy of Cuba in peril by transforming slaves into valiant combatants, and ones capable of launching an attack against whites. It is then unremarkable that in the stories that circulated following the British assault, enslaved men were represented as loyal to their white criollo (if not Spanish) masters. They fought on the side of the crown and without ever questioning their enslaved status, thus also remaining the property and at the mercy of white vecinos and men like Velasco. The tales highlighted the centrality of slavery and the importance of racial hierarchies amid the social transformations that had already altered Havana's landscape. They also allowed white criollos to assuage fears over the possibility of a successful black or slave revolt, especially amid a growing Atlantic climate of revolution.[66]

The participation of these men did not make their living spaces any less expendable to the colonial system of defense. Governor Prado issued an edict ordering that the extramuro neighborhood of La Salud de Guadalupe (divided into two barrios, La Salud and Guadalupe) and the barrio of Jesús, María y José (Jesús María) be set aflame in order to prevent British soldiers from hiding within their structures. Next, parts of the city were flooded with water from the Zanja Real, causing outbreaks of yellow fever among British soldiers and residents.[67] Each side blamed the other for the destruction of these areas. Either way, the drastic measures had little effect on the direction of the war, but destroyed the living spaces of extramuro residents, particularly those located immediately adjacent to the walls. In this way, the administration rendered expendable its extramural subjects while the territorial reorganization that would follow extended the crown's reach into the very landscapes it had previously excluded.

The war came to an end in February 1763, when officials signed the Treaty of Paris and returned Havana in exchange for Spanish Florida. The crown lost no time in immediately launching an investigation into the events that led to capitulation.[68] The junta convened for that purpose found Governor Juan de Prado deficient in his military responsibilities, and he was unceremoniously dragged back to Madrid and sentenced, as were other officials whom the crown blamed for handing the city over to the British.[69] The assault and subsequent capture of Havana—precisely what the walls had been built to prevent—should have exposed the failure of the existing system of defense. As early as 1674, critics of the walls had informed the king of their many defects, including the fact that they had not been built to the desired height and their baluartes were not of sufficient height to be militarily useful, causing the distance of artillery fire from the baluartes to be ineffective.[70] This paled in comparison to the scathing assessment that military engineer Antonio de Arredondo would later provide. Arredondo criticized the outdated military theory that had informed construction and leveled the same criticism of the too-short baluartes, but in addition he stated that the outline of the wall was defective and that a new enclosure should be planned far from the urban population, with seven new baluartes, moats, and a covered entrance. Debates over the new plans went on for four years, but in the end the crown abandoned the idea, and by 1740 construction was declared complete.[71] Instead of serving as a reason for demolition, the inefficiency of the walls created a new incentive for fortification. Even as the junta was in the process of deciding the fate of the officials recalled to Madrid, new officials appointed for the purpose of preventing another such episode were making their way across the Atlantic.[72] Among them were Havana's new governor, Ambrosio Funes de Villalpando (Conde de Ricla), Field Marshal Alejandro O'Reilly, and director of engineers Silvestre Abarca.

The new plan consisted first and foremost of repairing the damage to the city. El Morro Castle and Castillo de San Salvador de la Punta were once again priorities, as well as repairing the ancient Fuerza and the baluartes that the British had shelled at La Chorrera, San Lázaro, and Cojímar. Once the repairs were under way, officials turned their attention to the construction of new structures based on the British offensive. To eliminate the military edge that the heights of La Cabaña had given the British forces, the fort San Carlos de la Cabaña was built. A new fort (the Castillo de Atares) also now guarded the Real Arsenal (royal shipyard), which had been moved to the southern point of the city in 1734. Repair of the old structures and construction of new structures created a fort city that again appeared impregnable. The Conde de Ricla advocated expanding militarization and "arming the colonials" as the only method by which Spain might resist another attack.[73] Having a colonial militia with privileges such as the *fuero militar* (military privileges), Ricla reasoned, would prevent another embarrassing military display by co-opting the interests of colonial subjects and ensuring the legitimacy of colonial rule. Not surprisingly, by 1763 the number of men mobilized in Havana was tantamount to the number of civilian men residing within it, which also contributed to the city's expanding demographics.[74]

Changes also affected the organization of extramuro space. Illegal constructions were clustered around Havana's defense structures, namely the Campo de Marte (the military field that lay immediately west of the walls). Under the new plan by Abarca, construction near defense structures was again prohibited, including the areas adjacent to the city walls as well as the Campo de Marte, to allow for the more efficient defense of the city. In 1764, the area next to these structures where residents were prohibited from building was increased from 300 to 1,500 varas.[75] The prohibition effectively displaced the squatter settlements built with guano that had earlier appeared in adjacent areas. Large tracts of land in what had been strategic defense areas prior to 1762 were again confiscated (at times without restitution) in order to ensure the safety of the city. To aid the militarization effort, the Spanish crown issued royal decrees in 1784, 1788, and 1790 that allotted a total of 290,000 *duros* to the military effort in Havana (compared with a total of only 146,000 duros for the fortification of Santiago de Cuba).[76]

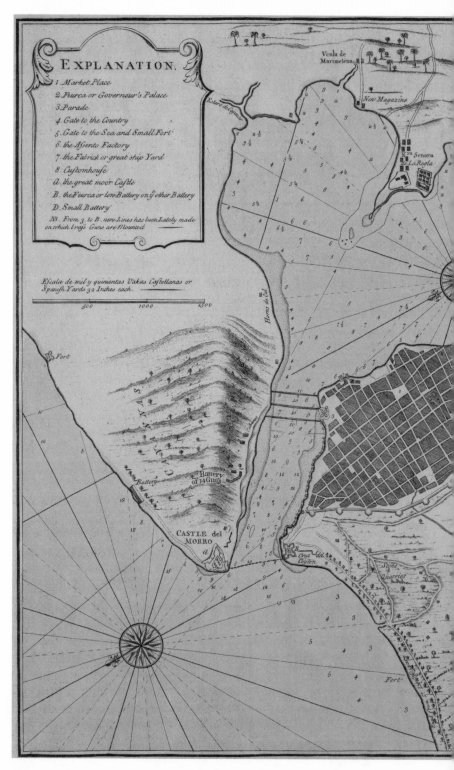

EXPLANATION.

1. Market Place
2. Feurca or Governour's Palace
3. Parade
4. Gate to the Country
5. Gate to the Sea and Small Fort
6. the Assento Factory
7. the Fabrick or great ship Yard
8. Customhouse
a. the great moor Castle
B. the Feurca or low Battery on if other Battery
D. Small Battery

NB. From 3. to B. new lines has been lately made
on which brass Guns are Mounted

Escala de mil y quinientas Vakas Castellanas or
Spanish Yards 32 Inches each.

500   1000   1500

FIGURE 6. *A New and Correct Chart of the Harbour of Havana*, c. 1762. Courtesy of
the Library of Congress, Geography and Map Division.

A

New and Correct Chart of the
Harbour *of* HAVANA *on the*
Island *of* CUBA *with a Plan*
of ye City &c from an Actual
Survey by Captain
James Phelps
1762

Ventas le
Guasabacoa

Puerto de Guasabacoa

la Doctora

Old Magazine

el Ingeny

Rio Vyano

Isla de mageres

DOCK
YARD

Arroyo de
Palo

New
Bridge

GUADALUPE

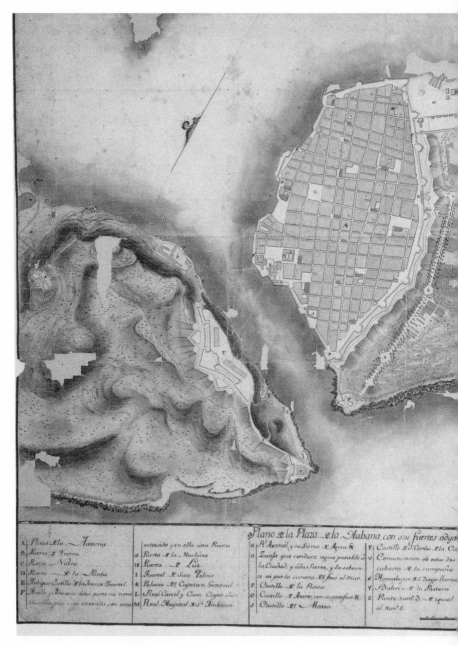

FIGURE 7. *Plano de la plaza de La Habana, con sus fuentes adyacentes, barrios extramuros, y sus inmediaciones*, 1785. CUB-107/10, Servicio Histórico Militar, Archivo General Militar de Madrid. Courtesy of Ministerio de Defensa, Instituto de Historia y Cultura Militar.

Barrios extramuros y sus ynmediaciones.

Salinas artificiales	g Hospital de San Lazaro	q Barrio extramuros del Horcon	de la Chorrera en la embocadura del
Reales almacenes de la Casablanca	h Casa de Beneficencia	r La Puente nueva	Rio de este nombre, distante una
Almacen de la Real Marina	i Terreno cenagoso, causado por los	s Santuario de Nra. Sra. de Regla	legua del Morro, y es la mesa a
Bateria de Sta. Clara en Punta Brava	derrames de la Zanja	t Poblacion de Regla	que pasible de estas ynmediaciones.
Bateria de San Nazario	m Barrio extramuros de S. Lazaro	u Arrecifes de Peña muy escabrosos	y Fuerte el Principe
Reales Molinos de Tabaco nueva	n Sa. de Guadalupe y de la Salud	en toda la costa	z Canteras q se sellenan con mampos
mente construidos	p Sa. de Jesus Maria	x Camino que va a la Torre y Bateria	& Real Factoria de Tabacos.

While expenditures and improvements to existing structures were significant, the regulations reinforced and extended earlier land-use patterns. Land expropriations continued, this time with a reminder by Abarca of the usufruct nature of resident holdings, though the warning of course was directed only to those with legal titles to begin with or those who had not lost their extramuro land (where renewed fortification and militarization efforts were concentrated) to denouncers decades earlier. Much like the litigation that resulted from the crown's land confiscations when construction of the muralla began, the cases would tie up courts for decades.

The fact that vecinos were able to once again take their claims to court for compensation illustrates competing claims between vecinos and the crown. The vecinos' claims were likely the reason that in 1779, the crown shifted from confiscation and restitution to purchasing solares outright. Once restitution was officially instituted for confiscated lands, vecinos who held legal titles in the extramuros and saw portions of their land confiscated ended up being the indirect beneficiaries of colonial policy, as decades later they were also able to profit by selling or renting their property at exorbitant prices during a period of land shortage and increased urban density and regulation. After 1763, those without legal claim to land in the extramuros are relatively invisible in the copious suits that militarization produced. Many had already been displaced by the earlier construction of the muralla or else had seen their lands denounced and their titles transferred to vecinos who could afford to pay the new taxes or make the mandatory improvements to the land. The cost of making said improvements may have far surpassed the real value of the land on which the population of pardos and morenos resided.

The church had been exempted from many of the early reorganizations, but it would not be spared again. This was a new era of political enlightenment: already the Jesuits had been expelled from all Spanish territories (1767), and the Conde de Ricla, eager to comply with his orders to fortify the city but minimize the cost, was ready to use church lands to do so. Although events were certainly tinged by this political climate, which affected the entirety of the Americas, there was also a historical precedent for how events unfolded in the post-1763 era. The proposal to construct La Fuerza and the Plaza de Armas centuries earlier had also involved a petition by the governor that the land should come from church holdings. The governor at the time had proposed that the church be demolished in order to allow for the more important military construction, though the crown rejected that earlier proposal.[77] Bourbon administrators and an enlightened monarch, however, would not be as sympathetic to the church this time around. According to Sherry Johnson, the military hospital and barracks came from the friars of San Isidro, and the San Juan de Dios hospital lost a portion of its land to the militarization effort.[78] While renewed concern with militarization provided the Conde de Ricla with the perfect excuse to expropriate church lands, it was certainly just that—an excuse. The church in Guadalupe, for example, had been demolished and the parish moved away from newly valuable land a full year before the British attack. Not surprisingly, all the church confiscations occurred in the extramuros. By contrast, intramuro church and convent land holdings were untouched by the militarization campaigns. These land confiscations illustrate that if we broaden the temporal boundaries of to include the years before and after the sugar boom and fall of Havana, the continuity in land-use patterns becomes clear. Land scarcity and the cabildo's loss of power, for example, both predate the military reorganization of 1763.

Several factors further exacerbated the diminishing availability of land and housing in the post-1763 era. The number of jobs that the militarization project created and the prosperous environment resulting from sugar and tobacco enticed newcomers to settle in Havana. Events in Europe also contributed to this trend. The growth of sugar and tobacco in Cuba coincided with the decline of industry in Spain, bringing with it a diverse immigration from areas of the peninsula previously not well represented in Havana. *Rascos, navarros,* and Catalans all became part of the post-1763 landscape.[79] Soldiers, too, contributed to Havana's population increase. The crown reorganized its military strategy and sent companies of carefully selected men from Spain's provinces for the future defense of the city. The men reinforced Spanish sovereignty by diminishing the power of the local militias and acting as royal representatives. They also increased the number of immigrants; many of them, having enlisted at a young age and for a period of up to eight years, decided to stay in the city.[80] Then there was also the increase that occurred as a result of the natural movement between the islands, the mainland, and North America. The independence war in North America caused immigration across the islands, Cuba included.[81] The increase in population as a result of all these factors increased density in and around the city, where the number of inhabitants rose drastically after 1763. The 1791 census placed the population of Havana and its extramuro barrios at 44,337 people, and this did not take into account military recruits and foreign visitors. By 1810, the population had more than doubled, to 96,114 in the unified city.[82]

Given the increase in demographics, it is unsurprising that as late as 1772, eight years after the original prohibitions were issued against construction around the Campo de Marte and other defense structures, squatter settlements were not only still present but also developing along the outskirts of the military field. Residents continuously petitioned the Spanish crown for special permission to build in these areas. At least on a few occasions, the crown granted petitions for temporary housing, although it shifted these to the area of Tallapiedra, on the southern end of the city in the extramuro barrio of Jesús María.[83] But while a few permits were granted, most housing units near military areas were illegally built and easily demolished. Following what seems to be the widespread violation of the new ordinances, the prohibitions against construction were reissued in 1773 and 1779. By 1788, noncompliance had encouraged the colonial administration to institute a fine of twenty-five ducats and a sentence of six months of hard labor for anyone who constructed, rented, or was caught bringing materials for the construction of illegal houses in the Campo de Marte.[84] The implementation of these statutes regulated settlements and enabled the crown to remove potential residents from the extramuros with legal ease.

BUILDING THE EXTRAMUROS

The physical reorganizations that followed the 1763 peace treaty were echoed in dramatic social transformations. Already the region was a theater for European conflicts, and it had demonstrated that it was capable of producing shifts in global power and regional configurations. The Bourbon monarchy in Spain reacted swiftly to counteract the effects of the brief British administration, causing a shift in Bourbon economic and administrative policies. The British had introduced approximately ten thousand slaves to Cuba, significantly altering the demographic as well as the social and economic landscape. In their wake, the Spanish crown opened new ports for commerce, and taxes and fees that had been previously imposed on sugar were now replaced by flat rates. The earlier taxes on the importation of slaves were also eliminated. As a result, sugar exports had increased fivefold by the 1770s, and slave numbers dramatically increased between 1763 and 1789.[85] The concessions granted to residents, however, did more than just secure the sugar and slave society of late eighteenth- and early nineteenth-century Cuba. The responsibility for securing funds to oversee rebuilding and fortification efforts fell heavily on the Conde de Ricla, who distributed the cost among city residents after 1763. Even then, however, the wealthy elite stood to benefit, and in return for their compliance with new taxes and increased colonial oversight, the Conde de Ricla offered local wealthy families commercial privileges and military titles.[86] In Havana, the cumulative result of the eighteenth-century changes was the emergence of a new urban and landed elite with legal claims to the extramuros.

The flurry of post-1763 reforms introduced a new system of cataloguing both the intramuros *and* the extramuros, organized the public lives of residents through legal ordinances, and generated the landscape that historians Carlos Venegas and Julio Le Riverend characterized as one marked by the emergence of *"el orden urbano"* (urban order).[87] The 1763 plan to urbanize the city proper (approved six years later) was the first to reconsider the layout of the city since the Laws of the Indies.[88] First, in 1768 the two areas of the intramuros were formally divided into two *cuarteles* (districts), and each neighborhood was assigned a comisario de barrio.[89] Prior to 1760, the city had consisted of only two districts, Campeche and La Punta, but by 1783 it had been subdivided into eight separate areas. The new intramuro neighborhoods of Estrella, Monserrate, Dragones, and Angel developed in the area of La Punta, while Campeche on the southern end of the city now consisted of the barrios of Santa Teresa, San Francisco, Paula, and San Isidro.[90]

The composition of the city had also shifted as a result of ongoing social and economic transformations. In 1791, the population classified simply as "white" in the census outnumbered the population of enslaved and free people of African descent by 52 percent to 47 percent in Havana and the extramuros, but by 1810, whites were in the minority. The number of people categorized as white had registered a 73 percent increase in the twenty-one years between the two census counts, while the slave population in and around the city had registered an increase of 165 percent. The largest increase, however, was noted in the population of free African-descended people, which registered the largest increase in percentage.[91] While population increase affected housing within the walls, it also had a dramatic effect on the extramuros, as new neighborhoods composed primarily of free blacks were relegated to areas outside the muralla. The population in this area quadrupled in the generation after 1780, where most of the neighborhoods were composed of "nonwhite" inhabitants and where black residents far outnumbered whites.[92]

Colonial policing systems reinforced policía as the trajectory of urban growth. *Capitanes de partido* were responsible for overseeing the city's

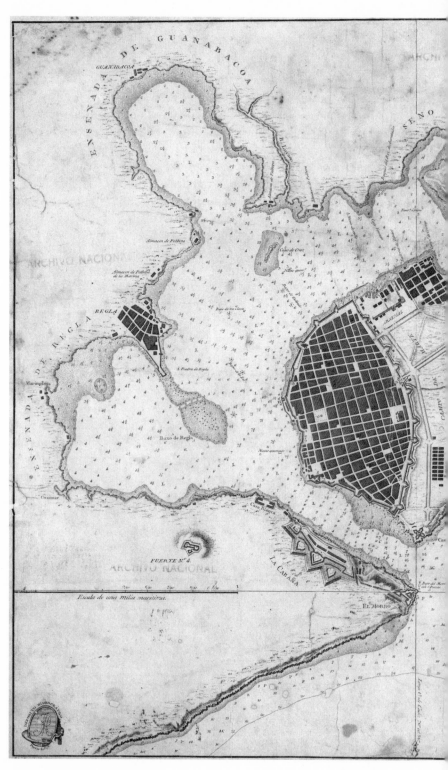

FIGURE 8. José del Rio, *Plano del puerto y ciudad de La Habana*, 1798. Mapoteca M-474, Archivo Nacional de Cuba (ANC), Havana.

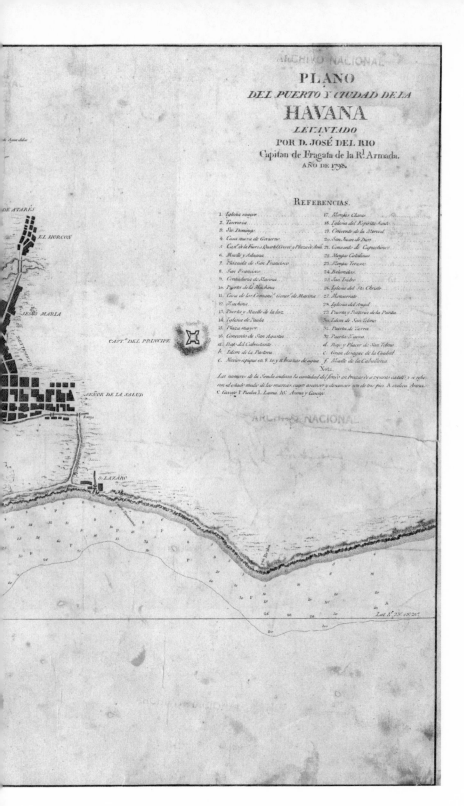

PLANO
DEL PUERTO Y CIUDAD DE LA
HAVANA
LEVANTADO
POR D. JOSÉ DEL RIO
Capitan de Fragata de la Rl. Armada.
AÑO DE 1798.

REFERENCIAS.

1. Iglesia mayor
2. Taverería
3. Sto. Domingo
4. Casa nueva de Govierno
5. Castl. de la Fuerza, Quartl. Genl. y Plaza de Armas
6. Muelle y Aduana
7. Plazuela de San Francisco
8. San Francisco
9. Contaduría de Marina
10. Puerta de la Machina
11. Casa de los Comand.e Genl. de Marina
12. Machina
13. Puerta y Muelle de la luz
14. Iglesia de Paula
15. Plaza mayor
16. Convento de San Agustin
a. Baxo del Cabestante
b. Idem de la Pastora
c. Navios que pican en 8, 10 y 11 brazas de agua

17. Monjas Claras
18. Iglesia del Espíritu Santo
19. Convento de la Merced
20. San Juan de Dios
21. Convento de Capuchinos
22. Monjas Catalinas
23. Monjas Teresas
24. Belemitas
25. San Isidro
26. Iglesia del Sto. Christo
27. Monserrate
28. Iglesia del Angel
29. Puerta y Batería de la Punta
30. Idem de San Telmo
31. Puerta de Tierra
32. Puerta Nueva
d. Baxo y Placer de San Telmo
e. Gran desague de la Ciudad
f. Muelle de la Caballería

Nota.
Los numeros de la Sonda indican la cantidad del fondo en brazas de a 2 varas castell.s y se refieren al estado medio de las mareas cuyo ascenso y descenso sera de tres pies. A indican Arena.
C Cascara. P Piedra L. Lama. AC. Arena y Cascajo.

CAST.o DEL PRINCIPE

DE ATARÉS
EL HORCON
JESUS MARIA
SEÑOR DE LA SALUD
Zanja
S. LAZARO

Lat.d N. 23° 08' 20''

districts and answered directly to the captain general.[93] They were responsible for maintaining policía by ensuring that residents complied with the ordinances issued by the crown. Besides dealing with gambling, prostitution, and other vices considered specific to urban areas, they were to control demographic and housing pressure in the city. Their positions brought them in contact with men recruited to Havana as part of the militarization effort, and mediating conflicts and disputes that arose among the population was part of their job, as was being vigilant and ensuring that conscripts, convicts, and royal slaves sent to labor on the fortification structures did not disappear into the growing city.[94]

The legal ordinances in place were an extension of the king's reach, especially into the extramuros. Vagrancy, and how the administration dealt with the growing issue, is an example of this. In 1765, a legal mandate allowed vagos to be apprehended and delivered to government officials, only to be placed in labor gangs working in the city's construction projects.[95] While vagrancy may have originally been an issue that concerned colonial administrators, its regulation was now directly tied to the success of the city's built environment. By 1769, a bounty system had developed that provided anyone who apprehended deserters, vagrants, and viciosos (people with vices; drunkards and such) within the city with a reward of eight ducats. If the culprit was apprehended in the suburbs surrounding the city, the reward rose to twelve reales, and it rose again to twenty-four reales for anyone who was apprehended beyond the city limits and throughout the island. One could effectively leave the city but remain a vagrant of it.[96] Forced conscription upon being mistaken for a vagrant, as well as simply being apprehended for the reward that a vagrant would bring their denouncer, was a constant threat hanging over the daily lives of the urban poor. Rising rent prices and the resulting high rate of rental turnover further left residents vulnerable to being mistaken for vagrants and forced to labor on one of Havana's new fortifications.

The sudden visibility of vagrants served a double purpose for the administration. First, it provided the free labor that Havana needed, along with the use of royal slaves. But vagrants also served to render visible an area of the map that the administration had earlier erased when the city expanded west. Construction of the walls and the restrictions governing realengo land were premised on the availability of solares in an area where residents were presumed to not exist. Once land scarcity and demographic growth made the area attractive, land denouncements resulted in the urbanization of the area outside the walls between the Zanja Real and the sea.[97]

Land scarcity was not just an extramuro problem. The limited availability of recreational opportunities within the walled city also provided
intramuro residents with an excuse to use the area outside the walls as a
respite from the cramped conditions of the city.[98] Already, residents of
the intramuros had taken to the wide calzadas that stretched from the
western Puerta de Tierra well into areas of the extramuros and had put
them to use as promenades. The royal shipyard had also become a sight-
seeing attraction for residents. Because of extant conditions, however,
the extramuros was a space where residential, recreational, and industrial forces competed. Decades later, the tensions would prompt Alexander von Humboldt to describe the city as one engaged in a virtual tug-of-
war over the accessible areas that lay closest to the walls. The tension
intensified to the point that there was an appeal to the crown to have a
moat constructed to surround Havana's military structures to keep not
just foreign enemies but also squatters at bay, a measure that if successful
would have turned part of the city of Havana—already a seemingly
impregnable fort—into a fortified island.[99] While no such proposal was
ever carried out, by 1799 a moat surrounding the military field *was* built
to further deter illegal housing construction. All illegally built homes (as
well as those that had been legally constructed) in the immediate vicinity
of the Campo de Marte were destroyed. With nowhere left to go but the
hinterland, squatters responded by simply picking up makeshift homes
and relocating to the south side of the Camino Real, clustered in full
view of the royal shipyard. In order for expansion to appeal to the land-
holding vecinos and merchant interests of Havana, it was necessary that
the area outside the city walls be symbolically incorporated into the city
and span the physical division that the city walls now imposed.

Colonial officials accordingly extended the crown's authority into the
outlying neighborhoods of Havana. Under the administration of the
Marqués de la Torre, the first plan of public works was implemented; it
affected the administration of both areas. The plan consisted of a series
of citywide measures to "beautify" the city and its surrounding areas.
Beginning in the late eighteenth century, it implemented a system through
which it could begin to look after the daily upkeep of Havana. In 1771,
it created a regular schedule for the cleaning of city streets. It also under-
took a project of systematically numbering houses and naming the individual streets that had snaked their way anonymously throughout the
city, with names known only to those living in the vicinity. A system of
public lighting was also instituted in 1773, and the administration took
charge of overseeing the construction of public fountains throughout

both Havana intramuros and extramuros in 1787, with the dual purpose of getting rid of dark corners in the city and offering residents the opportunity to participate in a new and modern environ. The measures effectively extended the administration's reach into the extramuros and reinforced the existing connection between royal sovereignty and the urban, built environment. When the Iglesia Parroquial Mayor was relocated to the site of the Jesuit church,[100] the move attracted wealthy landowners who constructed a number of new homes in the surrounding areas of Havana. It was during this era that the architecture of Havana typically associated with the colonial era first emerged, financed in part by the sugar revenues of the expanding economy. The *portal* (doorway) that would come to exemplify nineteenth-century architecture, for example, made its first appearance in the new buildings and wealthy homes then under construction.[101] The association of colonial Havana with the sugar revenues of the late eighteenth and early nineteenth centuries thus stems not only from the success of the economic transformations of eighteenth-century Cuba but also from the organization of the city already under way, a product of the confluence of eighteenth-century forces.

Among the more salient projects initiated under the plan of public works was the 1772 construction of the Alameda de Extramuros, located to the west of the wall at Tierra.[102] The wide avenue would become popular as a promenade for the middle classes and represented a critical step in the transformation of the extramuros into an official and elite space. In the promenades of the extramuros, intramuro residents were able to engage in the recreational and social activities lacking within the walls but essential to the creation of an urban(e) culture in the city. The new social opportunities created by the extramuro promenades were depicted in a new genre of illustration (paintings, lithographs, and watercolors) that emerged during the early nineteenth century. In the *Vista del paseo extramuros de La Habana* (View from the extramuro paseos of Havana), by Hippolyte Garneray, the *alameda* (avenue) is represented as a space of affluence where women (accompanied by escorts) can partake in the recreational activities of the city. Carriages typical of late eighteenth- and early nineteenth-century Cuba called *volantes* are illustrated driving along the promenade chauffeured by elegantly dressed black drivers.[103]

The new spaces of the extramuros present an organized and ordered view of the city in stark juxtaposition to the visibly cramped and disordered spaces of the intramuros.[104] Depictions of Havana intramuros by the end of the eighteenth century showcase an inversion in the use of urban public space. Havana intramuros, once an elite colonial space,

FIGURE 9. Hippolyte Jean Baptiste Garneray, *Vista del paseo extramuros de La Habana*, 1830. Courtesy of the I.N. Phelps Stokes Collection, Miriam and Ira D. Wallach Division of Art, Prints, and Photographs, The New York Public Library; and the Astor, Lenox, and Tilden Foundations.

was becoming an area notable for the failure of the same politics of order that the administration attempted to promote in the city and its outlying arrabales. Hippolyte Garneray's depiction of the everyday activities that took place in the bustling town squares of intramuro Havana, *Vista de la plaza o mercado príncipe de La Habana* (View from the plaza or main market of Havana), presents the plaza as a veritable cauldron of social and racial mixture.[105] The well-kept square is surrounded by the homes and buildings of the colonial elite, with facades constructed in the architectural style of the period. From the balconies of these buildings, young Spanish women sit dressed demurely in *mantillas* as they peer onto the scene unfolding below them, where well-dressed white men and a few women stroll past rows of makeshift wooden huts congregated in the middle of the square. These were perhaps drawn to be or to resemble the wooden *barracones* (barracks) that existed at the time near the port, where enslaved men and women were held. In the work, rows of young black women sit outside the wooden structures in a scene in which segregation is both gendered and raced.[106] Unlike their counterparts in the extramuro promenades, the women are confined to the margins of Havana's social spaces. Like the extramuro illustrations, the social space that black Havana residents inhabit is one in direct opposition to that of the Spanish elite women.[107] Social space and practices in colonial Havana, then, were outgrowths of the colonial governing practices that constituted race through the inscription and organization of the landscape.

Instead of concern about marauding bands of pirates gaining access to the port, colonial attention by the close of the eighteenth century revolved around other, more subtle threats emanating from the sea.

FIGURE 10. Hippolyte Jean Baptiste Garneray, *Vista de la plaza vieja o mercado príncipe de La Habana*. Original housed at the Museo Nacional de Bellas Artes de La Habana.

Urban density in the intramuros made disease, an issue since the preceding century, particularly troublesome. Outbreaks of yellow fever were a constant concern for public health officials and often originated from infected ships and their crews.[108] Ships coming from areas where outbreaks of the virus had occurred or those that were suspected of carrying the disease were denied entrance into the port or were quarantined for a time period that coincided with incubation. In a routine practiced in cities with similar concerns, ships carrying those already sick were asked to circle the bay twice in order to alert authorities that they were carrying infected onboard. Officials would then pick up and safely transport the sick to the hospital across the bay, where damage might be lessened due to smaller and less dense populations, or where colonial officials cared less about the damage done compared to what an outbreak in the city might do.[109]

By the first decade of the nineteenth century, conditions drove Humboldt to describe Havana as a metropolis whose lack of hygiene was unparalleled in all of Spanish America.[110] Notably, he also pinpointed the space in which colonial officials might find redemption. He found in the clearing of land to the west of the walls and in the colonial government's trajectory of westward extramuro expansion that *"la civilización hace progreso"* (civilization is making progress). It was progressing directly into the wide-open spaces of the extramuros.[111] By the early nineteenth century, the image of the intramuros stood in direct contradiction with the fact that the area was still the place where the city's elite lived, worked, and conducted daily business.[112] It remained the primary location of all major commercial, business, government, and military interests. Merchants, shop owners, notaries, judges, military officials, and even *hacendado* (large landowner) proprietors of *cafetales* (coffee mills) and sugar ingenios still made their residence in the intramuros during the early decades of the nineteenth century, despite the administration's significant inroads into the extramuros. This contradiction can be explained by the continued liminality of the extramuros. Its persistent association with the urban underclass was not yet erased, and the area still continued to define the limits of an exclusive and secure space of Spanish civilization that began and ended with the walls. Even though the British attack had exposed the military futility of the walls, and the growing urbanization to the west of the structures had rendered the intramuro/extramuro division pointless in terms of safety, the walls remained important in distinguishing between a legal and extralegal urban body.

Once in place, the correlation between the extramuros and its black residents was a difficult one to erase, particularly given the demographic changes that the city experienced in the early nineteenth century. The relationship between race and demographics was reinforced by the colonial ban issued by the Marqués de la Torre in 1776. The regulation prohibited residents of the intramuros from constructing any future residential structures from guano, a relatively inexpensive building material popular among urban inhabitants.[113] It also gave vecinos two years to alter their establishments or else risk fines and demolition. Building materials in the intramuros varied, but many homes were constructed of *teja* (or else they were made *de alto*).[114] The ban on guano required the use of more expensive building materials and would have thus deterred lower-earning or marginal inhabitants from settling in Havana proper, relegating them to areas outside the walls and reinforcing long-standing residential patterns and segregation in the larger city. At the same time, the administration passed another initiative that illustrates the aggressive approach that it took toward land control. In 1776, most likely in light of the litigation nightmare that affluent residents had created, it reformed and reorganized extramuro land sales in order to control the graft and corruption by landholders who evaded the Real Hacienda.[115]

Havana's hinterland also posed a problem for administrators for other reasons. As with the hinterland of many other Spanish American cities, colonial officials associated the area with a lawless and growing *independista* cause. This was not the area of the large sugar estates on which the economy of the island rested, but rather the home of those individuals that resided in the "pincer space" between campo and city and whom officials described as fraternizing with persons of varying status and color.[116] *Cuadrillas* (crews) of deputized men combed the area in search of the vagos and lawbreakers that by 1811 had made the establishment of *pueblos* difficult. For those reasons, of the more than four hundred registered business and government officials in 1823, less than 7 percent resided outside the walled city. And those who did were largely the hacendados whose obligations regularly took them into the rural *campo* (countryside).[117]

The Marqués de la Torres's 1777 plan for public order reflects the growing concern over the power of the criollo elite and the danger that a new, developing class of affluent habaneros could pose should a separatist movement gain momentum in Cuba. The danger of this possibility was fueled not only by the North American independence movement but also by the independence struggles sweeping across Latin America and the Caribbean. After 1791, the magnitude of events in Saint-Domingue shook the very foundations of Cuban colonial society. More than just bringing in large numbers of white coffee planters who fled the struggle, unfolding events would also make Cubans question the sustainability of a slave society on an island where blacks outnumbered whites. To Cuban planters in the eastern as well as slaveholding areas of the provinces, the fear that an independence movement in Cuba would result in a St. Domingue-style revolution and strip Cubans of their property was certainly a real (if overly emphasized in the academic literature) possibility. The Havana police report for 1811 noted that an anticolonial coalition of "malcontents" led by criollos was an increasing danger in the city, and that an effort should be made to more tightly control the possibility of an anticolonial movement via the stricter enforcement of law and order.[118] By the time that land scarcity peaked (in the 1720s) and the walls stood in their most complete form (by 1740), Spanish ideas of order and policía had been fully subsumed into the city's built environment. By this time, however, the meaning of urban space had begun to invert. Instead of safeguarding the city from the perceived dangers of the extramuros, the walls gradually encroached upon the perimeter of the city and enclosed its residents.

Cuban writer Cirilo Villaverde marked the end result of this first phase of amurallamiento (1640–1720) in his novel *Cecilia Valdés* through Havana's temporal and spatially overlapping existence and within parallel spaces that the writer described as simultaneously composed of *"luz y sombra"* (light and shadow).[119] The shadow that the nineteenth-century writer attributed to the intramuros stood in stark opposition to the redemptive possibilities that administrators, residents, and visitors saw within the extramuros. City officials thus built roads, paseos, and the necessary urban structures to facilitate colonial claims to territory and incorporate the extramuros into the civilized urban body. The reinscription of this space with the signs and symbols of colonial rule effectively extended the administration's power beyond the walled city and into the cartographically blank spaces that they had previously produced. By the time the Marqués de la Torre ordered the first-ever census of Havana to be taken between 1774 and 1775, census takers placed the total population of the city at 51,307 residents, for the first time including residents living outside the city walls. Until then, these extramuro residents had been counted separately from their counterparts in government records.[120] Now, however, at the end of the land scarcity problems and as the walls neared completion, the decision to include the extramuro population within Havana's census count foreshadowed the 1807 legal incorporation of los arrabales into the legal urban body. The legal distinction had been a significant one; where once the projected perimeter of the walls excised peoples and spaces from a colonial body politic found within the safe spaces of the grid, the eighteenth-century transformations that the city experienced now ensured that intramuro enclosure contrasted markedly with the civilization that thrived to the west.

CHAPTER 3

Modern Space

Mas la Brisa soplando,
En la tabla y el guano
Se vá el fuego cebando
Y no hay auxilio humano
Que baste a su[o]focarlo;
Sin haber mas recurso que cortarle.

(And the breeze blowing,
On wood and guano
The fire grows
With no human help
sufficient to suffocate it;
Without any more recourse but to abate it.)

—Anonymous, Havana, 1828

On February 11, 1828, a fire burned in the outskirts of Havana in the extramuro barrio of Jesús María, one of several barrios now located outside the city walls. From morning until the early hours of the night, the blaze spread easily among homes still made of wood and guano. An alert system notified habaneros of the flames, and residents from various barrios rushed to the southern area of the extramuros armed with supplies to combat the flames lest the fire spread to adjacent homes and areas. Once the wind picked up, Captain General Francisco Dionisio Vives also rushed to the scene. Collective efforts extinguished the fire before it reached the intramuros but not before the fire effectively destroyed the neighborhood. When it was over, the neighborhood was in ruins.[1]

Fire was a constant threat hanging over the lives of residents. As in many other cities, overpopulation and flammable construction materials within tightly built areas often led to such disasters. The 1828 fire recalled for residents other instances in the city's history when the extramuros had burned. In particular, residents discussed the blaze that destroyed the barrio of Señor de la Salud in 1802 in connection with the unfolding events.[2] On that earlier date, the morena[3] Eusebia Espinosa, her husband, and their two children had watched together with twenty other families composed of morenos, pardos, and residents simply described as "criollo" in colonial documents as their homes burned to the ground. The barrio of Señor de La Salud was located to the west of the walls and was the northernmost of the three barrios of La Salud, Guadalupe, and Jesús María.[4] The Marqués de Somersuelos, captain general and governor of Cuba, had organized a quick response to the disaster. Three days after the fire occurred the families were sheltered in the city's barracones and government officials were kindly encouraged to contribute funds to the relief effort, resulting in a collection that reached into the thousands of reales.[5] Within eight years, the area had regained most of its residents and remained the largest barrio outside Havana, with 28,419 inhabitants (in 1810, Havana proper was approximated at 42,805 residents), even though the district had been subdivided into new administrative units and the building restrictions had been reissued in 1825.[6]

Whereas the colonial government had been a visible presence in the earlier effort to assess and control the extramural damage, by 1828 it was left largely to the Comisión de Extramuros (Extramuros Commission) to fend for those affected. In the wake of the 1828 fire, residents mobilized donation drives to rebuild the area and took charge of finding temporary shelter and relief for those affected. Religious organizations also intervened to help the displaced secure food and shelter, and individuals from the city, such as Cláudio Martínez de Pinillos, Juan José Díaz de Espada y Landa, and Bernabé de Corres, made donations and organized lotteries to help the victims of the fire. In Jesús María, residents noted the absence of colonial officials during the first critical hours of the blaze.[7]

Though fires were a "natural" part of urban living, by the early nineteenth century some of those fires, like the blaze that destroyed Jesús María, occurred with unnatural frequency and seemed to disproportionately affect the extramuros. While there is no direct evidence to support the idea that neighborhoods were deliberately set on fire, archival and other documents suggest that something was amiss in extramural barrios. In his 1945 doctoral thesis (recently rediscovered and reprinted), Juan M. Chailloux similarly suggests that solares burned when the administration strategically set fires as a means to the clear the land.[8] Take for example the fact that in the wake of the 1828 fire, Captain General Vives put a stop to resident rebuilding efforts, prohibiting structures until building

FIGURE 11. *Plano de los barrios extramuros de la plaza de La Habana con las calzadas y demas edificios,* 1783. Courtesy of the Archivo Histórico de la Oficina del Historiador de La Habana.

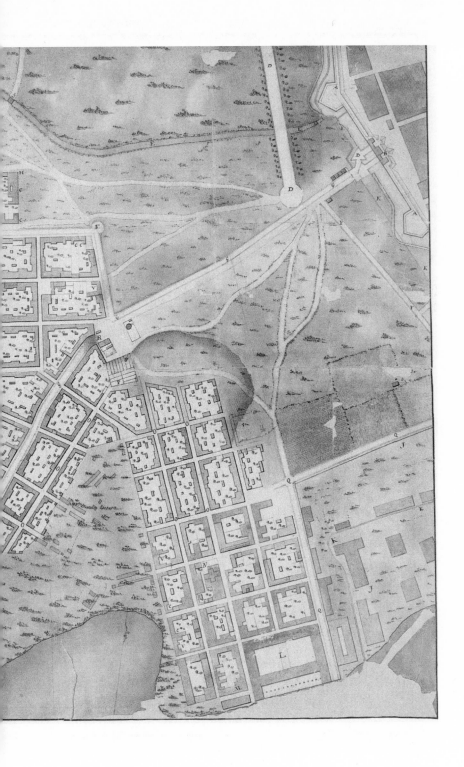

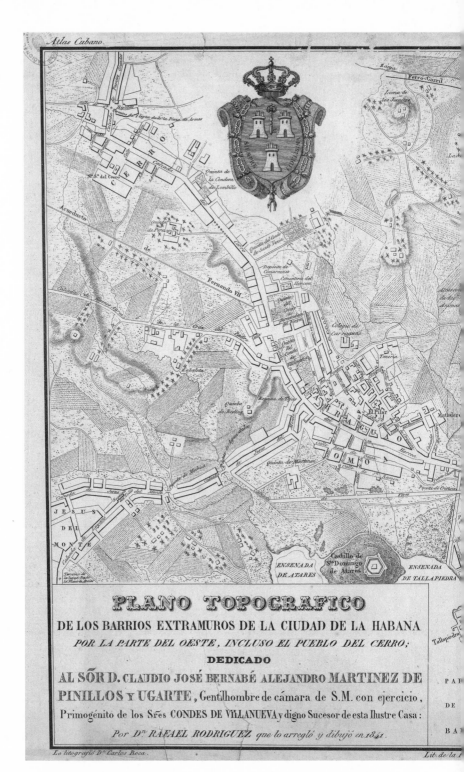

FIGURE 12. Rafael Rodríguez, *Plano topográfico de los barrios extramuros de la ciudad de La Habana*, 1841. Courtesy of the Biblioteca Nacional José Martí (BNJM), Havana.

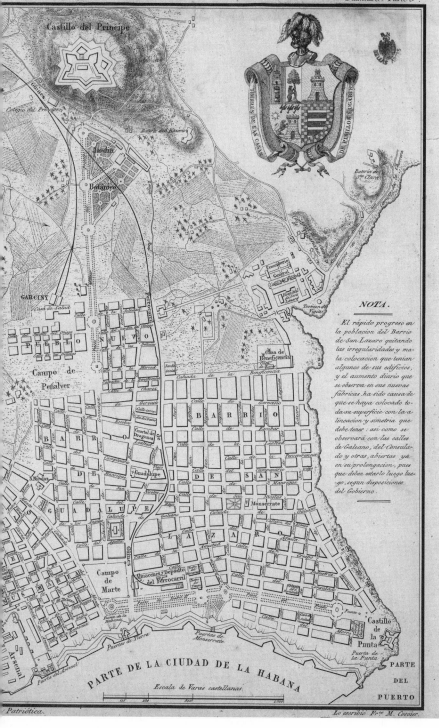

Castillo del Principe

Colegio del Principe

Batería del Nazareno

Jardin

Botánico

GARCINY

Casa de Salud

BARRIO NUEVO

Campo de Peñalver

Casa de Beneficencia de Luna

Calzada de la Beneficencia

BARRIO

Calle de Gervasio

Calle de Escobar

Calle de Lealtad

BARRIO DE SAN

Cuartel de Dragones

Guadalupe

Calle de Perseverancia

Calle de Campanario

Calle de Manrique

S. Nicolás

Monserrate

BARRIO DE GUADALUPE

Calzada de Galeano

LAZARO

Calle de la Amistad

Calle del Aguila

Campo de Marte

Almacenes y Deposito del Ferrocarril

Puerta de Tierra

Puertas de Monserrate

Arsenal

Puerta del Arsenal

Batería de Sta Clara

Cementerio General

Hospital de San Lazaro

Torreon de Vigias

Castillo de la Punta

Puerta de la Punta

El Morro

PARTE DEL PUERTO

ANDRES DE LAS CASAS — DE PINILLOS Y UGARTE

NOTA.

El rápido progreso en la poblacion del Barrio de San Lazaro quitando las irregularidades y mala colocacion que tenian algunos de sus edificios, y el aumento diario que se observa en sus nuevas fábricas ha sido causa de que se haya colocado toda su superficie con la alineacion y simetria que debe tener : asi como se observará con las calles de Galeano, del Consulado y otras, abiertas ya en su prolongacion, pues que deben estarlo luego luego, segun disposiciones del Gobierno.

PARTE DE LA CIUDAD DE LA HABANA

Escala de Varas castellanas.

125   250   500   1000

codes could be verified, ostensibly to prevent disasters like the one that had destroyed the barrio. He then went on to propose that the homes that had survived the blaze be demolished in order to standardize districts and barrios so that they might better fit with the newly designed areas of the extramuros.[9] Governor Vives's plan to rebuild would have thus erased the barrio's impromptu origins and divorced it from its existing extramuro population.

The drastically different responses between the two administrations is indicative of the political landscape and the physical changes that affected the nineteenth-century city. The city that Governor Vives presided over in 1828 was for the first time now composed of Havana intramuros and extramuros, in accordance with the 1807 edict that had declared los arrabales part of the legal urban body and had subdivided La Salud into districts that mimicked intramuro organization. By the time of the second fire, in 1828, colonial officials no longer made distinctions between intramuros and extramuros except as different areas of the same city.[10] The legal unification of Havana presented a temporary solution to the land scarcity issue of the eighteenth century, since unification and the decrease in the area of the military field ostensibly allowed the parceling and regulation of an increased area of land. Unification, however, did little to alleviate the tensions between the colonial administration and city residents, who were themselves divided along socioeconomic and political interests that affected their use of city space. The fire and the events that followed reflect a *"política del orden urbano"*[11] that was part of a larger, island-wide effort to better regulate the crown's colonial subjects amid the changing landscape that the age of revolution in the Atlantic produced in Cuba.[12]

The fire of 1828 and colonial attempts to regulate the extramuros came at the heels of social, political, and demographic changes. These forced colonial officials and residents to consider land development to the west of the walls in earnest. A new system of defense had displaced old militarization efforts but in the process had also exacerbated existing land scarcity problems and urban density. By the early nineteenth-century, the expansion of large-scale sugar cultivation and the growth of commerce and industry created lucrative business opportunities that in turn facilitated public works projects within the city and its surrounding areas. Sugar profits, for example, had already begun to finance construction of a distinctly Cuban architecture (the first that the city had seen) and helped Havana shed its designation as a colonial outpost designed to increase the wealth of Spain. While it would be a mistake to think that sugar, like militarization, provided the impetus for urban change, neither can its significance be ignored. From the port in Havana, sugar exportation more than quadrupled between 1786 and 1822, the formative years in which land-use patterns around the city underwent their most drastic transformation.[13]

Militarization, sugar, tobacco, and slave trading coalesced to constitute the urban landscape and mark the political topography of the city. This was a racialized process revealed through the built environment, the land tenure process, and shifting colonial policy and municipal governance. By 1810, the barrio of Jesús María had expanded to contain approximately 11,600 residents, making it the second-largest barrio of the extramuros, second only to the barrio of La Salud, the original and largest enclave outside the city walls.[14] In this emerging nineteenth-century context, land was still at a premium. Not only did the walls now encumber expansion and growth, but they were also at odds with the earlier directive that urged Havana residents to think of the city as a single entity. By 1811, only four years after the crown had declared both areas of the city (intramuros and extramuros) a single corporate entity, talk of demolition began to fill cabildo meetings.

Prior to the first decades of the nineteenth century, colonial city plans had largely erased extramuro spaces (and subjects) from the colonial grid. Unless they were nautical maps that privileged areas of the bay or military maps that focused on coasts, military structures, and fortification, the extramuros was largely expunged, with many of its living areas bereft of representation. After unification, however, extramural spaces and residents were rendered hyper-visible through topographic plans and the planning efforts and urbanization projects that spanned both areas of Havana.[15] New roads and paseos criss-crossed the urban body and inscribed a new Cuba upon the nineteenth-century landscape. The production of the modern, nineteenth-century city hinged on the administration's ability to implement the legal ordinances and spatial practices that governed the conduct and daily lives of residents. This was not, however, a one-sided project: Havana residents embraced the production of a new topography, moving through its spaces and politically imagining the city through cultural forms and expressions.

MIGUEL TACÓN: URBAN ORDER IN HAVANA

The early part of the nineteenth century coincided with the expansion of colonial record keeping and census taking. Between 1818 and 1868, meticulous records of the island's residents emerged to fill notarial pages. *Padrones* (municipal rolls), census records, statistics, and maps carefully recorded individual areas of the country and its residents.[16] This golden age of careful notation allowed the colonial government to regulate and more carefully extend its authority over different areas of life in the capital city. While the increase in record keeping had to do with the growth of the sciences in Europe, it was put to use in a decidedly advantageous way for the crown in the Americas; just as the first-ever census on the peninsula had carefully noted the number of Jews, moriscos, and conversos in an age when persecution was at its height, record keeping in Cuba was similarly used to keep track of individuals. The data accumulated drew for officials a careful picture of where and how the city and its residents expanded; it constituted a governing practice in which bodies, territories, and their regulation were central to the constitution of subjects and topographies.

The nineteenth-century unification of Havana also coincided with the era of Cuba's quintessential writers, thinkers, and philosophers. Many of them were criollos, and many made their residence in Havana. Men like José Antonio Saco (1797–1879) and Domingo del Monte (1804–1853) in the field of philosophy expounded on questions of contemporary concern. In the arts, Hippolyte Garneray (1787–1858) and Víctor Patricio Landaluze (1830–1889) emerged to document and visually illustrate the city and island. In the literary arts, Plácido (1809–1844), Cirilo Villaverde (1812–1894), and José María Heredia (1803–1839) all articulated an overarching "Cuban condition" that pitted the sugar and urban oligarchies alongside an urban rhetoric of expansion and development. It was in this context that the intramuros became the primary focus of the administration's attention under the direction of Captain General Miguel Tacón (1834–1838). Despite the shifting designation of intramuros and extramuros, it remained the area of residence for military and government officials. By 1834, however, many of its residents were fleeing into the "wide-open spaces" of the extramuros. Responding to this resident flight, Tacón openly criticized the trend toward extramuro migration. To counter it, three new buildings were constructed to house military and government officials within the walled city, thereby ensuring that the center of colonial authority would be kept intact.[17]

The push to *modernize* the city differentiated Tacón's approach to Havana from that of his predecessors; whereas the Marqués de la Torre had sought to beautify the city, Tacón worked to bring the area up to newly emerging standards of urbanization. Modernization became a defining ideology of the city from the transoceanic foundations of early European modernity. In the initial stages of contact, Havana constituted European modernity through the differentiated landscapes of the Caribbean that it helped produce, and the walls were an integral part of this process. The institutions of the city that governed and regulated urban life did so in contrast to the surrounding landscape and the emerging concerns with slavery and competition, and the walls helped assuage the conditions and fears that resulted from both. Modernization, on the other hand, was the transformative process produced by modernity, and it tied Havana to the expectations of urbanization.

With modernization measured in Western, U.S. terms, Tacón proceeded to tackle the issues of hygiene and sanitation as two of the most important components of modernization. His administration implemented a new trash collection schedule to deter residents from dumping their waste outdoors. The open-air markets and slaughterhouses of the city, responsible for much of the perishable waste in Havana, were also now the subject of newly proposed legislation. Slaughterhouses were made to comply with the new legislation, and "slaughterhouse experts" were brought in from the United States to provide hygiene consultations. New, more hygienic and efficient markets were created, including those of Cristina, Santo Cristo, and the famous Plaza de Tacón. In the last, all private vendors were grouped under a single market and forced to rent their space from the city, thus allowing the colonial administration to more easily regulate the vendors and extract a tidy profit for colonial coffers in the process.[18] Whereas the *mercados* (markets) of the intramuros had produced a revenue of about 8,712 pesos annually prior to 1834, these now provided the administration with a "liquid rent" of 45,900 pesos.[19] As an added bonus, the city retained rights to the land that the mercado operated on.

Other public and "necessary" buildings also came under colonial oversight. The two principal hospitals, the San Juan de Dios and the San Ambrosio military hospital, had long been a source of concern for colonial authorities because of the danger of infection. The San Juan de Dios provided little refuge for the city's poorest residents. In a report to the Tacón administration, Dr. Beltrán, one of Havana's public doctors, enumerated the conditions of the institution, including in his long list of complaints a lack of beds, overcrowding, poor staffing, and bad ventilation, which yearly contributed to the spread of disease within the hospital and posed a threat of the spread of infection outside it. During a meeting of the Real Junta Superior de Medicina y Cirugía (Royal Assembly of Medicine and Surgery) the year following Dr. Beltrán's account, the Tacón administration enacted hygiene measures to alleviate the problem, reducing the number of deaths by nearly 50 percent during the span of four years.[20]

Tacón's concern with hygiene had several infrastructural effects that brought the city more closely in line with urbanization and modernization standards. Intramuro streets were in deplorable condition, and many still lacked the paving that was increasingly common in the built areas of the extramuros. This meant that each year after the season's first rains, a mixture of mud and rock would be carried away from the city and into the harbor, and authorities were becoming concerned that the yearly debris would accumulate at the bottom of the harbor and hinder the flow of ships into the port. A more immediate concern, however, revolved around what the condition of streets would mean for the city and its residents. Mud and water collected each season in individual streets and often flooded them, a condition that was exacerbated by poor residential drainage systems (which often overflowed directly into city streets). The lack of sewers resulted in health hazards as raw sewage and bacteria accumulated and residents who traveled on foot were forced to wade in the filthy water.[21] To correct these and other conditions, the director of the newly created engineering corps, Félix Lemaur, was hired to oversee the building of a sewer system and the paving of streets in both the intramuros and the extramuros. At the end of the project, 3,270 varas of sewers had been constructed, and the administration had spent over one hundred thousand pesos for the project. Havana residents contributed approximately sixteen thousand pesos to the effort in the form of taxes. The result of these and other measures was a reduction of 16 percent in the number of deaths caused by bacterial illnesses in and around the city between 1835 and 1837.

Urban density and its consequences were also sources of concern. To combat the daily congestion of carriages on the southern side of the city, the administration installed a new gate leading to the paseos of the extramuros. The measure did more than effectively control traffic. A new promenade, the Paseo de Tacón (also known as Paseo Militar, Avenida de Carlos III, and Avenida de la Independencia), had been inaugurated in 1836 to provide intramuro residents with an area in which they could "breathe in the clean and pure air of the countryside" without traveling too far outside the capital city. The site also served as a foil to criollo spaces. The new paseo represented, according to Tacón, the transformation of a space that had been previously *"pintoresco"* (picturesque, or full of local color) into one that would harmoniously become part of a new urban landscape. Instead of providing residents with a rural respite from the city, as in the previous era, the new paseo was built to incorporate the green space that one might enjoy in the Cuban countryside with the added bonuses of modern decorations such as fountains and plazas. The Paseo de Tacón also functioned as a practical means of communication between the intramuros and the military fort at the Castillo del Príncipe, thus reinforcing the old connection between the administration and militarization.

Old ideologies still organized areas of the built environment, and new construction projects continued to highlight the importance of controlling resident mobility: it was the paseos and roads that now defined the outline of the city and forecasted its trajectory. To be sure, the Paseo de Tacón represented a significant step in developing the extramuros. Its importance, however, also lay in the fact that it forced the development of the marshland that surrounded it in order to provide access to city residents. The paseo and land development around it established the blueprint for nineteenth-century (and, arguably, twentieth-century) Havana. On a symbolic level, too, the project was an important one. The paseos of decades prior had reinforced the perimeter of the walled city and mimicked its enclosure, flowing as they did in the same direction as the city walls. By contrast, the Paseo de Tacón directed traffic directly into the extramuros. The importance of both these points cannot be overstated. What we see emerge with the first is construction of an urban infrastructure that would reinforce the land patterns of previous centuries. What emerged with Tacón, by contrast, was a new trajectory for the city. Where once the Spanish administration looked exclusively inward or to the Atlantic to chart and develop a space of civilization, Tacón looked outward and away from the colonial core, toward the extramuros and beyond, to create a modern, urban space.

As the old markers of distinction slowly eroded or otherwise became obsolete, new ways to designate areas of the city emerged around the idea—and, increasingly, the reality—of mobility. The 1837 building ordinances came on the heels of the infrastructural and symbolic changes that defined the Havana of Miguel Tacón. Composed of 467 articles, the ordinances were the first body of laws aimed at standardizing both the intramuro city and its extramuro barrios. The ordinances outlined a trajectory of urban development that now revolved around road construction. They established public highways and the infrastructural advancements to sustain them. In order to finance the project, the

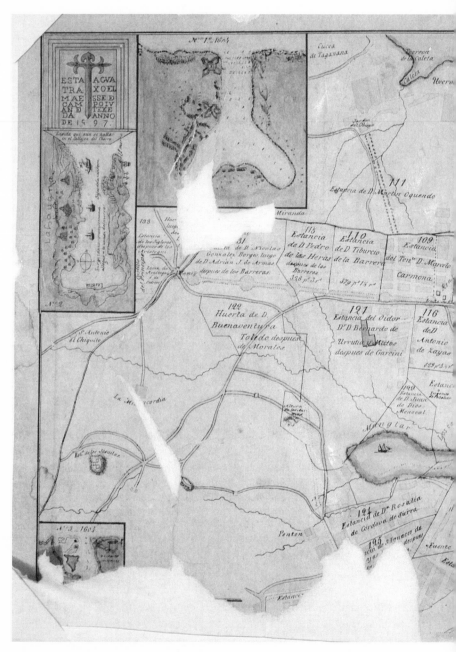

FIGURE 13. *Mapa ilustrativo de la obra titulada "Lo que fuimos y lo que somos,"* 1857. In José María de la Torre, *Lo que fuimos y lo que somos; o, La Habana antigua y moderna* (Havana: Librería "Cervantes").

Mapa ilustrativo de la obra titulada
LO QUE FUIMOS Y LO QUE SOMOS
ó la Habana antigua i moderna
Construido por el autor de la misma
Dn José Ma de la Torre
1857

ordinances also contained a proposal to force the expropriation of land in areas best suited to urban development.

Other innovations in transport and mobility followed. The 1837 introduction of the Cuban railroad united Havana with the nearby town of Bejucal with twenty-eight kilometers of rail and set the stage for future passenger travel.[22] Later, the inauguration of the Ferrocarril Urbano de La Habana in 1857, with animal-powered passenger lines to Carmelo by 1859 and to Cerro and Jesús del Monte by 1862, made communication and travel faster and more efficient. New modes of faster transportation also provided residents in the developing areas of the city outskirts, such as Cerro and El Vedado, with access to the intramuros, thus reinforcing their ability to function as practical and attractive areas for the affluent in the city.

The railroad and streetcar system, however, also had unintended consequences that affected how the city was governed. Between 1827 and 1847, urban growth was defined most of all by the *caseríos* (hamlets) and towns that developed next to steam-powered railway stops.[23] The new populations and unregulated areas that existed alongside more affluent areas did not go unnoticed for very long. In 1839, Cuban intellectual Tranquilino Sandalio de Noda proposed making all unplanned (or upstart) neighborhoods illegal. In 1839, Sandalio himself helped trace the design of new *poblaciones* (settlements), and later, in 1859, these were outlawed when a new measure mandated that all urban sprawl be subject to regulation by the city. New designations also emerged that allowed the administration to recognize and regulate new barrios more efficiently. In 1844, the Comisión de Estadística (Statistics Committee) was created, and it ruled that any grouping of houses under twenty in number would now constitute a "caserío" and that any grouping between twenty and one hundred would be classified as an *aldea* (small village). Anything over one hundred homes all grouped together would be allowed to stand alone as a pueblo.[24] Roads remained an integral part of this urban development. To connect the various zones of the extramuros to the core city, in 1840 large calzadas built by a corps of engineers were introduced.

By the close of the Tacón administration in 1838, government expenditures on public works projects had reached 2,087,520 pesos.[25] Amazingly, the number of square varas of new street that had been laid out reached 173,500. Once the physical and infrastructural changes to the city were completed, Tacón issued a series of decrees aimed at adjusting the behavior of residents to complement the new environment. The administration reissued the *Bandos de buen gobierno*, now enforcing the nightly curfew and stipulating the hour at which residents were required to retire indoors.[26] To ensure compliance with the new city measures, a *cuerpo de serenos* (nightwatchman corps) composed of four brigades was created and dispatched nightly into different barrios. Tacón also assigned a police inspector to each cuartel in Havana and uniformed soldiers to replace what he saw as a corrupt police force under the previous system of comisarios de barrio and *tenientes* created by the Marqués de la Torre. Their specific target were the twelve thousand men *"sin bienes ni ocupación honesta [que] se mantienen en la capital"* (men without means or honest labor that reside in the capital).[27]

The alleged deterioration of the moral character of Cubans—in the form of vagrancy—was also an issue of great concern to the administration. Vagrancy was the scapegoat illustrating the social conditions that prevailed among Cubans and that kept the island from achieving the modernized social advancements sought after and proposed by the colonial government. In Havana especially, such was the concern with moral character that in 1829 the Real Sociedad Económica de Amigos del Pais de la Habana put out a call asking that Cuba's foremost intellectuals address the moral conditions of the island, paying special attention to the issue of vagrancy and how to eradicate it. Cuban intellectual José Antonio Saco answered the call with his essay *La vagancia en Cuba* (1832), in which he used Havana as a case study to examine the root causes of vagrancy as a moral condition, recommending a series of measures to alleviate the problem.[28] Saco concluded that it was the social and cultural institutions of the island that were to blame. Gambling, the state lottery, billiards, dice, and the like, he claimed, all contributed to the cultural impoverishment of the population by leading individuals to a life of vice.

His conclusions are clearly marked by colonial notions of cultural capital, but his recommendations for the eradication of vagrancy convey a specifically urban notion of progress and modernity that also revolved around mobility. In his essay, Saco uses vagrancy to advocate for the construction of public works projects in Havana; he argues that among the principal problems enticing the rural population of Cuba into a life of vice was the lack of urban infrastructure to support the influx of people arriving into the capital city. Specifically, he found that the lack of roads connecting the core city and the Cuban hinterland prevented the rural population from developing the initiative needed to cultivate agricultural products for small-scale production. The lack of markets in which to sell their goods kept *guajiros* (peasants) lethargic and meant that those who did venture into urban areas did so without any means of support. According to Saco, "If there were roads ... many people might occupy themselves with the transport of agriculture, and since the numbers of these would grow with the construction of those [roads], there would necessarily be more employment. If there were roads, the men who did not find comfort in one place, and for which same reason are a burden to society, might relocate quickly and without great cost to another place where they might be offered jobs."[29]

Among the other recommendations proposed by Saco was construction of an orphanage and charity homes that would protect the poor and safeguard residents from vagrants seeking to take advantage of their goodwill. Both institutions already existed in Havana; the Casa de Beneficiencia (1794) oversaw both of these functions for the city when it united with the maternity home in 1852. The only recommendation left for administrators to implement was expansion of the city's infrastructure, something that the Sociedad Patriótica rallied behind.[30] Eventually, his insistence that the colonial government assume responsibility for the social conditions of the island and his political views on slavery would get him into trouble with the administration and force him into exile.[31]

The symbolic extension of colonial law into the newly developed areas of the extramuros soon followed. Most visibly, the jail, which had been situated within the Casa de Gobierno in the intramuros, now stood outside the walls and at the foot of the port. Its renovation and new location meant that it could now house two thousand individuals properly divided along gender, race, and class lines. As in previous eras, inmates were used in work programs, which drastically decreased the cost of public works projects around the city.[32] The new jail was not the only institution relocated to the extramuros. At the urging of medical professionals such as Charles Belot, all new hospitals were to be placed exclusively in the extramuros, with facilities required to undergo routine government inspections, thus relieving the intramuros of at least one reason for its poor hygiene and the rapid spread of disease.[33] The city's insane asylum was also moved to the foot of the Paseo de Extramuros, the area of the extramuros closest to the walled city, which had previously functioned solely as an elite and criollo space of recreation. The insane asylum now stood in view of the promenading crowds, as did the plaza for public executions (although according to official figures, the number of public executions decreased during Tacón's four-year administration). For affluent criollos, the symbolic dimensions of the relocations could not have been lost.

The administration also had recourse to more tangible and less symbolic measures of social control. Tacón reissued the bounty-hunting expeditions. Residents were also encouraged to become active participants in safeguarding public order, with the administration going so far as to encourage them to apprehend criminals and petty thieves.[34] The measures introduced to reduce crime and criminal activity in and around Havana had the desired effect of restoring colonial rule with habaneros, be they criollo or peninsular. When asked about crime and safety in Havana, for example, the Santa Cruz y Montalvo family responded by affirming that only since Tacón had violent crime around the city ceased to exist almost completely, especially crimes in broad daylight.[35]

Writing in the early 1840s, the Countess of Merlin (María de las Mercedes Santa Cruz y Montalvo) urged Captain General Leopoldo O'Donnell to reform the laws that governed the island and develop the symbols that would properly define it as the capital city.[36] The countess, like many of the affluent who resided within the intramuros, had a clear vision of the areas where urban development should take place. She noted that the post-Tacón development of the extramuro barrios of Jesús María and La Salud, where elegant *quintas* (a name that alluded to the Spanish homes of the peninsula) now took the place of *bohíos* (traditional thatched-roof homes made of wood, cane, or straw), gave the city an air of new and "flowering" grandeur.[37] The area immediately west of the walls thus held the potential not only to serve as a temporary respite from the cramped quarters of the intramuros but also to provide a permanent "release" for city residents. Given its proximity to the center of colonial activity and its ability to accommodate affluent criollos increasingly out of place in the cramped colonial center, its value was rapidly increasing. The alamedas and paseos surrounding the city had proven a great success in attracting an affluent crowd away from the dense city center despite the improvement in urban infrastructure that the administration had made. And as outbreaks of yellow fever and malaria continued to escalate at alarming rates, intramuro residents increasingly looked outward to find a clean, "pure" area to reside in. In the letters that the Countess of Merlin sent to Paris, she describes the intramuros as a space from which residents were forced to seek respite in the "clean air of the countryside."[38] Her views were shared by the likes of Alexander von Humboldt and Cirilo Villaverde. The move to depict the area outside the walls as laden with a pastoral tranquility in stark contrast to the intramuros is poignantly illustrated through the many descriptions of the city.

In the work of the Cuban writer Cirilo Villaverde, the juxtaposition of urban and rural illustrates the changing view of the intramuros. In his masterpiece novel *Cecilia Valdés,* Villaverde associates the *zonas campestres* (rustic zones) with the peripheral character of Isabel, the sweet, virginal criolla in whom redemption from the impurity of the city and its vices may be found.[39] Isabel is the prototype from which criollos drew the noble guajiro as a symbol of Cuban difference from Spain. Ironically, habaneros' experience with the guajiros who showed up in Havana from nearby rural areas was anything but harmonious. But Isabel's character was nonetheless an important symbol of a burgeoning Cuban identity forged away from dense urban centers.

It was not simply an affinity for "nature" that attracted Villaverde to the Cuban countryside, but rather the association of the intramuros with a colonial administration already out of favor in the rest of the Americas. Between the intramuros and the Cuban hinterland, Villaverde crafted the character of Cecilia Valdés. Cecilia, the protagonist for whom the novel is entitled, resides in a markedly different space than the intramuros and extramuros. She is the *mulata* who belongs to neither area but travels freely between the colonial center and the urban periphery. She represents a third and liminal space akin to the parallel cities of Havana's intramuros and extramuros.[40] As a mediating zone, this third space is neither Spanish nor colonial, neither urban nor rural, but rather one forged in the in-between spaces outside of the city but *within* the empire.

SOCIAL CONTROL

The mid-nineteenth-century trend toward social control and urban regulation was in part a reaction to new concerns arising from the growth in the social position and political inclusion of once-excluded colonial subjects. The demographic composition of the city had changed drastically from the era when military concerns predominated. When Miguel Tacón transferred his duties to the new administration of Joaquín Ezpeleta in 1838, he mentioned the organization of the city only with respect to its demographics, noting the peninsular and criollo enclaves and the rural character of the people who now lived far into the extramuros.[41]

Since the 1762 British occupation of the city, the revolt in Saint-Domingue, and the expansion of sugar production, Cuba had undergone significant demographic changes. As the production of sugar expanded, so too did the number of slaves imported.[42] The demographic impact was such that as the white population showed a steady decline as a percentage of the total population between 1774 and 1827 (from 56 percent of the population in 1774 to 44 percent in 1827), the proportion of the enslaved population increased markedly (from 26 percent in 1774 to 41 percent in 1827).[43] From 1827 onward, however, the racial balance in Cuba once again shifted as whites regained a racial majority on the island, increasing slightly to 47 percent of the population by 1846 and to 57 percent by 1861. Notably, the gain occurred at the same time that the enslaved population was decreasing in relative proportion to that of whites and, significantly, during the same time that the free black population, for the first time in Cuba, showed a steady and sustainable increase.

The increase in a free African-descended population preceded a momentous phenomenon in the history of Cuba: the gradual decline of the institution of slavery that took place from the mid-nineteenth century onward. On sugar estates, where slavery was heavily concentrated, the disintegration of the institution was visible in the variety of workers employed; there were slaves, "paid" slaves contracted out either by their owners or on their own volition, and employed free blacks, whites, and Chinese laborers.[44] Urban slavery similarly showed visible signs of decline. In cities throughout Cuba, a black bourgeoisie developed with access to power and capital. In Havana, for example, free blacks who were able to accumulate substantial amounts of wealth were not uncommon; in 1828, José Oñoro was a foreman on the docks and the owner of four homes in Havana and eight slaves. Similarly, José Agustín Ceballos, also of Havana, was in charge of 160 workers and owned his own business transporting goods (an enterprise facilitated by the advent of the railroad). He also owned his own home and seven slaves. Félix Barbosa was the successful owner of a funeral home in Havana. When he married, his fiancée brought with her a dowry of five thousand pesos, plus a home and numerous slaves, thereby substantially increasing Barbosa's wealth.[45] By 1844, the number of people of color in Havana who could be counted among the black bourgeoisie had increased markedly. Slaves, on the other hand, were becoming an increasingly valued commodity in both urban and rural areas; as the trade and institution showed signs of decline, the price of slaves increased, from 400 pesos in 1820 to 600 and even 700 pesos in 1850.[46]

While the effects of demographic changes were most dramatically felt in the sugar-producing areas of the island, urban areas were also affected by the swift demographic changes and the growth in the number of African-descended people on the island. By 1825, for example,

28 percent of the enslaved population of Cuba lived in cities; by 1855, they constituted 42 percent of the adult labor force of Cuba's urban areas.[47] In Havana alone, four thousand slaves labored in the cigar factories of the city, while another four hundred worked as skilled laborers in trades and as artisans.[48] And as the number of Africans and their descendants increased as the institution of slavery declined, the proportional number of the free black population in urban areas also increased. Such was the rise in number that the colonial administration in Havana, like city residents themselves, was forced to grapple with the social position of blacks, both enslaved and free, and to respond to *black* criollo claims for access to city space and resources.[49] The old colonial concerns of the previous century, such as poverty, vagrancy, and the menace stemming from rural and extramural areas beyond Havana, were still a concern. However, these concerns were now compounded by the visible threat that black criollos (more so than slaves) posed to the social order that had been so carefully instituted in the Havana of Miguel Tacón.

The overall stagnation of slavery, the increase in the monetary value of slaves, and the rise of an upwardly mobile black population did not immediately affect social categories. It was not until the 1842 *Bando de gobernación y policía de la Isla de Cuba* was approved that social categories in Havana became subject to scrutiny and redefinition. Until then, the trend toward order and standardization was most visible in the regulation of Havana's physical environment; the number of hectares approved for urbanization, for example, by 1850 had surpassed the number approved in the entire century preceding it. By 1842, however, at the suggestion of Captain General Gerónimo Valdés, a new set of government regulations was published by the colonial government. The *Bando de gobernación* introduced new measures not only relating to the modernization of the island (such as public order, health, hygiene, and public safety) but also dictating activities in the private lives of Cubans.[50] Religious observance (including the activities that could and could not be undertaken on Sundays), public morality, and, especially, entertainment all fell under new colonial scrutiny.[51]

The *Bando de gobernación* addressed the old problems that threatened social order (poverty, vagrancy, and the extramuros) before moving on to preempt the threat posed by the upwardly mobile black population of the city. Local enforcement of the new measures became the responsibility of the comisarios de barrio and *capitanes de seguridad* (security captains), who were in charge of individual districts within Havana and its barrios extramuros. Ensuring security in Havana's living areas was especially important. Comisarios regulated housing by compiling censuses for the district to which they were assigned. When new residents arrived they were responsible for reporting to the comisario within a twenty-four-hour period. When household numbers increased or decreased by either birth or death, residents were also required to report the change. Failure to do so resulted in a fine of four pesos levied upon vecinos. Landlords were also responsible for reporting the names of new tenants or else be fined four pesos. Owners of lodging houses were to provide the comisarios with a list of their clientele on a nightly basis, including the name, profession, and nationality of each lodger, or else suffer the higher fine of ten pesos.[52] Under a special article, those who rented rooms to blacks were advised to pay special attention to legal status and permits to ensure that these were not forgeries.[53]

The effort to track the composition of each barrio disproportionately affected the living spaces of impoverished Cubans. Subletting, for example, was grounds for immediate eviction, whether the renter had sublet the entire property or was merely renting a spare bedroom for extra income. Landlords' rights were reasserted throughout the new ordinances, giving them the ability to evict any tenant immediately after a second missed rental payment or when a tenant made *"mal uso físico o moral"* (ill use, physical or moral) of the property. Landlords and their properties were also protected from squatters, an issue still of concern in urban areas.[54] Furthermore, *ciudadelas* and *casas de vecindad* (low-income and high-density dwellings) specially set up for the urban poor were subject to even more stringent regulation. Owners were required to keep the inner portion of their buildings well lit at all times. The lanterns to be used for this purpose were to be maintained on the inner side of building doors (and thus inaccessible to the passerby) and were required to give enough light so that "from the street may be visible all that happens within, to be prorated by the residents of the rooms."[55]

Other means of control involved assigning certain activities to specific areas of the city. On the calzadas of Monte, San Lázaro, Luyanó, and Reina, *"tiendas, posadas y tabernas"* (stores, lodging houses, and taverns) were allowed to remain open until midnight instead of being subject to the 11:00 P.M. curfew imposed on these establishments throughout the rest of the city. They were allowed to reopen at 2:00 A.M.[56] Not only did the lax regulations provide colonial officials with a way of policing areas of the city over which they would have otherwise had little control, but they also directed "activities of the night" to these barrios and away from other, more exclusive areas. Other measures were more specifically aimed at deterring the impoverished from settling in the capital city. A prohibition against guano, wood, and straw houses was once again asserted, this time at the threat of a one-hundred-peso fine and immediate demolition. For Havana specifically, the area bordered by the Casa de Beneficiencia, Belascoain, Puente de Chaves, and the canal and extending to the harbor was designated as the limit of the Havana población, within which the guano, wood, and straw homes were prohibited and any structures deemed to be *insalubres* (unhygienic) would not be allowed to remain.[57]

Any plot of land on which a building was demolished for violating the *Bando de gobernación,* if it could not be rebuilt by its owner in accordance with the regulations, would be forcibly sold to whoever was able to properly rebuild. Furthermore, any structure planned in urban areas had to have been previously approved by the *comisarios de ayuntamiento* (municipal deputies) and the *comisarios de obras públicas* (public works deputies).[58] The *bando* (proclamation) thus ensured that the homes of the impoverished within key areas of Havana would be demolished, paving the way for structures that more accurately reflected a colonial and ideal vision of the city. Other measures were passed to ensure the permanence, safety, and livability of proper urban spaces. Residents were required to contribute to a fund to maintain the night watchmen's corps and the firefighters' corps in order to avoid the fires that had destroyed the barrio of Jesús María less than two decades earlier.[59] An alert system was also devised, and residents of neighboring barrios were required to join in the relief should their help be necessary to contain the flames.

Much like private dwelling spaces, open and public spaces also came under increased scrutiny. Affluent criollos in the extramuros became the specific targets of social control. Strict regulation of the paseos provided residents with a model of acceptable behavior on the nightly walks. Article 49 of the *Bando de gobernación,* for example, specified the activities allowed on the paseos of Havana and the personal conduct of strollers. The *Bando de gobernación* prohibited any person from taking a stroll *"sin farol"* (without a lantern) in urban areas. All, that is, except those individuals *"de gerarquía y distinción"* (of hierarchy and distinction), a definition that was left to the discretion of city officials and local comisarios to determine.[60] While the qualifying characteristics may have been open to interpretation, certain peoples and occupations were specifically written out of this category. Black residents, for example, were subject to the nightly curfews. Access to city space was similarly limited for members of other groups. Street vendors not only were required to obtain permission from the city council to sell their wares but also were forced to seek permission from comisarios and capitanes before they were allowed to change residences, making it easier for city officials to control the social demographics of each neighborhood.[61] Under Article 85 of the new ordinances, lifestyles contributing to the impoverishment of urban space, such as vagrancy and begging, were strictly prohibited.[62] The article went on to authorize residents to arrest beggars and deliver them to their respective comisario, who would then hand them over to the Casa de Beneficiencia.

Mobility in the form of traffic (both pedestrian and otherwise) was thus once again the subject of vigilance and regulation. Volantes and *quitrines*[63] utilizing the promenades after dark (when it was customary to do so in order to avoid the heat of the day) were required to keep the top portions of their vehicles open so that all passengers were visible.[64] The article also set the rental price of volantes at four reales per hour or else per trip around the paseo.[65] On the Paseo de Isabel II, specifically, the *Bando de gobernación* stipulated the order in which vehicles should enter the paseo. The street closest to la muralla served as the street used to access the road, whereas the new calzadas provided an exit.[66] The traffic that entered the city from the countryside was to do so only through the gates at Tierra and Arsenal, on the west and southwest sides of the city. An additional gate, at La Punta, could be used by all other traffic.[67] Deterring rural traffic to the west and southwest of the city meant that the barrios adjacent to this side of la muralla (such as Jesús María) would experience the full congestion of the rural traffic. The population of Havana residing away from these barrios, such as in the old colonial core, would be spared the noise, clatter, and smell of the traffic.

As its name suggests, the *Bando de gobernación* dealt specifically with governance. Control of changing demographics on the island as a whole and in Havana specifically became one of the ordinances' primary goals. Decades later, political concerns over the power of criollos would underpin the administration's actions in Havana, but at this earlier juncture officials channeled concern with the island's changing demographics into a concern with black criollos who were either born free or manumitted. In public spaces especially, colonial administrators were vigilant. Employers (or slave owners) had to register the names, addresses, and legal status of the black men and women who used the promenades, along with the number of the volante in which they drove or sat, or else suffer a fine of twenty pesos.[68]

Many of the "public order" articles of the *Bando de gobernación* register a mid-nineteenth-century concern with the opportunities for both the upward mobility and social freedom that had historically existed in Havana for black residents. Both posed potential problems for the administration, though for different reasons. Article 87 of the bando expelled black cabildos outside the walled city, warning comisarios to be especially vigilant of the homes in which members resided. *Cabildos de nación* were black mutual aid societies active in Cuba since the middle of the sixteenth century, when the associations' membership revolved around ethnic affiliations and identities (either real or imagined). By the middle of the nineteenth century, the organizations functioned as social aid clubs and put on elaborate and visible celebrations during feast days and other holidays.[69] The *Bando de gobernación* limited cabildo celebrations to Sundays and special feast days. And under no circumstances were members to venture out into the city dressed in attire that marked them as *negros de nación* (African-born blacks, usually enslaved), or the cabildo itself would be fined the sum of ten pesos. Furthermore, any parts of the cabildo's costume that could be used as weapons—namely sticks, spurs, or machetes—were strictly prohibited.[70] The regulation on celebration and dress divested members of the most significant markers of cabildo identity. Whereas in rural areas ethnic clubs would be suppressed for their potential threat of insurrection, in Havana these were encouraged—within acceptable limits—as part of a larger effort to control the black population.

Popular representations of black Cubans during the mid-nineteenth century typically fell into one of two extremes.[71] As in the illustration by Fréderic Mialhe, blacks either were depicted as socially outside an urban public sphere or were featured in positions in which their social threat was neutralized. Men depicted on the paseos of Havana, for example, were often enslaved or else the servants employed as the drivers of volantes, appropriately attired in dress befitting modern Cubans. In Hippolyte Garneray's nineteenth-century illustration *Vista del paseo extramuros de La Habana,* black representation is similarly regulated, with slave and servant (in this case, as the volanate driver) providing the only two spaces of representation. The ordinances of the *Bando de gobernación* thus correlate with the representation in Garneray's and Mialhe's illustrations. In a more concrete fashion, together they suggest an acceptable form of social blackness that provided the African-descended with the only strategy for entering (both literally and symbolically) the walled city of Havana.

Through the administration's 1855 *Ordenanzas municipales de la ciudad de La Habana,* Havana was divided into six districts.[72] The six dis-

FIGURE 14. Fréderic Mialhe, *Día de reyes*, 1853. Courtesy of
HistoryMiami Archives and Research Center, Miami, Florida.

tricts and their respective areas organized areas of the city in both the
intramuros and the extramuros. Many of the measures stipulated in
the municipal ordinances rearticulated the measures already in effect
for Cuba. Others, however, imposed new restrictions upon the city and
especially the free black population. Attire, for example, was once again
made a particularly important marker for delineating social class. However, the municipal ordinances approached the issue differently than
had the *Bando de gobernación*. In the bando, the emphasis was on
black Cubans as cultural others (as in Mialhe's illustration) or else as
belonging, as the term *negro de nación* suggests, to an African instead of
a Cuban public sphere. In the 1855 municipal ordinances of Havana,
however, the emphasis on dress revolved around punishing "whoever
uses dress belonging to ... another class or category other than his
own," who for this offense would "pay from five to ten pesos' fine and
[would] be subject to prosecution if the object of the costume should be
criminal in nature."[73] For colonial officials who deliberated over the
ordinances for well over a year, the emphasis lay in criminalizing not
what stood out as other but rather that which attempted to impersonate
the *familiar* and which thus fell outside the two polar extremes represented in popular depictions. The municipal ordinances also more strictly
regulated the space and movement of black Cubans. Not only were
cabildos still excluded from the walled city, but, under Article 65, they
were only allowed to reside in homes outside the walls that had been
specifically designated as cabildo residences by the governor of Havana.

Failure to comply would again result in a fine of up to five pesos and immediate eviction.[74]

Black Havana residents who aspired to upward social and economic mobility found their opportunities significantly restricted by the new ordinances. Among the more coveted jobs in Havana was employment on the docks. Through these jobs men could increase their pay and status by rising to the level of foremen. Joining the colonial militia as well provided social and economic opportunities. Both opportunities, however, were severely restricted after the 1842 bando, which outlawed the service of blacks in the military and imposed new restriction for black employment in the port.[75]

Despite the more rigid control of space and people implemented by the municipal ordinances, in 1861 another legislative measure was passed. The *Ordenanzas de construcción*, like the municipal ordinances before them, were aimed at filling the gaps left in the previous legislative measures. In this case, once the municipal ordinances were in effect, the city government decided that only by regulating the urban environment could the project of properly creating a cohesive city be carried out. The intended effect of the ordinances, according to Governor Antonio Mantilla, was to inform the population of the urban *"medianerías y servidumbres"* and to familiarize individuals with their rights and responsibilities as members of the legal urban body.[76] The stated goal of the Construction Ordinances of 1861 was to achieve the following:

> A concentration of population: its boundaries [of the población] will be standardized; isolated constructions will not extend to far points or those not meant to be settled; the numerous vacant lots in attractive locations will be built upon; the regulations of the public police will be better carried out, and all this without contradicting, as truly progressive it may be, the tendency to expand the population, and not restrict the right to build new neighborhoods for those who have a rigorously legitimate right to do so, and have put together the means and resources under the new conditions of projects of such importance.[77]

The Construction Ordinances of 1861 addressed all aspects of public works projects and the physical environment, from major issues such as construction of public and private buildings and the standardization of streets and sidewalks to more practical aspects such as the institution and standardization of proper measurements for walls and windowsills, as well as mundane issues such as the proper lighting of private homes. Furthermore, they emphasized the need to concentrate on the unification of the two Havanas into one single modern body. To achieve this goal, the ordinances used the ideas embedded in the compendium of laws governing the capital cities of the United States and western Europe. They were meant to endow the municipal government of Havana with a similar ability for regulating urban growth and the city's existing population.[78]

In October 1859, the administration issued a royal decree creating a corps of municipal architects in all the major cities. By the time the Construction Ordinances of 1861 were passed, the architects no longer served as merely an advisory corps to the governor and city council. At this later date, they labored beneath their own regulations, the *Reglamento para los arquitectos municipales de La Habana* (regulations for municipal architects of Havana) in order to ensure full compliance with the Construction Ordinances of 1861. Henceforth, it was the corps of municipal architects who were in charge of demarcating the lines of solares and dividing those that were ready for construction; most importantly, they were also in charge of setting the price of urban lots for sale in Havana. They were required to live within the city and perform their duties at a salary of three thousand pesos annually.[79] Passage of the Construction Ordinances of 1861 and the professionalization of architecture that went along with it was the final step necessary in preparing the city for unification.

The significance of the legislative measures lay not only in the potential effects that they exercised over the landscape of the city but also in the fact that they appeared to seal off any alternate modes of urban possibilities between 1842 and 1862. Not surprisingly, problems associated with rapid urbanization were staunchly criminalized under the drive for social control. Vagrancy provides an example of this. While Saco had once recommended social reforms to treat beggars and vagrants, after the new legislative measures passed, "treatment" was exchanged for criminalization. In 1844, a census was taken of all free black men in Cuba who could not provide proof of residence, employment, or other means of livelihood. These men were to be brought in front of a vagrancy tribunal and sentenced as criminals.[80] In 1857, under the direction of Captain General José de la Concha, vagrancy was further criminalized with the construction of two correctional facilities, one in each department of Cuba, built especially for the purpose.[81]

Respite from the concentration of government control nonetheless existed within the tightly regulated confines of urban areas, Havana included. Celebrated Cuban anthropologist Fernando Ortiz conducted extensive ethnographic work on what he termed *"el hampa afrocubana,"* or the underworld of a sector of the free black population. In *Los negros curros,* Ortiz describes the evolution of a specifically urban subculture that flourished in Havana from the late 1830s through the middle of the nineteenth century, whose members were commonly referred to as *negros curros.*[82] While not part of the criminal underworld that Ortiz would go on to later describe in *Los negros brujos,*[83] they nonetheless posed a threat to social categories in Havana. The fact that they did not conform to the polar extremes in popular representations of blacks in Havana (such as in Mialhe's or Garneray's portrayals) meant that they existed in a space beyond the social control of the legislation being passed. These spaces were confined to areas of the city previously discussed as the working-class enclaves located outside las murallas: Jesús María, Regla, and Guanabacoa.

In *Los negros curros,* Ortiz situates curro subculture in historical perspective by locating it within the national developments of Cuba. That is, he sees the evolution of a black underworld as a response to colonial rule and the mid-nineteenth-century expansion of the institution of slavery. This position allows Ortiz to argue that the defining characteristic of the curro was precisely his free and urban status, developed as a foil to his enslaved counterpart, who was more rigidly controlled by the colonial government in rural areas of the country. According to Ortiz, "el hampa" in Havana thus constituted a free space for African-descended Cubans that was somewhat akin to the cimarron enclaves of rural areas.

Documentation suggests that the evolution of the curro had local roots. The urban subculture referenced by Ortiz was one specific to Havana and one not easily replicated in other towns and cities throughout Cuba. The signifiers of curros' class, as well, were ones unique to the city and specifically addressed by the municipal ordinances. When these forbade individuals to dress outside their class, they directly affected the population of curros, for whom attire blending "African" and "Spanish" clothing was the primary marker of status. The purpose behind their attire was to both emulate and draw a difference from urban whites. In the visual representation of the curro, however, what is accentuated is not the curro's ability to emulate white habaneros but rather the outrageousness of his attempt to do so.[84] The representation of his character in Victor Landaluze's print *Los curros negros* may well have been part of the response to the negro curro, who, while inhabiting a socially marginal space, was nonetheless a black criollo first and foremost and thus a figure endowed with the legal rights afforded to all vassals of the crown and residents of the city and who was furthermore divorced from any association with the institution of slavery. While his presence may have constituted an affront to the larger colonial structure in light of the institution of slavery, the evolution of his character in the urban public sphere also reflects a concern with the upward mobility and social class of the free African-descended population in Havana. Even after the curro "disappeared" from the landscape, he remained an active character in popular culture and representation.

Black representation in Havana, beginning with the curro and culminating with the Cuban *teatro bufo*,[85] illustrates the process through which blackface and blackvoice performance served the popular function of socially excising upwardly mobile African-descended people from the urban public sphere. Theater scholar Line Real describes the Cuban concept of *choteo*, a process of ridicule that achieves its goal by inverting social hierarchies, as an integral component of blackface, and specifically bufo, performances in Cuba.[86] The parody of blackness, however, did not prohibit the redefinition of black identity. Rather, the image communicated was shaped and molded not only by its representation but also by the audience's expectations.[87] For blackface performance in Havana, the audience's expectations evolved from its initial portrayal in the 1830s to the latter stages of the bufo in 1868, the same time period during which the city was undergoing a legislative drive for urban order. At the same time that writers and audiences were working through the drive for social control in the city, they were also molding a representation of blackness that, while not meant to be a "true" depiction, was shaped by the shift in what city residents would have recognized as acceptable "black" behavior.

The defining episode of the bufo stands as an illustration of how this process worked. During the summer of 1869 at the Teatro Villanueva in Havana, a diverse group of theatergoers were gathered for a blackface performance of *Los negros catedráticos* (The black professors). One of the actors broke from the script and during the performance shouted "long live the land of sugar" into the audience, a statement that was inflammatory because of its improvisational nature and the space in which it was shouted. Theater performances required approval from the colonial censors, and improvisation was strictly prohibited by both the *Bando de gobernación* and the municipal ordinances. To make matters worse, the audience responded with a shout of "¡que viva Cuba libre!" The incident escalated inside the Villanueva until the colonial guard, also present at the performance and provoked by the demonstration, opened fire upon the crowd and wounded several of the audience members. Albeit not about race, the incident demonstrates the symbiosis present in the forging of social meaning in the bufo. The 1869 incident is also important because it marked a pivotal event for the history of the bufo, effectively transforming the genre into a pro-independence cultural expression and divorcing it from the local, urban context that had created it. In the literature that surrounds not only the bufo but also black representation in mid-nineteenth-century Cuba, the incident at the Villanueva has served to solidify the relationship between the theater and the growing momentum of the independence movement.[88] The emergence of a criollo literary movement that supported the idea of independence but expressed concern with the potential displacement of racial categories further reinforced this correlation.[89]

In the blackface and blackvoice genre from which the characters of the bufo emerged, "working through" the potential displacement of race involved articulating and rearticulating the markers of nineteenth-century conceptions of race itself. The process began by revisiting the characteristics developed during the expansion of the slave trade that came to define racial and ethnic difference among enslaved people in Cuba. In representations of blackness, categories were defined significantly by the linguistic characteristics of black Cubans. At the bottom of the racial hierarchy was the *negro bozal*, a slave whose description can be found in the first edition of Esteban Pichardo's *Provincial Dictionary of Cuban Voices and Phrases*, published in 1836. In it, Pichardo describes a bozal as someone recently arrived from Africa and distinguished by the following linguistic pattern: "a disfigured Castilian, without numerical agreement or conjugation, without hard R sounds, S or D endings, frequently exchanging double Ls for Ñ, the E for the I, the B for the V, etc.: a jargon made increasingly confused the more recent his immigration."[90]

By the time the third and final edition of the *Provincial Dictionary* was published in 1875, almost forty years after the original, the emphasis on linguistic assimilation in the definition of a bozal had disappeared. At this later date, the term indicated a foreign rather than a specifically black identity and included recent Chinese immigrants.[91] The replacement of black Cubans by "foreigners" occurred after the first war of independence. This suggests that it was the growing momentum of the independence movement, in which black Cubans occupied an integral position, that affected racial markers. As the possibility of independence became a reality, the onstage representations of blackness underwent a shift that mirrored the transformation of Pichardo's category. But in its representation during the 1830s and 1840s, blackvoice and blackface drew heavily from Pichardo's initial description of the bozal; that is, the unassimilated slave of rural Cuba.

The transatlantic slave trade and the late abolition of slavery provided habaneros with the initial stock characters from which to draw the negro bozal in blackvoice and blackface. In 1838, one playwright in particular emerged as the defining voice of Cuban satire, popularizing the use of blackvoice before blackface made its debut on the theater stage. Bartolomé Crespo was born and educated in Galicia, Spain, but had followed the waves of Galician immigrants arriving in Cuba during the mid-nineteenth century. Despite his peninsular origins, Crespo was politically sympathetic to the emerging independence movement in Cuba. Upon arrival, he began work as a newspaper columnist at the Havana newspaper *La Prensa,* a serial decisively partial to the separatist struggle.[92] While at *La Prensa,* he published a series of letters and plays under various pseudonyms and soon introduced the "alter ego" that he created in mock imitation of the Cuban bozal. His name was Creto Gangá. The name holds strong allusions to a bozal identity and became his trademark signature in Cuban blackface.[93]

The most famous of Crespo's plays was entitled *Un ajiaco, o La boda de Pancha Jutía y Canuto Raspadura* (A Cuban stew, or the wedding of Pancha Jutía and Canuto Raspadura), which was published in regular installments in *La Prensa* before finally making its theater debut in 1847.[94] The play evolves around the wedding celebration of two slaves. The miscommunication that surrounds the planning of the event is the source of the play's humor, albeit a humor that is contingent upon the audiences' understanding that a bozal—and not just a slave—represents a cultural outsider in the sphere of Cuban society. In a reading of the play, Jill Lane notes that the name of one particular bozal is transformed into various mutations—from Alfonso to Idelfonso to Lifonso and then Alifonso—with the effect that by the end even Alfonso himself is no longer able to properly pronounce his own name.[95]

The play utilizes a distinct and accented Spanish to approximate the dialects and languages of Africans recently sold into bondage and to demonstrate their inability to grasp Cuban culture.[96] The humor of the play and its use of ridicule has been the source of its varied interpretations by literary scholars. Vera Kutzinski, for example, argues that by writing in blackvoice, Crespo effectively removed himself from social accountability and thus gave free reign to his critique of Cuban society. The "freedom" that blackvoice provided also allowed Crespo to articulate an early

anticolonial and abolitionist sentiment from within that same society.[97]
This is also an argument made by Cuban theater scholar José Arrom,
who contends that blackvoice allowed Crespo to openly satirize colonial
slave society during a historical moment when he would have either
been restricted by the colonial censors or punished.[98] Other studies of
Crespo read his actions as a reflection of an inner knowledge or understanding of Cuban blackness, a claim that is in line with the literary tradition in Cuba at this time. One scholar, for example, claims that "in order
to cultivate his style he must have intimately known those whom he represented with so much sympathy" and credits Crespo for bringing blackness to the foreground.[99] Because the expected reaction was laughter at
the expense of colonial society, the literature that surrounds Crespo's
work has largely overlooked the double-edged sword of ridicule. But by
conflating foreignness and blackness, Crespo effectively circumvented the
discourse of racial mixing by excluding black Cubans from the emerging
society.

The monologue below, taken from the purposefully awkward stan-
zas of "Wedding Song," in the last act of A Cuban Stew, illustrates the
manner in which the bozal fell outside the Cuban cultural sphere:

> *Married couple:* Little black most fortunate . . .
> Blessed white hour
> That brought him to me in this land
>
> The land of whites is glorious
> When good masters are found
> Mine are Christian
> And like sugar itself.[100]

In the short piece, gender agreements have been confused, numerical
agreements are faulty, *e* sounds have been substituted for *i* sounds, and the
s sounds from the ending of Spanish words have been eliminated. The language conforms closely to Pichardo's definition of a bozal. Given that the
play debuted in 1847, however, we also see how the momentum of independence marked the production. Its treatment of slavery, for example,
reaffirms the belief in the benevolence of the Cuban institution popularized
in the postindependence period. It places the blame for the cruelty of slave
owners on the immigrants who arrived in Cuba in large numbers during the
middle of the nineteenth century. The words from "Wedding Song" spoken
by the bozal slaves assure slavery a benign place in the historical memory of
the nation even as it creates the image of an institution out of place in the
emerging society. The construction of black Cubans as cultural others as a

result of slavery was in poignant contrast with the simultaneous attempt to portray all Cubans—blacks included—as part of a newly emerging society in the latter half of the nineteenth century. Imbued with this early nationalism, the name of the play itself, "un ajiaco," or "Cuban stew," serves as a metaphor for the racial mixing that Fernando Ortiz later coined in his ethnographies.[101] The "stew" is one concocted through the array of harmonious relationships between the vastly different characters—bozales, Cubans, peasants, and Caribbean islanders.

While the bozal was used as a medium to poke fun at the strange and the foreign, he was not the figure who most clearly threatened Cuban society. Rather, as a colonial official poignantly noted, "There is little to fear from the *negros bozales* because of their grand stupidity, but the [*negros*] criollos who by and large know how to read and write, and who are in possession of trades and arts, and among whom there are many who are the owners of large amounts of capital . . . [they may] deliver the final and perhaps irreversible blow [to colonialism]."[102]

Other elements more in line with the aspirations of an upwardly mobile black population were also ridiculed. The idea that black upward social mobility was ridiculous grew out of the sentiment that it was tantamount to an aspiration toward whiteness. The poem below, "Que se lo cuente a su abuela," or "Let him tell it to his grandmother," was written by the black poet Plácido (Gabriel de la Concepción Valdés). In it, Plácido ridicules the social aspirations of one particular black Cuban by equating them with a desire for whiteness:

> Don Longino is always exclaiming:
> —"I am of pure and noble blood,"
> With a greater passion
> Than the rind of bacon,
> And with his olive face
> That indicates his African ancestry
> Deluded he proclaims
> To be of excellent parentage!
> *Let him tell it to his grandmother.*[103]

The "don" that prefaces Longino's name is indicative of his high standing in Cuban society. The fact that he is a *mulato* is evident by the reference to his olive skin, which "betrays" his African ancestry. Don Longino's characterization as "cetrino," however, does not only allude to his racially mixed background, since "cetrino" can also be read as "sallow" instead of "olive," indicating the unhealthy coloring of his skin as well as the use of chemical skin lighteners.

The well-known Conspiracy of La Escalera and its consequences for upwardly mobile black Cubans provides evidence of the very real reactions to their threat against the social order. In 1844, the colonial government claimed to have uncovered an antislavery conspiracy among the enslaved and black population, supported by the black military regiments of the government. The numbers published by the military commission to prosecute those connected with La Escalera note that over seventy-nine individuals were sentenced to death, among whom there were thirty-nine slaves, thirty-nine free blacks, and one person classified as white. Among these were several of the prominent black writers from the western areas of the island, including Plácido. In addition, 435 people fled into exile after mass persecutions meant to uncover the plot affected members of the arts movements.[104] Colonial inquiries into the nature of the conspiracy and its membership led to the voluntary exile the following year of 739 people, most of whom belonged to the upper echelons of black society. Among them, members of the Havana black elite were well represented; the individuals mentioned earlier, Félix Barbosa and José Agustín Ceballos, as well as several others, were executed or died while still in prison.[105] The fear that surrounded the events not only settled the question of slavery but also virtually eliminated the arts movement among the upper strata of black Havana residents.

The later development of another character of theater performances, the black *catedrático* (professor), provides a window into the ensuing backlash. The catedrático illustrates that the redefinition of blackness in and around Havana mirrored the colonial administration's concerns and its legislative attempts to restrict black mobility. With the introduction of this character, the emphasis in black representation shifted from ridiculing Cubans of color for falling outside the Cuban cultural sphere to specifically ridiculing urban blacks who aspired toward upward social mobility. This new representation of blackness debuted in 1868 with the opening of the play *Los negros catedráticos,* written by Francisco Fernández and performed by the theater company known as Los Bufos Habaneros. The date is cited as the official beginning of the Cuban bufo, with performances now exclusively in blackface.[106]

What is particularly striking about the catedrático is that unlike the bozal, he could not be marked as a cultural outsider by virtue of being either African or enslaved. The catedrático parodied Cuban blacks who, like their white counterparts, were Cuban-born, free, and urban. The lexical confusion that is part of the catedrático's character, as with the bozal, served to minimize the threat that black upward social mobility posed and thus to construct him as a cultural outsider. According to Matías Montes, because of the threat that assimilation posed, Cubans of color were cloaked in "lexical distortions" that functioned to reassure white elites and middle-class audiences that "purity"—both linguistic and racial—would remain unattainable for black Cubans.[107] Scholars of the Cuban bufo have traced the linguistic roots of the genre's mimicry of black speech and found that it closely resembles the dialect of Galician Spaniards.[108]

Unlike a bozal, the catedrático was a black criollo and was thus far more dangerous to existing racial hierarchies than the Cuban "negritos" that appeared before him. The representation of urban, upwardly mobile, free, Cuban-born blacks was created at a historical moment when a new class of black habaneros, like the curros, had a legitimate and legal stake in the environment of Havana and who, because of the changes affecting the landscape, were now forced to inhabit a marginal space within it. The limited space available for social mobility as a result of the stringent ordinances in the urban public sphere was the cause of the verbal disconnect and incoherency of the catedrático's speech in the literary arena. The result was a character whose use of language, like that of the bozal before him, made him the object of public ridicule. While the bozal and the catedrático appear to inhabit opposite ends in the spectrum of black representation, the catedrático effectively serves the same symbolic purpose as Crespo's bozal: he functions to limit the social possibilities of free black habaneros.

By 1875, the definition of the catedrático had been codified in Pichardo's dictionary, described as a black Cuban who, through verbal affectations, aspired to a higher social status.[109] Black representation may well have assuaged racial fear as the question of independence intensified, but in its inception it reinforced the exclusionary nature of what it meant to be habanero. In its early incarnation, blackvoice and blackface representation defined who would be excluded from the emerging society that, as far as the colonial administration was concerned, began in Havana and radiated to the provinces. Depictions reflected the parameters of Havana's society as well as the popular concern over black social mobility.

The unprecedented construction and road and infrastructural developments that occurred to the south and west of the city made possible the renewed urbanization outside the walls. These projects occurred at the same time that administrators worked to define the parameters of the city. Both were part and parcel of a two-part plan to organize the social and political topography of Havana and were embodied in the 1855

Havana municipal ordinances and the Construction Ordinances of 1861. The ordinances were arguably the most important legislation to affect the city of Havana and constituted watershed moments in the city's history.[110] The legislation radically altered the physical landscape and proposed new trajectories of growth and social regulation. It also masked racialized struggles to redefine the terms of colonial civilization. The emergence of the modern nineteenth-century city thus still hinged on exclusion, but whereas colonial administrators, cartographers, and planners had once excised people and places from the city proper, the extramuros and extramuro residents were now rendered hypervisible in the colonial attempt to order, modernize, and fold the area into the legal urban body.

CHAPTER 4

City

The renovation of the geometric plan that will soon be under way . . . will mark the three or four main highways that will interlink *la ciudad antigua* [the old city] with *la ciudad nueva* [the new city].

—*Ordenanzas de construcción para la ciudad de La Habana*

In his introduction to the Construction Ordinances of 1861, Governor Mantilla celebrated the city's "policía urbana" for propelling Havana *"al alcance de los adelantes modernos"* (in the reach of moderniza-tion).[1] In the same document, he also went on to describe the city in the following manner:

> A widespread settlement, irregular and without any fixed boundaries; long streets, tortuous and uneven, and of multiple widths, lacking pavement and without borders, in its major parts: entire neighborhoods without design, without sewers, with drains spouting infected waters onto public highways and turning them into stinking and unhealthy swamps; plazas without regu-larity, without trees, without *portales* here, or with portales there . . . wooden houses, deformed, dirty, and in ruins, next to new buildings, elegant and even grand, give, in effect, to he who steps onto this ground for the first time, a very different idea from the one formed of *la culta y opulenta Habana.*[2]

Mantilla blamed the ever-deteriorating ideal of "la culta y opulenta Habana" on the city administrations that came before him. One year earlier in an address to the city council, Dr. Nicolás José Gutiérrez had cited "the lack of hygiene measures that were not thought of or taken into consideration at the outset of public works projects, and that were not later implemented as preventative measures when the population began to grow" as the culprits behind the deplorable conditions in which parts of the city lay.[3] He claimed that the lack of foresight in the initiation of public works projects was the primary reason behind the outbreaks of disease that devastated the city on an almost yearly basis.[4] When describing the conditions of Havana, Mantilla alluded to the same lack of proper planning. He went on to note that the poor planning had resulted in a form of "anarchy" in the physical environment of the city, which current administrators were being forced to contend with.[5]

Making this matter one of pressing concern was the image of Havana outside Cuba. In 1862, representatives of the crown described the city as a capital unlike any other in Latin America, where urbanization promised modernity, and the defining characteristic of the island was *"el elemento civilizado"* (the civilized element). The cultural changes that had affected Havana during the middle decades of the nineteenth century were similarly impressed upon visitors. Foreign travelers and visitors to the city described residents who appeared to be "as polished and well dressed as [those] in the most civilized cities of Europe," with the upper echelons composed of a people who were "exceedingly refined, and well educated either in the United States or abroad."[6] The splendor of city residents was linked to the city's built environment and lauded in the memoir written by Samuel Hazard, in which he described the newly built Calzada de Galiano, located in the outskirts of Havana beyond the paseos of the extramuros, as a "handsome paved highway, with long rows of well-built, striking looking houses, most of them with pillared fronts."[7]

The urban structures that invited similar commendations had been built during the early decades of the nineteenth century. Amid the well-developed physical environment of Havana and its well-established high society, however, there remained the pervasive issue of social spatialization to contend with. The noticeable presence of urban poverty and overcrowding within *all* areas of the city, including those well built and new, was the last culprit to invite criticisms from abroad.[8] Samuel Hazard noted this in the travel accounts that he left behind of his visits to Havana, as did numerous others, including Rachel Wilson Moore, who described Havana's "grandeur and squalid poverty intermingled to the greatest extent we ever beheld."[9]

By the 1860s, the colonial administration was in the process of trying to eliminate such criticisms while boosting its own legitimacy among city residents. For Benjamín Vallín, the Spanish envoy to Havana, the steps that the colonial administration was taking to ensure that "civilization" thrived on the island implied the possibility for political reform and the continuation of Spanish rule in Cuba.[10] When juxtaposed with the threat of an independence struggle, political reform through urban change seemed an appealing compromise for Spanish officials and some of their well-off criollo counterparts.[11] Urban development opened up a myriad of possibilities. For North American visitors, urban development around the trope of "civilization" meant that the city could function as both a familiar and exotic locale, satiating visitors' desire for the "picturesque" customs of the island while simultaneously offering services comparable to those available in the United States.[12] The steady growth of tourism that Havana experienced during the same years in which it saw the greatest extent of urban development was not insignificant. Havana received five thousand North American visitors annually by midcentury.[13] Foreign immigration peaked during these same decades. Immigrants entered the country, perhaps for the similar sense of possibility, and established mutual aid societies in and around the city that further maximized the promise that Havana seemed to hold.

The different possibilities that civilization held for royal officials and city residents were not always mutually irreconcilable or even contradictory, even as they offered alternatives previously not considered. For example, the jump in tourism and foreign immigration both increased revenues for the city and provided residents with different cultural and political exchanges, just as the port always had; it also fueled in some the desire for political reform in Cuba instead of independence at a time when the economy remained strong. The idea of "civilization," however, also allowed for irreconcilable visions of the future to emerge among competing interest groups in Havana. For the criollo and peninsular administrators of the city, "civilization" and "possibility" during the latter decades of the nineteenth century implied urban trajectories that were dangerously at odds with one another. In this case, the schism that occurred in Havana's administration reflects the larger phenomenon unfolding within the political trajectory of the island—that is, the political struggle over independence that shook the Cuban countryside between 1868 and 1898. While the armed conflict was concentrated in the rural areas of the island, it nonetheless left a physical imprint on the topographical arrangement of the city. It affected Havana by irrevocably altering the trajectory of urban development on which the city was poised after the 1861 ordinances.

ON THE VERGE OF POSSIBILITIES

By the decade of the 1860s, Havana had emerged onto the international scene as a cosmopolitan city. Its role as civilizing agent had been well established, particularly after the revolt in Saint-Domingue. Improvements in notation, census taking, and cartography allowed the colonial government to exert a newfound control over the island and its people and to further centralize power in Havana.[14] Adding to the overall sense of growth and prosperity were the strides that the colonial administration had made in developing the city. Between 1850 and 1862, more hectares were approved for urbanization than had been developed during the entire century prior.[15] The area of the extramuros, where much of this new development had taken place, now far surpassed that of the city proper. By 1860, the population outside the walls had reached 122,730, compared with the 46,445 inhabitants of the intramuros.[16]

While areas of the extramuros were now well-established middle-class enclaves instead of the havens for the urban poor that they had been in decades prior, the demographics were constantly in flux. Peninsulares arriving in vast numbers during the nineteenth century increased already fraught political tensions in the capital. By 1860, immigration numbers from Spain totaled one hundred thousand in Cuba. And between 1868 and 1894, despite the reality of war, another four hundred thousand Spanish immigrants entered the island.[17] Unlike immigrants in the earlier decades of the nineteenth century, when most Spanish immigrants arrived from Andalusia, Castile, and Extremadura, these new arrivals hailed from such places as Galicia, Asturias, and the Canary Islands, causing a transformation not only in the overall demographics of the city but also within the Spanish population already present.

Despite changes that increased the potential for urban friction, several developments had taken place during the mid-nineteenth century that allowed colonial administrators to position Havana and its inhabitants for a return to Tácon-style urbanization. First, the division between high and low culture previously subsumed into the built environment was now reinforced through such things as print media. And although it remained a contested terrain, the rhetorical and symbolic exclusion of the "undesirable" members of the public sphere—urban blacks, guajiros, and the urban poor—had proven a popular process with city residents. The symbolic exclusion of these individuals was followed with an attempt to spatially exclude them from the more desirable areas of the city via the 1861 construction ordinances.

In his introductory comments on the ordinances, Governor Mantilla did not dismiss the advancements in urban planning made decades earlier. Rather, he protested the manner in which public works projects had isolated portions of the city from one another. The new challenge facing administrators at this juncture of the city's history, as mentioned briefly in the previous chapter, was how to devise a way to *link* the dual cities. This was a far cry from the project of *creating* a cohesive urban body on which the Tacón administration had embarked. Complicating this process was the fact that "moderna" and "antigua" Havana were no longer easily identifiable: no longer could either be said to lie solely within the intramuros or extramuros. In fact, by the mid-nineteenth century, the ability of the walls to differentiate between desirable and dangerous areas and populations had all but disappeared.

The walls that surrounded the city proper had long ceased to provide Havana with any practical benefits; instead, they served a symbolic purpose in the minds of colonial officials and city residents. The military concern that once served as the impetus for their construction had been removed by the decline of both the Spanish and British empires, as well as by an overall shift in the Spanish ideology of conquest and colonization and the independence of the Spanish mainland.[18] On a more practical level, amid the city's continued population growth the walls were proving to be an even greater encumbrance to urban development. Commerce grew during the mid-nineteenth century, and the city was becoming increasingly congested not only with pedestrians but also with merchant traffic, the majority of which entered and left Havana through the gates of La Punta and Monserrate. The administration installed nine doors at various junctures along the walls to encourage the dispersal of traffic, but congestion continued to be a noticeable problem. Pedestrians, mounted horsemen, volantes, carts, and *carruajes* (carriages) all congregated at the city gates and made congestion within the walled city a growing problem.[19] The scene was one impressed upon visitors, who commented on the difficulty of maneuvering through the narrow and congested streets of the intramuros.[20]

In an effort to create physical space and relieve the obstruction of city streets and points of entry, a plan advocating the complete removal of the city walls gained popularity among city administrators. The crown had considered such a plan in 1839, when it contemplated selling portions of the wall in order to increase revenue and maximize city space. Although the initial plan was never carried out, the idea periodically resurfaced until it was brought up again as an extension of the 1861 city ordinances and the new reorganization of the city that the ordinances proposed. The plan for demolition was finally approved in 1863, once the director of the Office of Public Works, Cuban engineer Francisco de Albear y Lara, supported it.

FIGURE 15. Demolition of the city walls, c. 1870. Courtesy of the
Archivo Nacional de Cuba, Havana.

Demolition of the ancient city walls continued from 1863 to 1875.
The decision to bring down the walls allowed—finally—for the physical
unification of the city through the incorporation of the extramuros into
Havana proper. In a symbolic capacity, the decision also served to "lib-
erate" the core city from its physical confines, thereby positioning
Havana for what seemed to be yet another phase of rapid urban development branching immediately west and south of the core city. The area
of land that was cleared once the walls disappeared consisted of twenty-
six hectares, measuring 1,700 meters in length. In real terms, this translated into an area the equivalent of eighteen city blocks in length and
four city blocks in width that would suddenly be made available.[21]

The colonial administration introduced a system of urbanizing *repartos* (neighborhood divisions) as a result of the premium land suddenly
made available (in coveted areas of the city) after the 1863 decision. The
reparto system provided an official means of designating different areas
of Havana. The neighborhood created in the wake of demolition was
Reparto Las Murallas, so named by the architects charged with designing the new neighborhood, Juan Bautista Orduña and Manuel Portilla y
Portilla.[22] Heavy construction in Reparto Las Murallas took place
between 1865 and 1883, a period that spanned the entire length of the
first war of independence (1868–1878) as well as that of the interim
government in Cuba between the first and second wars (1895–1898).
The political tensions mounting on the island during the period in which
the Reparto Las Murallas came under heavy construction not only left

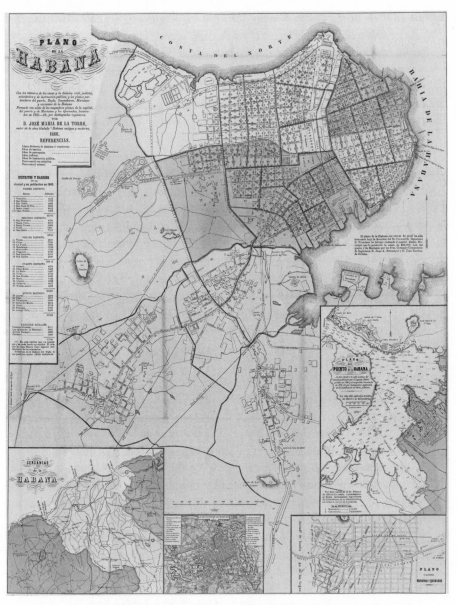

FIGURE 16. José María de la Torre, *Plano de La Habana con los números de las casas y la division civil, judicial, eclesiástica, y de instruccion pública,* 1866. Courtesy of the Biblioteca Nacional de España (BNE), Madrid.

its imprint in the urbanization plan but also radically transformed the nature of the historical struggle over urban space. The "war" against the residents of the extramuros that Alexander von Humboldt had described in 1828 was still taking place in the very same spot where Las Murallas was being created. Ironically, however, *"los habitantes de los arrabales"* (the residents of the suburbs) now constituted a radically different population than the excluded members of Havana society previously described by Humboldt.[23]

Interests in Reparto Las Murallas now included peninsulares and criollos invested in the growing independence movement (for different reasons) as well as private land speculators looking to profit from property sales. The colonial administration's investment in the reparto, too, was now much different than it had been four decades earlier. At this point in time, the potential cost of an independence struggle outweighed the benefits of the symbolic reinforcement of colonial rule, a decision that would also affect urbanization of the reparto. Construction of the neighborhood would thus mirror the political developments caused by the independence struggle gaining strength in the countryside, leaving a visible imprint in the new reparto as well as on the city as a whole.[24]

THE STRUGGLE FOR INDEPENDENCE IN HAVANA'S REPARTOS

In stark contrast to the Cuban countryside, Havana remained intact during the physical violence of war. The political struggle that led up to the independence wars, however, nonetheless marked the people and neighborhoods of the city. As the base of the colonial administration, the city was the space where political struggles were performed, while decisions affecting urban development during the latter decades of the nineteenth century were made with the politics of independence in mind in a way that earlier developments in Havana's neighborhoods were not.

The urbanization of El Vedado provides an excellent counterpoint to the development of Reparto Las Murallas. The difference between the design and use of each neighborhood draws attention to the growing impact that the independence struggle had on the topography of Havana. El Vedado (literally meaning a territory that is forbidden, preserved from construction, or residing at a lower geographic area) came into existence in 1858, when the city council approved the parceling and sale of the estate El Carmelo. The initial plan was introduced by the Conde de Pozos Dulces as a means to establish a reparto that would serve as a model of hygiene and urbanization. That El Carmelo was chosen for this honor speaks both to the fact that only far to the west of the colonial core was land available for development and to the fact that by midcentury, the extramuros had achieved a complete inversion of its former status. One year after the plan was drawn, owners sold the neighboring farm of El Vedado, and the two areas were joined to create the first urban residential neighborhood in Havana. The neighborhood officially came into being in 1860 and was designed by engineer José Yboleón Bosque. It stretched from the Almendares River, located to the west of the city, all the way to Calle Infanta in the east. Calle Infanta served as the western boundary to the developments that had been built during the early to mid-nineteenth century. The area of Havana that lay between Calle Infanta in the east and Calle Monserrate to the west was the area formerly known as the extramuros. The two streets split the city in a symmetrical north-south fashion.

El Vedado is perhaps one of the best examples of the array of ideological influences affecting the city prior to the struggle for independence. The designs of engineer José Yboleón Bosque were influenced by the designs of Spanish engineer Ildefonso Cerdá, whose work on the Ensanche of Barcelona is reflected in the square and compact nature of the residential blocks of El Vedado.[25] The neighborhood also exhibits characteristics in its aesthetic designs and in its use of space similar to those present in the garden city designs of Frederick Law Olmsted in the United States. José Yboleón Bosque designed the neighborhood of El Vedado to contain a maximum of 160 inhabitants per hectare, leaving between 30 and 35 percent of all neighborhood space clear.[26] When compared to the almost 325 inhabitants per hectare that the intramuros housed, the spatial difference would have been obvious even to the most casual observer.

There were also other physical characteristics specific to the neighborhood. Streets in El Vedado measured sixteen meters in width and avenues measured fifty meters. Each house was required to contain a five-meter garden in the front yard. On the street, the pavement was tree-lined. Public parks as well as recreational areas were also built into the neighborhood. Climate considerations were integrated into the built environment, and the direction of the day and night breezes were taken into account when the avenues were constructed so that the neighborhood would benefit from the ocean breezes. Its two main avenues, Paseo and Prado, were oriented toward the coast to allow for the breeze to cool the neighborhood, making this area of the city significantly more comfortable and cooler than the compact areas of the core city and the extramuro development that lay to the west of where the walls had stood.

Although the original neighborhood plans drawn by the Conde de Pozos Dulces were virtually unaffected by the politics of the early separatist movement, the neighborhood's future development was markedly affected by the onset of the independence struggle. Without financial subsidies from the colonial government in the years that followed its construction, El Vedado suffered the financial fate of many of its residents, among them the most prominent members of the criollo "sugar aristocracy" who made up the population of the lavish neighborhoods on the outskirts of the city.[27] While this sector of the population was certainly well off during the first half of the nineteenth century, the deteriorating conditions of the countryside took an increasingly harsh economic toll on its members as the armed struggle continued. The standstill in El Vedado mirrored the urbanization standstill taking place throughout Havana. The vacant lots peppered throughout the neighborhood once designated for the construction of stately mansions were now left bare; they were soon overrun by weeds or else ended up as dumping grounds for urban waste by neighborhood residents. The housing regulations that had been specified in the original plans were also ignored as the population in the new reparto experienced increasingly harsh financial times with the full onset of the independence wars. Lots meant for single-family homes were used instead by residents to house two and three families in an attempt to alleviate their economic situation, or else the portales of each home, in direct violation of housing regulations, were used to establish small businesses with which to subsidize the family income.[28]

After the death of the Conde de Pozos Dulces, El Vedado resident Dr. Manuel Varona Suárez emerged as a leader in the development of the neighborhood. He established the Asociación de Propietarios, Industriales y Vecinos del Vedado y Príncipe (Association of Property Owners, Entrepreneurs, and Neighbors of El Vedado and Príncipe), which oversaw the reparto. The association established different bodies to handle the reparto's administration, including police, firefighters, and sanitation. They also ensured that each home lived up to the urban potential of the neighborhood by being properly numbered, its lots properly marked, and its trees and shrubbery well cared for. As far as urban development was concerned, the association sought to expand its goals of hygiene and urban progress not only in El Vedado but also throughout all of Havana. It initiated urban works projects that included

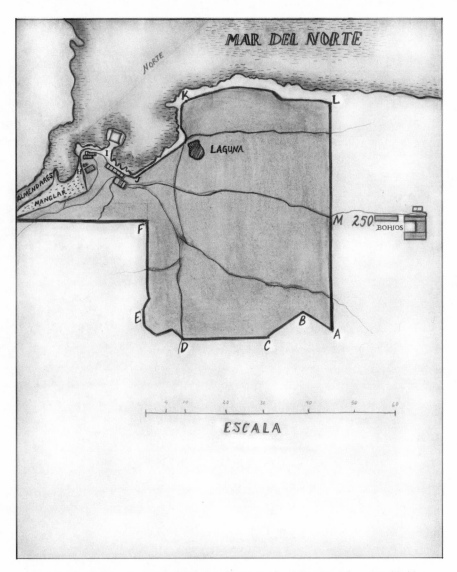

FIGURE 17. El Carmelo (later El Vedado). Illustration by Sylwia Kusiak; original held at the Biblioteca Nacional José Martí, Havana.

FIGURE 18. District 9 of Havana (El Vedado). Courtesy of the Biblioteca
Nacional José Martí, Havana.

support for the extension of the former Alameda de Paula (which would turn into the seaside wall of Havana, the malecón), seaside baths for the impoverished, and *centros de socorro* to aid those in need. Most importantly, in its support of the physical development of the city, the association served as the unofficial watchdog that ensured city compliance with the 1861 city ordinances, relieving the colonial administration of this task and establishing itself as a central player in urban affairs.

The association's growing importance in urban government coincided with the colonial administration's reprioritization of the war at the expense of urban development. Unlike El Vedado, Reparto Las Murallas reached urban maturity during the years immediately leading up to the struggle for independence. Mounting political tensions and the recent demolition of the city walls provided the necessary ingredients for Reparto Las Murallas to function as a theater in which different interests could express their political ambivalences and claim part of the new territory. Immediately after the 1863 demolition of the walls, for example, the colonial administration replanned the three *plazuelas* (small squares) that stood at the entrance of the city gates at Monserrate. These were subsequently converted into the Plaza Isabel II and then later into the Parque Central. The city park covered the length of four city blocks: Calles Prado, Neptuno, Zulueta, and San José, in what became the center of Havana. Construction came to an end in 1877, at which time the park's "modern" adornments (such as streetlamps) were shipped from the United States in emulation of New York City's Central Park.[29] Construction of the Parque Central by the colonial government, however, by no means meant that the space was a colonial enclave. On the contrary, in 1871 eight medical students were killed in the park by the Spanish army for political crimes against the colonial government; after their deaths, they were memorialized with garden plots in the same location.[30]

The symbolic dimensions of the neighborhood were amplified by the fact that Reparto Las Murallas was located in an "in-between" space *between* those areas of the city already in use as either criollo or Spanish spaces. To the west of Las Murallas lay Cerro and El Vedado, both of which had been developed with the specific objectives of their criollo residents in mind. To the east of Las Murallas lay the shrinking enclaves of Spanish colonial power: the Plaza de Armas, the stately mansions that surrounded it, and the developments made by Tacón. To the south of the city there remained the surviving remnants of Havana's lower classes, although many of these enclaves had also undergone urban renovation that changed their use value in decades prior.

Creating further ambivalence as to who would inherit the reparto were several distinguishing characteristics of Las Murallas. Unlike Cerro or El Vedado, Reparto Las Murallas had not been created as a means to provide wealthy habaneros with either an urban respite from the city center or a residential alternative to the cramped intramuros. Instead, the late and almost accidental creation of the neighborhood in the middle of the already developed and established city allowed for various interpretations to emerge regarding its potential uses. The vacant spaces surrounding the four main arteries of the extramuros, Belascoaín, Galiano, Reina, and Monte, housed communities of competing interests. Furthermore, because the 1861 city ordinances had been drafted prior to the decision to demolish the walls or construct the neighborhood, the space that Reparto Las Murallas occupied was not affected by the strict zoning laws that regulated other areas of the city, thereby opening it up to a multiplicity of construction possibilities.

As in the rest of Havana, the use of space in Las Murallas was significantly affected by the impending threat of an independence war and became largely a political struggle between criollos and peninsulares. Once demolition of the walls was begun and then interrupted by the outbreak of the first struggle for independence in 1868, the crown quickly approved the sale of hectares in order to raise funds for the war effort. By the mid-1880s, the economic conditions of Havana were such that the colonial government was forced to sell even more land in Reparto Las Murallas, this time against the wishes of the city council, which proposed instead that the area be utilized for the construction of government buildings to service the city and increase its revenues. Among its proposals was the plan to relocate the University of Havana and construct a tax office in its place. Instead, the colonial government sold much of the area to private individuals, who then developed the reparto according to a new vision of entrepreneurial "urban possibility" made feasible by the struggle for independence. Foreign-owned hotels became one of the new symbols of Reparto Las Murallas. The Pasaje Hotel was the first to open its doors in 1876, soon followed by the Plaza and the Quinta Avenida Hotels in 1879. The Roma and Telégrafo Hotels followed in 1880. The demand was such that by 1899, twenty-five new hotels were fully functioning in Havana, many of these located within the new reparto.

The demand for new hotels reflects the ways in which foreign land speculators responded to the growing business of tourism. Immigration similarly created new demands that altered the urban topography. Private hospitals and mutual aid societies in predominately peninsular and other immigrant areas were constructed as an alternative to the medical care that was provided in Havana's existing hospitals. The Beneficencia Catalana (Catalan Charity) and the Asturian and Galician centers were some of the new landmark services available in Reparto Las Murallas.[31]

With the colonial government no longer able to support the type of expansion that it had engaged in only a few years earlier, during the midcentury (1850–1862) urbanization boom, urban development came to a standstill as the administration indefinitely postponed new projects. Such was the extent of the economic strain that even those projects already approved and under way were suddenly halted. The 1862 plan by Cuban architect Saturnino Martínez to create the new avenue of Serrano became one of the casualties of the crown's new economic policy. The plan would have joined the Plaza de Armas, in the core city, with the Paseo de Isabel II, in the extramuros. Construction of this avenue would have not only demolished every block between Calles Obispo and O'Reilly, but would also have served as a reinforcement of the modern and ordered trajectory introduced by the 1861 city ordinances. The construction of Serrano Avenue, the relocation of the university, and the new colonial tax office would have served to reaffirm a sense of colonial authority in Havana.

Among the principal concerns emerging along with the urbanization of the new repartos was once again urban order in the forms of sanitation and hygiene. In 1879, the new Junta Superior de Sanidad de la Isla de Cuba (Sanitation Committee of the Island of Cuba) was created to oversee hygiene and sanitation across the island. The committee was based in Havana, and its members were selected from among colonial government officials, medical doctors, civil engineers, merchants, veterinaries, architects, and other professionals. The committee enacted citywide measures to ensure that outbreaks of cholera and yellow fever in Havana were eradicated or at least contained within specific areas of the city. In 1882, a resolution was introduced to clean the harbor in Havana in the hopes of eliminating bacteria that could lead to disease.[32] When an outbreak occurred in Colón in 1890, it was published in the newspapers and the neighborhood was quarantined to avoid the spread of disease.[33] Boats entering the harbor and coming from regions believed to be sources of infection were also quarantined, and passengers and their baggage were fumigated. Funeral homes, stables, and other establishments considered unhealthy were transferred to the outskirts of the city, away from the majority of inhabitants.[34]

While mortality rates in the city remained relatively stable during the first half of the nineteenth century, the numbers show a dramatic increase from the 1860s onward. In fact, a similar rate of mortality had not been seen in Havana since the first years of the nineteenth century, prior to the hygiene and sanitation ordinances passed by Tacón.[35] Whether due to the onset of war or the outbreak of viruses (or the conditions caused by war, as troops entering the city were often seen as a source of contagion), the increase in mortality rates was enough to put into question the efficacy of the colonial administration in Havana. Concern over sanitary conditions extended to newly built areas in the city outskirts and its criollo residents.

During the earlier part of the century, when the extramuros still resided in a marginal space within the city, the city's hospitals, insane asylums, and garbage dumps had been transferred there. During the latter half of the nineteenth century, the relocation of the stables and the funeral home, although not in the immediate vicinity of El Vedado, joined earlier developments in providing a constant source of worry for residents of this neighborhood. This trend would continue well into the final years of the nineteenth century, when rural and hinterland townships served as a dumping ground for Havana's sick. In Marianao, for example, a special hospital was built during the 1895 war of independence to move those with contagious illnesses away from the population of Havana.[36] While urbanization of El Vedado had come about as a backlash to the poor hygiene and virus outbreaks of the walled city, neighborhood residents now had to contend with the presence of these establishments in their vicinity. The fear of epidemics was such that even in El Vedado, residents took precautions to build their homes on higher ground in the belief that this would provide them with some measure of protection against contagion and disease.

The construction and use of space in each neighborhood serves as a visual articulation of the differences emerging in the new society. With the establishment of El Vedado and Cerro, the urban periphery became a space for the criollo sugar aristocracy and its merchant classes. The core city and the area where the extramuros had once stood, by contrast, served as a place of marginality and dislocation. Peninsulares, for example, composed a large part of the newly established residents of Las Murallas. Peninsular immigrants who had relocated to Havana owned many of the tobacco factories that flourished in the area during the 1880s. Galicians and Catalans made up the large majority of the proprietors of the 134 tobacco factories that ringed the core city.[37] Such was the initial integration of peninsulares into the vicinity of Las Mural-las that the presence of a single pro-separatist symbol was enough to incur the wrath of the Spanish Cuerpo de Voluntarios, the military unit organized to control the pro-separatist strain in Havana. In 1869, the Cuerpo de Voluntarios looted the lavish private residence of Miguel Aldama once they discovered that he was sympathetic to the separatist movement. After the residence was destroyed, it was converted into a tobacco factory.

Violence was only one of the markers that colonial rule was waning. By 1867, only one year prior to the colonial decision to halt land urban-ization in Havana, one of the emblematic institutions of mid-nineteenth-century modernization disappeared. The Centro de Estadística was dis-banded immediately before the first struggle for independence in 1868, permanently reversing the nineteenth-century trend toward quantifica-tion and notation. And although the census was published as scheduled in 1867, it did not live up to the standards of the previous publications. Cuban productivity also declined, in rural areas especially, due to the destruction of land, crops, and equipment. The rural populations dis-placed by war migrated to urban areas, where they competed with urban workers (and, after 1886, with the former slaves freed by emancipation) for already scarce jobs and places to live. In Havana, twenty thousand workers were unemployed. Of those who were employed, many were paid in depreciated wages or, if employed as public officials, were often-times not paid at all as the colonial government itself felt the strain of the economic depression, exacerbated by the war effort.[38] The strain on resources led not only to the suspension of public works but also to the suspension of the urban services that had previously legitimized the colonial administration. Trash collection, urban lighting, and similar services stopped. The depression also affected some of the long-estab-lished institutions of importance in Havana. The Caja de Ahorros liqui-dated its assets, and the Banco Industrial and Banco de Comercio, for example, closed their doors.[39]

Following the Pact of Zanjón (1878), which ended the first war of independence, scarce credit, high unemployment, and migration to urban areas all affected urban living. The price of urban property in and around Havana remained high. A two-bedroom home in Havana, for example, might rent for up to three ounces of gold—not script—monthly.[40] Despite the increase in available land following demolition of the walls, the hous-ing situation for most habaneros did not significantly improve. The number of residents looking for housing actually *increased* during the interim years between the two struggles for independence as a result of economic decline in rural areas. The solution to this problem was the rise of single-room dwellings serving as alternatives to single-family residences, the cost of which was in the realm of twelve pesos monthly.[41]

Popular stories circulated around Havana during this period of urban dislocation among the renting population that warned against the pitfalls that such an arrangement could have. Potential landlords and those looking for housing were painted as potential victims of the real-estate market. Families who rented rooms in their homes were warned against the possibility of the "problem tenant" whom they might encounter. In popular writer Francisco de Paula Gelabert's short story "Se alquila un cuarto a un matrimonio sin hijos" (Room for rent to a couple without children), the husband and wife, who decide to rent out a single room of their home, are taken advantage of by a couple appearing to be the perfect tenants. In the end, the renters refuse to stay in their designated area of the home or to pay the agreed-upon sum, and they end up causing such an altercation that the police have to be called in to intervene.[42]

For those seeking more affordable accommodations, Gelabert's stories point out that the move into more affordable neighborhoods may come at the cost of one's honor and respectability. In "Las que andan como locas buscando casa" (The ones going crazy looking for a house), the protagonists are three women: the matron of the home and her two single daughters. They embark on a search for new accommodations after being surprised by their landlord with a rent increase. While they find more affordable neighborhoods to live in, they also find that the population that resides in these is decidedly of ill repute. After a series of misfortunes befall their search, they give up when they meet a young black woman residing in one low-income neighborhood who alludes to the sexual favors she is forced to trade for housing. The three women, who maintain their honor even though they are poor, retreat back to their more expensive dwellings.[43] The abundance of such stories suggests that the struggle over urban housing had definite ramifications for social order, and implicated the colonial government, which was unable to sustain it.

As rent prices remained high and the stream of new arrivals continued from the rural areas of the island as well as from abroad, city administrators had to contend with other, more pressing concerns. First, not all who searched for affordable housing had the option of finding it or of returning to the places from which they hailed. A large number of those without options were the rural migrants increasingly dislocated by the wars of independence who looked to urban areas in search of economic improvement. But as they arrived in Havana, they found unaffordable rent prices, few available dwellings, and an increasingly sparse periphery in which to settle. The political consequences of this situation would become apparent once the independence struggle again gained momentum.

SPACES IN-BETWEEN

While the issues that worried administrators revolved mostly around political tensions with criollos, not all threats to public order were the result of political divisions. There were other, everyday concerns that also hinted at the unraveling of a colonial order based exclusively on the sustainability of an urban project. Occurrences such as the sacking of the Aldama residence and the violent repression from the Cuerpo de Voluntarios were not enough to deter most criminal activity from taking place. The nature of criminal activity in and around the city during the last decades of the nineteenth century reveals the different ways in which the physical city served as a public forum for individuals to make their grievances known.

Civil order was suspended in Cuba during the first war of independence, between 1868 and 1878. In its place, law enforcement responsibilities were transferred to the Comisión Militar, under whose discretion the administration of individual municipalities was placed. When the war ended with both parties agreeing to political reform under the Pact of Zanjón, however, civil order was reinstated and the administration of the colonial government reorganized. The government reorganization affected Havana first by forcing the incorporation of two of the rural *cercanías* (neighborhood outskirts) into its new municipality. The 1878 constitution stipulated that every unincorporated suburb of a large población be immediately incorporated into its nearest municipality. Not coincidentally, the measure would have allowed the colonial government to gain tighter control over the largely unsupervised rural zones of the country.[44] The move was in all likelihood an attempt to maintain stricter vigilance over the rural areas of the country. The new legislation meant that Havana incorporated two more barrios into its municipal territory, which now included the core city, the barrios extramuros, and the previously unincorporated and largely rural areas that surrounded it.

New law enforcement bodies were also created and the 1878 Ley Orgánica de Ayuntamientos was passed. This was arguably the single most influential piece of legislation to emerge from the treaty with respect to the administration of municipal governments. The Ley Orgánica transferred oversight responsibilities from the military commission to the municipality. The actual powers that municipal governments were endowed with, however, remained unclear. In order to alleviate this uncertainty, in 1881 the colonial administration commissioned publication of a government guide detailing the exact nature and extent of the responsibilities conferred upon municipal and city governments, including the specifics of what *orden pública* (public order) entailed in the postwar period.[45]

Despite the array of law enforcement bodies in the city, the primary responsibility for maintaining public order in each neighborhood rested with the small corps of inspectors and *celadores* (guards) assigned to a neighborhood beat. The relatively small area of the neighborhood that each team—composed of one inspector and one celador—was tasked with policing allowed each of these men to forge close relationships with the residents of his assigned barrio. The information that inspectors and celadores were privy to ranged from the mundane, such as who was having intimate or extramarital relationships with whom, to the politically sensitive, such as whose relatives were visiting Havana and from where as well as the political leanings of individual residents.[46]

Special regulations endowed alcaldes with the authorization to take extreme measures for the protection of public order, including the ability to suspend civil government and call upon the full force of the colonial military establishment.[47] Reunions of any kind and freedom of the press also rested within the discretion of the municipal governor.[48] In Havana, this translated into an immediate censoring of the press and those newspapers that were perceived as seditious in nature, including ones that used the deplorable conditions of rural migrants on the Havana outskirts to point out that "real" habaneros would soon find themselves in similarly dire straits should the economic situation continue to escalate. *La Lucha,* for example, pointed out that soon, peasants fleeing the war would not be the only ones going without food, as the effects of the war were being felt in Havana.[49] The newspaper was among the censored.

Under the government reorganization, each of the six provinces in Cuba had a civil governor who answered directly to the captain general of the island. Each province was further divided into municipalities (which then also had a municipal governor who answered to the provincial governor), and each municipality was subdivided into various barrios that also had their own *alcalde de barrio* (neighborhood governor). As the highest-ranking supervisor within each neighborhood, the alcalde de barrio was charged with a variety of duties to ensure public safety—a concept that was now correlated directly with colonial order. Among his new duties was the collection of *cédulas de vecindad* (akin to neighborhood IDs) that accounted for each resident of a neighborhood, including foreigners and immigrants. After each cédula was taken, identity cards were issued that allowed residents to travel freely and legally throughout the island.[50]

The census and identity cards provided colonial administrators with a picture of neighborhood demographics, which subsequently facilitated the job of law enforcement bodies. The administration's concern with accounting for the political ideology of habaneros stemmed from the fear of incidents that would disrupt the political stability of the capital city, before this moment largely unscathed by the violence of war. Collection of the cédulas and assignment of identity cards was thus a serious part of the duties of each alcalde, and the colonial government was keen on prosecuting individuals for noncompliance or falsification of identity papers, especially once the armed struggle commenced anew.[51] The task of collecting cédulas and familiarizing oneself with barrio residents fell on the Policía de Gobierno y Orden Público, which was also in charge of overseeing and maintaining public order (in rural areas, it was the *guardia civil* that shared this same responsibility), and it did so with the help of other law enforcement bodies such as the Cuerpo de Voluntarios, *policía de seguridad, policía municipal,* and the still-standing cuerpo de serenos. Each barrio was further patrolled by the inspectors and celadores who reported criminal activity in each neighborhood to its alcalde.

By colonial decree, censors were to review editions of each newspaper and report criminal activity to the magistrates.[52] In reality, however, more criminal accounts were reported in the press than were thereafter prosecuted by colonial authorities.[53] Archival records indicate that the criminal activity prosecuted between 1868 and 1898 was primarily arson, homicide, and robbery committed in the vicinity of Havana and thought to have a connection to the independence struggle. Criminal acts of a similar nature but with no visible ties to the independence movement were, however, also prosecuted.[54] Evidence of "petty" criminal activity can found in numerous newspaper accounts.[55] A possible explanation for the government's focus on anticolonial activity and the censor's unwillingness to follow up on certain crimes, besides the obvious reason of war, is the divergence of interests between government officials and the press. The colonial government's decision to prosecute only those crimes that threatened its immediate survival, rather than the criminal activity of petty thieves and criminals, is an understandable one given the extant political context. The interests of the Havana press, however, were different. Newspaper editors were not simply interested in reporting the activities that threatened colonial order but also in reporting those incidents that threatened the immediate physical and material safety of residents. For this reason, newspaper accounts and popular stories dwell not on the fires that were scorching the rural areas surrounding Havana or on the nature of homicides committed during the last years of colonial rule but on the escalation of everyday "petty" crime committed in and around the city.

To be sure, petty criminal activity was not a new development in Havana. Prior to the demolition of the walls, criminal activity within the intramuros was one of the driving forces behind the development of the extramuro neighborhoods of Cerro and El Vedado. The rise in certain types of criminal activity between the 1865 creation of Reparto Las Murallas and the second war of independence, however, served to undermine the already unstable authority of the colonial government. An analysis of José Trujillo y Monagas's accounts as celador of the barrio of San Francisco (located in the intramuros) between 1866 and 1869 and later as sub-inspector of the third district of Havana (and finally as its inspector) reveals the extent to which law enforcement officials were caught between the anticolonial concerns of their superiors and the everyday needs of barrio residents.[56] Whereas superiors were concerned with maintaining public order for the purpose of avoiding an outbreak of separatist violence in the capital, the barrio residents were concerned with the threat stemming from an overall rise in criminal activity and the alarming growth in public crimes such as robbery and charlatanism.

As the colonial government became increasingly concerned with the extent of anticolonial demonstrations around Havana, they were also aware that the nature of criminal activity in the capital was changing. José Trujillo y Monagas describes the changes that he witnessed with regard to the nature of criminal activity since the outbreak of the first war of independence.[57] What we see develop in his accounts is the emergence of banditry as the method of choice for perpetuating criminal activity in and around Havana. While banditry was certainly a source of concern in rural areas surrounding the city such as the neighboring provinces of Pinar del Río and Matanzas, Havana saw a rise in the overall activity of rural bandits *within* the city.[58] Trujillo y Monagas's account described the new phenomenon as caused first by the different opportunities that existed for criminals in the capital; bandits fleeing prosecution in rural areas could more easily hide themselves in the busy streets of Havana. The high number of merchant traffic moving through the city on a daily basis also provided bandits with a means of permanent escape. In and around Havana, infamous bandits were rounded up and captured. In 1867, two well-known men, one of whom took on the name of El Habanero, were captured in the Mercado de Cristina. In 1868, Ramón Carranza y Rubio, a.k.a. el Mono, was captured for crimes and robberies committed in Havana. In 1874, Antonio Díaz was killed by Inspector Trujillo on a public street after alluding capture. And in 1875, the infamous Felipe Quiñones y Ortega was taken in by Trujillo, as was the rest of his band. He was later executed at La Punta for his various crimes.[59]

What concerned colonial officials most was the escalation of *"cierta clase de delitos que se cometen en las grandes poblaciones"* (certain types of criminal acts that are committed in large urban areas).[60] At first glance, Havana would appear to be no different than other urban areas in its increase of criminal activity specific to large cities. However, the same lack of social segregation that had previously shocked North American tourists would play a significant role in undermining colonial authority. The heterogeneous population of the city's neighborhoods was proof of the inability of the colonial government to contain criminal activity—so often associated with race and class but now also associated with wealthier criollos—to specific areas of the city. For example, in 1865 Reparto Las Murallas had been a meeting ground for the city's different interest groups. The 1869 incident at the Teatro Villanueva, however, illustrates that the theater, once located in a "safe zone," was now located in an area of Havana increasingly under competition from criollos, peninsulares, and the colonial administration. Furthermore, the criminal accounts of Trujillo illustrate that by 1881, the administration had all but ceded control of this reparto, something evidenced by Trujillo's comment upon his pursuit of another well-known bandit. When the inspector finally managed to capture the man on the outskirts of Reparto Las Murallas, he commented on the luck of having captured him prior to his actual entrance into the heart of the neighborhood, as the bandit would have certainly escaped given the criminal element that resided there.[61]

The rapid urbanization of Reparto Las Murallas, the growth of the tourist market, and an influx of foreign immigration and displaced laborers contributed to the rapid change in the landscape at the same time that the independence struggle was slowly chipping away at the colonial government's legitimacy. The result was an increase in the public and political nature of criminal activity. Robberies took on a political significance when a representative of the colonial government was robbed at gunpoint, in broad daylight and in front of the Plaza de Armas. Rare, however, was the occasion when these types of crimes took place in the isolated areas of the city, as criminal accounts illustrate. Rather, the criminal activity found more profitable outlets in busy environs and within the safety of the heterogeneous population within Reparto Las Murallas.

The new emphasis on public space extended to the new criminalization of activities not previously seen as criminal. José Antonio Saco's groundbreaking essay in 1832 on vagrancy, *La vagancia en Cuba*, had argued that vagrancy was an indicator of the larger issue of moral breakdown caused by the growth of cultural vices such as gambling.[62] Saco advocated the use of government programs such as the Casa de Beneficiencia to alleviate the problem and provide alternatives to those who would otherwise suffer from what he described as a social ill. Measures implemented by the government during the decades leading up to the administration of Miguel Tacón were based upon a similar view. While the stated goal of government legislation was to deter vagrants, it did not do so through criminalization. Vagrants apprehended by private citizens or public officials in Havana during the 1830s were either taken to the Casa de Beneficiencia or made to labor on public works projects. In the latter decades of the nineteenth century, however, vagrancy was looked upon not merely as a social ill but as a criminal one. At this later date, vagrants apprehended in Havana as well as in other provinces of Cuba were tried in criminal courts and sentenced accordingly. Individuals as young as fifteen, for example, instead of being placed in asylums, as advocated by Saco in earlier decades, were now tried and sent to correctional facilities especially designed to house them.[63]

An old development took on a new significance between the end of Trujillo's term and the renewed outbreak of war in 1895. At this later date, not only were rural bandits using Havana as a base of operations but also a few were actually emulating their rural counterparts. The habanero emulation of *rural* criminal activity took the form of celebrating not, as one would expect, the emerging heroes of the independence movement, who hailed from the rural areas of the country, but rather the heroes of the banditry underworld, who were increasingly able to elude the government authorities. The 1896 criminal accounts left behind by Eduardo Varela Zequeira, a newspaper reporter for the Havana daily *La Lucha,* illustrate this emerging phenomenon. Varela recounts the experiences of the *inspector de policía* Juan Cuevas and his celador Tomas Sabaté under the direction of the chief of police and public order, Tomás Pavia.[64] Charged with patrolling the intramuros, the pair would go on to recount time and again their encounters with known bandits hiding in Havana as well as their encounters with new bandits, some of them lifelong residents of the city, who came to emulate the more-celebrated bandits operating in the countryside.

The timing of this new development was auspicious. The "ruralization" of Havana contrasted markedly with how visitors had described the city in previous years. Even when visitors commented on what they saw as uncivilized elements blemishing Havana's landscape, these were usually limited to a criticism of the city's lack of racial and class segregation. The presence of negros, pardos, and mulatos among the city's legitimate residents undermined Havana's worldly reputation among the city's visitors and, by extension, a population in Havana that increasingly measured its own social and economic accomplishments by Western standards. By the latter decades of the nineteenth century, however, the problems affecting the city and the colonial administration also included the intrusion of the countryside into the modern capital. While the wars raged on in the rural areas of the country and Havana remained seemingly intact, the increased competition over city space and resources marked a powerful shift between colonial officials and the residents of the city. The meaning of this would unfold fully with the onset of the final war of independence.

PART TWO

Colonialism's Aftermath

CHAPTER 5

Empire's End

Not only the *(re)concentrados*
don't have meat
we see that we are left without it
in Havana.

—Anonymous, Havana

This refrain, captured in the pages of a Havana newspaper, rang through the streets of the city during the last years of the nineteenth century. Its significance would have immediately resonated with city residents. Cubans who lived through the wars of independence (1868–1878, 1879–1880, 1895–1898) were aware of the policy of *reconcentración* implemented by the Spanish military and the effects that it was having on cities across the island. Reconcentración was the colonial government's attempt to control the tide of the independence wars by forcibly relocating the Cuban peasantry to the western areas of the island around the towns and cities that remained under Spanish control. In reality, however, reconcentración amounted to a death sentence for the 155,000 to 170,000 Cuban guajiros subjected to the orders, and it irrevocably disrupted the lives of those in urban areas compelled to receive rural migrants.[1] Although most Havana residents witnessed little of the fighting that devastated the Cuban countryside and suffered even less of the infrastructural destruction during the thirty-year armed struggle, this did not lessen the impact of the war. Instead, residents experienced the struggle through the deteriorating conditions of the city and the demographic shifts caused by the war, all of which cast a long shadow over the efficacy of colonial rule.

Havana had not experienced issues of food scarcity since the middle of the sixteenth century, when the city's position in imperial trade networks and the administration's intervention bolstered its legitimacy among residents and visitors alike. Two centuries later, the anonymous resident who now wrote about the scarcity of meat in the city was inadvertently writing about the seeds of colonial discontent. In the refrain he not only pointed to the diminishing availability of goods and services as a result of the armed struggle raging in the Cuban countryside, but was also drawing a distinction between himself as a resident of the city and those who arrived in Havana only to be excised from the urban body politic. It was not a distinction that hinged on class or displacement, but rather one that took geography as the starting point for distinguishing between individuals with legitimate access to the city and its resources, and the wartime conditions of the island made these distinctions especially salient. It was the unmet expectations of Havana residents, forged over centuries of urban colonial rule, which would foreshadow the end of colonial government in Cuba.

WAR AND COLONIAL RECONCENTRACIÓN

The forced removal of peasants not only underlined existing differences between urban and rural Cubans but also brought people to the city under a shroud of criminal suspicion. The colonial government had pursued reconcentración because it associated the countryside with the rebel insurgency, and that association implicated guajiros as potential rebel combatants in the war. Unlike insurgents, however, reconcentrados had not volunteered to fight in the independence movement, so their status as wards of the colonial government also made them immediately suspect to those who supported the cause of Cuba libre. During the period leading up to independence, guajiros found themselves inadvertently associated with both sides of the political struggle and thus the easy political targets of everyone. The mass relocations and the conditions under which peasants arrived further created lasting and raced associations between the eastern areas of the island and disease, which went on to render reconcentrados incapable of belonging to "la culta Habana" and reminded residents of the internal threats that civilization in Havana faced.[2]

The first bando of reconcentración to affect the western provinces was issued on October 21, 1896.[3] For the insurgents and colonial administrators, command over the Cuban countryside and control over the rural population were key components of the struggle that they were fighting. The colonial policy of reconcentración had been introduced as a military strategy during the earlier Ten Years' War and was practiced in other areas of the Spanish empire. Spanish general Félix de Echauz y Guinart had published a report during the Ten Years' War against the Cuban insurgency in which he detailed the actions necessary to ensure a Spanish victory, and neutralization of the rural population by reconcentración was central to his plan.[4] He pointed out that the natural resources found in rural areas enabled insurgents to survive for long periods of time and that access to the coastlines facilitated their ability to procure reinforcements from abroad. He urged Spanish officials to seal off the coast while "tearing up the country" in order to have any hope of defeating the rebels.[5]

The Spanish decision to implement reconcentración in the fall of 1896 would certainly prove the efficacy of the military strategy. The independence forces of generals Antonio Maceo and Máximo Gómez had already captured the eastern parts of the island, and by January 1896 they had also invaded the western provinces. Part of the new Spanish offensive included support for Spanish general Arsenio Martínez Campos's earlier proposal to reconcentrate the Cuban peasantry in town and cities, though the general warned that the policy's success would hinge on the funds and manpower available to colonial administrators and that it might well spell disaster for the Cuban peasantry, stating that "their misery and hunger would be horrible."[6] By February 1896, Martínez Campos's inability to repel the Cuban insurgency resulted in his replacement by General Valeriano Weyler, who became the primary author behind the military offensive that included the reconcentración of western Cuba. Weyler's command of western Cuba drew from the vigilance of the administration in Havana. When it was time for him to name the officials in charge, he named Tomas Sabaté, the barrio inspector who had gained a notorious reputation among city residents, to the task of maintaining order within the reconcentrado camp in Havana.

The aggressive reconcentración in Pinar del Río in 1896, the precursor to that in Havana, was significantly influenced by the belief (harbored by both sides) that the rural population would play a key role in this war of economic destruction. The Cuban Liberation Army had already evidenced its willingness to use the rural population to its military advantage. On July 1, 1895, Máximo Gómez had decreed that all Cuban labor from which the colonial government could derive profit should cease immediately. Those who failed to follow the order would have "their sugarcane . . . set on fire and their processing plants demolished."[7] The proclamation was no doubt a powerful factor in Weyler's decision to counter by rounding up the rural population in the western provinces. According to the October bando, guajiros had eight days to report to a specific locale and were expressly forbidden to bring foodstuffs, farm animals, and other possessions. Anyone found in the affected areas after an eight-day grace period would be reclassified as a "rebel auxiliary" and treated as a captured member of the insurgent army.[8] More relocation orders soon followed. On January 15, 1897, Havana and Matanzas fell subject to the orders, as did Santa Clara two weeks later. Additional proclamations amplified earlier ones, forcing reconcentrados as well as guajiros voluntarily fleeing the countryside to arrive en masse and await resettlement instructions. Those who arrived on the outskirts of Havana came from as far away as Pinar del Río and Matanzas and brought with them news and information that spread panic among the city's population. The countryside was rapidly deteriorating, they claimed, and sugar mills were rumored to be "ablaze in the province of Matanzas."[9]

In the province of Pinar del Río, insurgents burned half of all standing towns after Maceo entered in January 1896. Juan Alvarez, one of Maceo's company commanders, reportedly burned not only vacant homes in the countryside but also those occupied by guajiros. Some forty homes were torched in this way in the suburb of Luis Lazo in Pinar del Río alone, and inhabitants were forced to flee to towns and cities before the forces of Antonio Maceo.[10] The actions of the insurgent army had a similar effect on the Cuban countryside. As the colonial government focused its efforts on reconcentrating the rural population around towns and cities, the insurgent army quickly if inadvertently deconcentrated the Cuban countryside. Instead of forcibly relocating individuals, however, the insurgent army ensured that a steady stream of rural migrants would arrive in urban areas when unauthorized theft occurred or when guajiro homes and fields were set ablaze. To justify their actions, insurgents looked to stories of guajiros who had "gone to the city with the soldiers" or else had sold food and livestock to the inhabitants of towns and cities, thereby helping to sustain the colonial administration.[11]

The leadership of the CLA seemed to understand that it could not take on the responsibility of clothing, feeding, and otherwise caring for the large numbers of guajiros who, in part because of the scorched-earth policy that both armies pursued, were finding it difficult to feed and care for themselves. Gómez also understood that the only option for this population was to seek shelter in urban spaces, where they would quickly become the problem of the colonial administration and help divert colonial funds and resources away from the war being waged against them. Guajiros fleeing to towns and city centers could also be counted on to relay information to city residents who might have otherwise remained ignorant of events occurring in the countryside. Reconcentrados were quite literally the vehicles of the insurgency, which was unable to get to the city by other means. Their physical presence called into question the power of the colonial administration by illustrating the inability of the government to meet even the most basic needs of its subjects, both in the city and outside it. Migrants and reconcentrados thus threatened to undermine the appeal of Spanish colonialism by exposing the perilous condition of the country's economic foundations and the impotence of the colonial government to control the situation.

The Cuban insurgency understood something else: if a new republic was to rise from the ashes of destruction, Cuba's urban areas would need to be disassociated from the Spanish. As the locus of civilization under centuries of Spanish rule, Havana was a key component of colonial rule and stood in the way of the formation of *Cuba libre*. The symbolic division of the island into a rural "republic in arms" and its contrasting "urban colony" mobilized the dual and founding tropes of colonial rule in Cuba. Colonialism had been predicated on the joint abilities of Havana residents and colonial administrators to carve a civilized space from an uncivilized region, defined by walls and protected from external threats. By the time reconcentrados and other migrants stood on the outskirts of the city and insurgent forces threatened to overrun Havana, the crown's inability to secure the basic needs of its subjects had already undermined the future of its hegemony in Cuba.

COLONIAL RULE IN THE CITY

The precarious position of the administration was apparent in the declining condition of Havana. Visitors to the city did not fail to notice or comment on the circumstances under which colonial employees labored. U.S. women's journals, weekly magazines, and newspapers all published accounts of the war in Cuba and used the age and gender demographics of the reconcentrados, the plight of the rural population, and the inhospitable environment of the city to lobby for U.S. intervention.[12] Even before military intervention occurred, accounts of the insurgents and the deserving population of reconcentrados stirred many to action: the Ward Line steamers in New York volunteered to transport all charitable goods collected by the Red Cross to Havana free of charge. Without the cooperation of the shipping line and others like it, the prohibitively high costs of shipping would have likely prevented the work of the Red Cross and the distribution of goods in Cuba.[13] By the final years of the nineteenth century, receipt of these goods was crucial to the survival of Cubans, including urban dwellers. Economic transactions in Havana, for example, were increasingly carried out in gold, silver, copper, and the occasional U.S. dollar. Although the war had made colonial script unstable, colonial employees continued to be paid, when they were paid at all, in the depreciated currency. As a result, many could be found begging for alms on Havana streets. This is perhaps not surprising given that bank notes issued by the colonial government in 1896 had lost 96 percent of their value by the end of the war.[14] After 1896, city residents experienced the war on far different terms than their rural counterparts. Unlike the guajiros, who continued to experience the war through personal losses and the relentless destruction of the countryside, habaneros experienced the war through the changing urban landscape.

General Weyler's failure to ameliorate the perilous and public conditions of the reconcentrados or to shift the tide of the war resulted in his replacement by General Ramón Blanco in October 1897. One of Blanco's first decisions was to ascertain the number of individuals displaced from the countryside and living in towns and cities before moving to end the reconcentración. He ordered provincial governors to provide numbers for the reconcentrados in each district and to account for the conditions in which they lived. In Pinar del Río, 47,000 people were reportedly part of the reconcentración out of a total population of 226,692, and 50 percent of the reconcentrados were believed to have perished. Matanzas reported a total of 99,312 reconcentrados out of a total population of 273,174. The mortality rate in the province was placed at 26 percent. Santa Clara, which served as the front line for much of the period, suffered 140,000 reconcentrados and a 38 percent mortality rate among them.[15] While the provincial governor of Havana did not report numbers, data is available from the reports prepared by the U.S. government in January 1899. Approximately 150,000 individuals,[16] many of them women and children, had been reportedly reconcentrated to the province of Havana, which at the time had a total population of 235,981 individuals.[17] In the four-month period from August to December 1897, 1,700 individuals entered the Havana camp known as Los Fosos (the ditches). By December 1897, 460 of the new arrivals were said to be dead or dying from disease and starvation.[18]

The strained resources of the colonial administration could not meet the expenses of both the armed struggle and the reconcentración. Under

Weyler, much of this responsibility had been shifted to local government and private individuals. Cultivation zones, for example, were a crucial component of making the reconcentración feasible in the western provinces. The zones were envisioned as a way to facilitate the administration's ability to feed reconcentrados (or rather, to allow reconcentrados to feed themselves), but they also functioned to strategically further the colonial government's war efforts. Reconcentrados with suspected ties to the CLA were denied provisions as a way to punish and deter future insurgents.[19] Because they were administered by the colonial government and run by municipal juntas composed of a military commander, judge, alcalde, and urban residents, the zones were also looked at suspiciously by insurgents, reinforcing the correlation between urban spaces and colonialism and causing frictions to erupt between reconcentrados who labored in the zones and members of the insurgency. After Blanco's arrival, insurgent suspicions increased further when the administration suspended the orders of reconcentración.[20] As part of the suspension, the administration agreed to provide work opportunities in the sugarcane fields still under cultivation, including daily food rations. It also agreed to furnish reconcentrados with civil and military protection and guaranteed their treatment at the hands of the Spanish planters.[21] The precarious position of reconcentrados became evident when the administration acknowledged their need to carry arms in order to defend themselves and their property.[22] Exactly whom they were defending themselves from, however, was a question with perhaps too many possibilities to answer.

Outbreaks of disease after the orders aggravated living conditions and contributed to the stigmatization of guajiros in the city, despite the many outbreaks that Havana had experienced during the long history of colonial rule. In Havana, the sanitary inspector of the United States Marine Hospital Service (USMHS) noted that outbreaks of smallpox "increased very considerably" among the civilian population.[23] This came as no surprise to the servicemen stationed at the USMHS, whose job it was to inspect port cities and who had declared Los Fosos a "pest hole." One serviceman noted that on the day he inspected Los Fosos, "there were 500 people found in and around the building, and of that number over 200 were found lying on the floor sick and dying . . . the emaciation of their bodies . . . startling." The USMHS believed that 1,190 of the 1,700 guajiros assigned to Los Fosos had perished.[24] The dependence created by the reconcentración, the escalation of the war, and outbreaks of disease meant that by the end of 1897, the number of dead had increased from 6,730 to 18,123.[25] Starvation, anemia, and intestinal and other diseases had a devastating effect on the population congregated in and around towns and cities. Disease had the tendency to follow the same course as the insurgent army and to travel through the same rural areas. Smallpox infections increased in the eastern areas of the island along with the fighting, and epidemics tended to move westward. Indeed, the insurrection actually altered the spatial dynamics of disease and introduced new epidemics into areas previously immune to outbreaks.[26]

The spread of disease, despite its erroneous association with reconcentrados, played directly into the strategy of insurgents and worked to discredit the colonial administration. The dramatic increase in cases of yellow fever, at least, was the result of the large number of new arrivals in the Spanish army. Cuba's longtime residents had developed immunity to the disease as a result of having contracted it as children, when its symptoms were so mild that it often went undetected.[27] Many of the young men sent to fight in the Spanish war effort, however, suffered the same fate as had other European soldiers sent to the colonies, succumbing to disease long before they witnessed any of the fighting. The island's Junta Superior de Sanidad, which convened regularly through 1896 to discuss the spread of contagious disease, also noted that colonial soldiers were the primary reason for the growing number of deaths in Havana.[28] Before reconcentrados and rural migrants became the chief sanitary concern for the administration, the sick and dying Spanish soldiers produced the perception of urban disorder that would later implicate the colonial administration's ability to rule.[29] Moreover, the deadly outbreaks of disease, specifically the smallpox epidemic of 1896–1897, devastated Havana residents unaccustomed to dealing with epidemics of this magnitude since the end of the earlier Ten Years' War, and certainly not in every environ of the city.[30] The epidemic spread outside Havana and infected areas along the northern coastline, including Matanzas, Sagua La Grande, and Pinar del Río. When the disease resurfaced a year later, it was clear that the city was the source of the contagion.[31]

To city residents, the epidemic implicated the population of reconcentrados. Where once outbreaks of disease had been contained, they were now traveling the same path as the war. The USMHS further reinforced this belief when it concluded that "the localities affected most are along the bay, near the wharves, and in the suburbs. Here, on the one hand, are segregated the poorer classes, in overcrowded and unsanitary dwellings, and, on the other, the refugees from the country. The unusual

epidemic is mostly due to the great influx of these refugee country people."[32] The USMHS's statements as the war continued reveal the growing belief among U.S. administrators and Cubans alike that, as the war
continued, reconcentrados and displaced guajiros were to blame for the
outbreaks of contagion. The displaced found themselves at the center
of other controversies that reinforced the belief that the population was
a dangerous element in the city. Necessity-driven criminal activity in
Havana such as the theft of food and animals dramatically increased
along with criminal activity in general.[33] The work of Cuban scholar
Yolanda Díaz Martínez shows that crime rates almost doubled during
the first years of the reconcentración in Havana province and did not
return to prewar levels until the end of the U.S. military occupation in
1902. While the increase in theft is not surprising given the lack of
resources available, there were, of course, other reasons for the increase
in crime. Men, women, and children broke with colonial laws because
enforcement was now lacking. Crime in the city signaled the weakening
power of the colonial administration and its inability to enforce public
order.

Once the orders to end the reconcentración were amplified in March
1898, fully ending the policy, reconcentrados found themselves facing
many of the same perils that they had previously encountered. With the
aid of the Board of Reconcentrados, private charities, citizens, and
church officials, each municipality was responsible for relocating the
rural population living in their respective areas. The danger of returning
home, however, was not lost on reconcentrados. Rumors circulated that
Spanish soldiers indiscriminately shot guajiros outside former camps
and that guajiros were dying for lack of food and water in the Cuban
countryside.[34] Reports from colonial administrators corroborate the
rumors, although they assign blame to the insurgency forces.[35] The
uncertainty of who was responsible for the murders suggests that both
armies were perceived as potential aggressors and that both sides saw
reconcentrados as enemies "more or less disguised."[36]

Despite the dangers, government administrators found ways to
encourage those who remained in towns and cities to return home.
The military governor of Marianao, for example, not only issued an
order providing for the return of the displaced guajiros but also was
prepared to extend his protection, five hundred dollars to be distributed
among the returning families, and free rail tickets.[37] The declining condition of the city played a key role in official attempts to relocate guajiros to the countryside. According to USMHS observers in Havana,

"The streets and pavements reek with human excreta, both solid and liquid matter being scattered around indiscriminately. . . . An inspection of the principal markets developed the fact that meats exposed for sale were not protected from the filth floating in the atmosphere."[38] Other reports blamed deteriorating conditions on the unproductive newcomers, especially those with physical conditions that prevented them from working or leaving the city. One observer noted that "cities, overfilled with men, women, and children without work, were unable to sustain a population of consumers who produced nothing."[39] Given the perils of the countryside and the unwillingness of some reconcentrados to test their luck, the Board of Reconcentrados distributed emergency provisions such as food, clothing, and medicine and established food kitchens to aid those in need.[40]

Emergency help also arrived from expected sources. The United States, always an interested party where Cuba was concerned, now rallied to the aid of the reconcentrados. International indignation at the conditions that the war had created had escalated since Weyler first implemented the reconcentración, and indignation now prompted the American Red Cross, directed by Clara Barton and working under the direction of the U.S. Department of State, to lead the relief efforts. The result was the Central Cuban Relief Committee. In January 1898, it began to collect food, clothing, medical supplies, and money to ship to Havana.[41] By February, an estimated forty thousand dollars in aid had arrived in Cuba, including forty tons of food.[42] When the USS *Maine* blew up in Havana Harbor, however, its relief efforts were indefinitely postponed, and many of the provisions sat in the harbor and in padlocked warehouses pending the U.S. decision about its future position in Cuba. By the second week of April, the Red Cross was forced to evacuate in fear of an imminent declaration of war.[43]

The long-awaited declaration of war brought with it a naval blockade and had disastrous consequences for the rural population, especially those on the outskirts of Havana. Los Fosos, as well as the four other camps in Havana province, doubled as prisons, hospitals, and orphanages and served as makeshift refugee centers. In an ironic shift of fate, the centers of forced confinement now became makeshift sanctuaries for guajiros living in urban centers. Those who decided to "relocate" to the countryside amid the worsening conditions radically altered the demographics of the island. Railway stops became popular living quarters for former reconcentrados, as rail tickets were relatively easy to obtain for those who wished to reach the interior of the island and makeshift towns provided access to travelers who might offer alms. Railway stops also became the pragmatic end points of the journeys "home" that many guajiros found themselves incapable of finishing. In the town of Jaruco, some twenty miles east of Havana, thousands of reconcentrados turned the railway stop into an overnight refugee center.[44] The Red Cross reported that "Jaruco is one of the great points of devastation; it is said that more people have died there than the entire town numbers in time of peace. . . . Everything is scarce and dear; even water has to be bought."[45]

The small pueblos located south and west of Havana, as well as in the city's center, served their intended purposes.[46] The towns of Santiago de las Vegas, San Felipe, Bejucal (at the time Santiago), Jaruco, and Guanajay had been founded by royal grants in the middle of the eighteenth century as part of the island's system of military defense. While their presence has often been erroneously attributed to the rapid economic growth of the eighteenth century, the towns were meant to insulate Havana from outside invasion by creating a protective barrier between the city and the hinterland. At this later date, the towns served to draw migrants away from Havana on their journeys to and from the city. By the end of the reconcentración, these guajiros found themselves in "in-between" spaces around the city: they were neither defeated colonialists nor triumphant victors, and they further underlined the ambiguity of the land system of defense that still surrounded the city.

In 1862, the crown's military budget was 23,689,609 pesos and was the second-largest expenditure in Cuba.[47] Only the treasury, responsible for paying colonial administrators, spent more funds before the war effort. Prior to the first war of independence, the crown continued to emphasize the island's defense, and this included continuing to fortify Havana. Yet discussion of the walls at this juncture of Cuban history, as we saw in preceding chapters, took on a significantly different tone than had the earlier debates. The earlier plan by Antonio de Arredondo was meant to prevent precisely what occurred in 1762, when the British overtook the city by land. The plan was created in the midst of changing military defense theories, while the 1763 plan by Silvestre Abarca, implemented soon after the capture of the city, was part of a larger military effort to refortify Havana immediately after the attack.

Nineteenth-century plans, however, had neither of these impetuses behind them. Drafts of plans to extend the walls emerged anew as early as the administration of Miguél Tacón, and serious consideration was given to a plan by Juan María Muñoz and Matías Letamendi in 1840 and 1844 that included building new walls on Calle Galiano, in the extramuros, in order to incorporate the existing urban population into the proposed enclosure.[48] The plan was followed in 1855 by yet another draft, this one approved by royal order and designed by Juan Ramón Carbonell, Júan Alvarez de Sotomayor, and Francisco Javier Zaragoza only eight years before the engineer Miguel Portilla y Portilla drafted his plan to begin demolition. The debates and proposals would extend through the nineteenth century and continue even as demolition took place. The crown appointed a committee composed of two military colonels (Colonel Gautier and Colonel Castillo) to study the effects of moving the walls west of the city as far as the Almendares River, which would have effectively extended the walls to the existing urban limits. Reconsideration plans stalled until the outbreak of war in 1868 hastened debates. At this time the practical considerations of building new walls to encompass the limits (formal or otherwise) of the city's perimeter made the proposals unfeasible. The city limits had reached to the Calzada de la Infanta by 1874, and by 1881 the new limits extended to the district of El Vedado.[49] Not to mention that construction would leave the city exposed and vulnerable should another war break out; since the first project had taken almost a century to complete, this consideration was not insignificant.

The correlation between construction of walls and the rising fear that an *internal* aggressor would threaten the city became even more explicit with the outbreak of the war in 1895. Instead of new walls, a fortified defensive line to the west of the city, the Mariel-Majana Fortified Military Defensive Line, was constructed and maintained. This was not the only defensive position taken by administrators. Construction between 1868 and 1895 included the Santa Clara Battery, near the La Punta fort, where its location on a high coastal area again was meant to prevent access to the city by sea. Other batteries along the coast were improved, and military quarters (in Dragones) were rebuilt after the old quarters sustained damaged in a fire almost two decades earlier.[50] The colonial administration focused on fortifying the city even though the 1868 war was waged primarily in the eastern areas of the island, and it was these areas that the armed conflict most directly (and physically) affected. The beginning of Antonio Maceo's western offensive, however, changed that. The presence of troops in Matanzas some hundred kilometers from Havana was destabilizing enough already. And then insurgent forces avoided facing a Spanish offensive by entering Havana province from the south, taking with them the towns of Guara/Melena del Sur, Güira de Melena, Alquízar, Ceiba del Agua, Vereda Nueva, and Hoyo Colorado. By the time the insurgency reached Marianao, Spanish army headquarters in Havana had gone on full alert. It was this move by the insurgent forces, and their presence in Havana province, that led to the resignation of the Spanish general Martínez Campos, the commission of General Valeriano Weyler, and the reconcentración effort that was pursued with full force after 1896. The focus of the military effort that included the consideration of extending or rebuilding the walls was ostensibly protecting the urban base of the Spanish administration. By the end of the nineteenth century, however, the external threat that the crown was facing was not from competing empires, pirates, or corsairs. Rather, the threat came from its eastern subjects. The answer to *whom* and *what* the walls protected had a far different answer in the nineteenth century than it had in previous centuries of Spanish rule. Fortification may have prevented Maceo and the insurgency from gaining access to the city, but it would not prevent the introduction of the "western invasion" of the war effort that officials so clearly feared, or the resulting disintegration of colonial rule.

RECONCENTRACIÓN, MASS DEPARTURE, AND COLONIAL DISINTEGRATION

The correlation between geography, race, and empire was one forged through centuries of colonial rule. For habaneros, the cinturón azucarero was the mythical home of Cuban guajiros. These were the men and women of Garneray's depictions who embodied the soul of the Cuban *manigua*, the pristine and lush countryside that had little to do with the urban production and culture of Havana except as an extension of the island's economy. It was this area that embodied the spirit of emerging Cuban nationalism, and the fact that the concept was one located away from the city from which Spain ruled was fitting. The insurgency and the colonial administration were located in two distinct geographic areas for Cubans, and by the end of the nineteenth century, it was widely understood that the guajiros of the countryside were not only Cuban but also white by virtue of geography, history, and tradition. By contrast, the women and children who arrived in Havana as wards of the Spanish administration were not. Cubans in the western provinces had already begun to associate the armed insurgency with the black, *mambí* battalions from Oriente, leading to the popular perception that towns and cities were being overrun by a "black invasion" from the east.[51] The correlation was one that was easily extended to the displaced guajiros. Not only did Cuban peasants make up much of the rank and file of the Cuban Liberation Army, as did Cubans of African descent, but they also arrived in towns and cities as a result of the ruined countryside, which followed the same course as the CLA. Outbreaks of disease seemed to ominously follow both migrants and insurgents, further sharpening the raced and decidedly negative perception of the Cuban peasantry.[52]

That disease and blackness both were associated with the arrival of rural migrants can be explained by the more complicated relationship that habaneros had with the eastern areas of the island. The pervasiveness of racism extended to members of the Cuban insurgency. It is true that the Cuban Liberation Army boasted a significant number of black and mulatto leaders: Antonio Maceo, José Maceo, Guillermo Moncada, Dimas Zamora, Quintín Bandera, and Flor Crombet were all honored members of the rebel insurgency, many of them from the significantly "blacker" areas of the island's east. This did not, however, insulate black officers and their troops from the racism of white officers and soldiers or from the regionalism that often equated Cuba's eastern provinces with blackness. Ada Ferrer's study of Quintín Bandera demonstrates that the latent racism present among members of the Cuban insurgency could lead to charges of "uncivilized" behavior being brought against black officers from Oriente; she highlights that black and mulatto soldiers in the rebel army also experienced similar acts of racial discrimination when they transgressed colonial racial norms.[53] Ferrer demonstrates how Cuban perceptions of "uncivilized" behavior were intricately connected to Cuban geography. This meant that as the CLA made its way from Oriente into the western provinces of Cuba, it had to combat the raced and racist perceptions of westerners, which is not surprising given Cuba's demographics at the time. In areas of Oriente, the population classified as "nonwhite" was listed as 63 percent, a significant contrast to the 32 percent in a place like Las Villas.[54] Thus, as the Cuban Liberation Army moved westward, they had to contend with Cuban concerns over the racial nature and direction of the war.

Insurgents and guajiros who found themselves associated with the CLA immediately aroused suspicion and racial stereotypes. Esteban Montejo, a former slave, guajiro, and soldier for the insurgents, recounted the racism that he was subjected to not just by members of the CLA but also by foreigners who reinforced Cuban beliefs that the insurgency was waging a race war against the "civilization" that colonialism had fostered. In one particular account, Montejo relates how his struggle with a

Galician man and a conscript in the Spanish army carried explicitly racial overtones. After sparing the man his life, Montejo was surprised when the Spanish soldier accused the insurgent army of being composed of "savages." As an explanation for the epithet, Montejo offers that "they started to think we were animals, not men—that's how they came to call us Mambises. Mambí means the child of a monkey and a buzzard. It was a taunting phrase."[55] Regardless of the term's origins, the encounter illustrates the centrality of race and racial perception during the wars. For mambís, racial identification provided a central component of their identity as insurgents, in part because of the significance placed upon it by Cubans, Spaniards, and North Americans. Ironically, just as foreigners had played a key role in the white perception of guajiros almost a century earlier, they now contributed to the black perception of insurgents and *orientales* (from the eastern area of the island) and associated the Cuban Liberation Army with a "savage" black constituency. To further complicate matters, few foreigners (or Cubans, for that matter) could or cared to distinguish between black members of the CLA, mambís, rural insurgents, peasants, and their white counterparts. Rather, designations were based on geography, history, and tradition—and the war and subsequent reconcentración had disrupted many of the historic understandings when it implicated displaced guajiros in the decline of the city, the spread of disease, and the increase in criminal activity.

The fear of Maceo's western campaigns had cast a shadow over the entirety of the Cuban peasantry, but peasants were not the only ones at risk of being suspected or accused of treason. Fear of insurrection, particularly where free people of African descent and slaves were involved, had previously shaken the foundations of nineteenth-century colonial rule in Havana. The Aponte rebellion in 1812 had made the fear and possibility of a black, island-wide, and potentially Atlantic rebellion a reality in Havana. The moreno José Antonio Aponte, not coincidentally from the neighborhood of Guadalupe, inspired the rebellion. The 1843 Conspiracy of La Escalera, too, brought the possibility of a black-aligned independence movement into the purview of the colonial administration and caused it to rid the city of those who, through discourse, art, or politics, questioned Spain's hegemony.[56] Slavery had ceased to be an organizing ideology by 1880, when the administration officially implemented the *patronato* (patronage) system that instituted free-born laws across the island and granted slaves their freedom after a six-year tutelage period under their existing masters. Independence, however, was an ever-pressing concern, though what is clear by colonial administrators' reactions to the western offensive is that the fears that drove the swift and brutal reprisals of habaneros following Aponte and La Escalera had not gone away with the end of slavery. Arguably, without slavery to organize concerns over the fate of the island, what Antonio Maceo's western invasion unmasked was racial fear over the future of the island's administration.

It was not just racial fear that underlined the disintegration of colonial rule. While the holding cells at El Morro Castle overflowed with dozens of treason cases, the arrest and transport of prisoners to Havana further brought the war into the city.[57] Their presence in Havana also brought their wives and daughters, who pleaded the cases of their loved ones with the colonial authorities. The addition of these women and children, many of whom had had few options but to heed Spanish bandos, contributed to the effect that Havana, by the end of colonial rule, was a city filled with women, children, and the old or infirm.[58] The hypervisibility of these populations alongside a visible lack of men did much to undermine the political and cultural capital of the city. No reliable data exists for the changing demographics of the city during the years of the war, and the last Spanish colonial census, published in 1898, offers little in the way of demographic information for the period. The census undertaken the following year by the U.S. government of occupation takes the Spanish numbers as its base. Instead, the visible changes were commented on by newspaper accounts, visitors, war correspondents, and city residents, and these only became more pronounced with the beginning of the U.S. military occupation that served to underscore the importance of the new political direction of the country after 1898.

CHAPTER 6

North Americans in Havana

To build . . . there is an enormous distance between
what you project and what you accomplish.

—Carlos Miguel de Céspedes

In 1925, the famed French architect J. C. N. Forestier arrived in Cuba.
Forestier came to Havana armed with a team of French and Cuban
architects and urban planners at the request of Cuba's minister of public
works, Carlos Miguel de Céspedes (1924–1933). He was there to design
a master plan for the ensache of Havana and to correct the "anarchical"
way in which the city had been allowed to grow.[1] Forestier's arrival
illustrates the ways in which the republican, twentieth-century city of
Havana was narrated as an outgrowth of new political processes. Likewise, Céspedes's characterization of Havana as the "Paris of the Caribbean" (a moniker that grew in popularity throughout the first half of
the twentieth century and that is often attributed to him) reveals the
ways in which Havana was again understood as a city on the brink of a
post-independence urban modernity.

A series of U.S. occupations (1899–1902, 1906–1909, 1917–1922)
marked Cuba's transition into the early republican period. These interim
years and the changes that took place in the city's political landscape
lent credence to the idea that a new urban trajectory had emerged for
the city of Havana. The processes of colonialism, independence, and
military occupation altered the physical geography of Havana. Urban
planning and city organization, however, remained to facilitate an
imperial project that drew on past colonial structures and Cuban elites
for legitimacy. During the brief period between 1899 and 1902 especially, when the legal and political structures of the island were

not yet consolidated, urbanization continued as the enduring theme of empire. The flurry of urban works projects undertaken during the U.S. occupation served to propose and communicate the limits of Cuban sovereignty while simultaneously reinforcing the power of the city, its residents, and their ability to legitimate the U.S. presence on the island.

While Cuba's thirty-year struggle for independence had permanently settled the question of Spanish colonialism, the issue of Cuban sovereignty remained largely unresolved. The United States intervened in Cuba in April 1898, after the destruction of the USS *Maine* in Havana Harbor, to a mixed reaction. Some members of the Cuban elite championed annexation, while others looked with skepticism toward the United States but welcomed intervention as a means to ensure mutually beneficial alliances. Others still wanted to see nothing more than the birth of a Cuban republic and the end of Spanish colonial rule. By the time the U.S. Congress issued the declaration of war against Spain on April 25, 1898, these choices were not all equal. Already the Cuban Liberation Army had imposed free zones in the eastern part of the island and in some areas of the western provinces, and had made significant inroads toward draining Spanish resources. The CLA had not, however, managed to occupy Havana and unseat the Spanish. This came as somewhat of a relief to the administration of U.S. president William McKinley, who looked warily at the tired contingent of Cuban soldiers and the ineffectiveness of the Spanish government as a potential drain on U.S. resources.[2]

Four months after the U.S. Congress declared war on Spain, Spain signed the peace treaty directly with the United States. The treaty bypassed the CLA and made it easier for the United States government to effectively exclude members of the Cuban army from shaping the political negotiations taking place. They were also largely excluded from the public celebrations of the revolution that José Martí had begun—that is, one shaped by the ideology, if not the practice, of an anticolonial and antiracist new republic.[3] Havana's continued importance in these unfolding events was clear. Its colonial designation as *"la llave del nuevo mundo"* (the key to the New World) was no less true at the end of the nineteenth century as it had ever been; control Havana, the actions of both governments seemed to suggest, and the rest of the island would soon follow. In fact, the political sway of the city stretched far beyond the island. Puerto Rico and the Philippines, likewise the final remnants of Spain's empire, were also implicated by the events taking place in the Cuban capital. No sooner had Spanish officials signed the peace treaty than guerrilla wars erupted in both these territories, and with that, the Atlantic and the

Pacific became amphitheaters of insurrection. Events had proven that Havana was important *and* permeable, and on the eve of 1898, the representatives of the U.S. and Spanish governments who brokered the peace agreement would have been keenly aware of that fact. The peace treaty was responsible for ending the war and permanently resolving the issue of Spanish rule in the Atlantic. Cuban sovereignty, however, was another matter altogether.

MILITARY REORIENTATIONS

For U.S. troops arriving in Havana, their first reaction to the city would have been a visceral one. The stench coming from the bay would have been compounded by the heat and humidity of the summer months; the salt from the sea would have stuck to their skin, and before they had time to take anything else in, their senses would have been accosted by the totality of the sights, sounds, and smells of the Caribbean city in the midst of war.[4] If they were familiar with urban areas especially, they would have noticed the lack of urban services and civil government; if they were not, they might have only registered a subdued chaos hanging over the city streets. Only after stretching their legs in the Plaza de San Francisco adjacent to the port would it have begun to dawn on the North American soldiers, themselves having arrived in Havana in segregated steamers and "white-only" railway cars, that they were staring at a city almost completely devoid of young men, composed primarily, as one U.S. official so deftly put it, of "women and children" and residents who were decidedly darker than the North American newspapers and U.S. media had led them to believe.[5]

When the U.S. Army Corps of Engineers conducted its first general survey of Havana shortly after the end of the war in January 1899, Major General Ludlow found it a city filled with the old, infirm, and destitute. Ludlow noted the reconcentrados who lingered in and around the city and whose presence clashed with the image of "la culta Habana" so extensively written about in previous decades. In his official reports Ludlow stated that "the physical condition of the city could only be described as frightful. There were several thousand reconcentrados in and about, who had been herding *[sic]* like swine and [were] perishing like flies." Because aid facilities such as Havana's Casa de Beneficiencia had been abandoned just as the colonial administration stopped providing services, city residents were left to deal with the needs of the city.[6] Ludlow noted that reconcentrados "were found dead in the streets and in their noissome quarters, where disease and starvation were rampant. Other thousands were lacking food, clothing, and medicines."[7]

It is perhaps not surprising, then, that sanitation, hygiene, and disease prevention became the immediate goal of public works projects. Outbreaks of disease had been rampant with the escalation of the war and tended to follow the direction of the conflict, such that from the eastern provinces and toward Havana the war and the army troops left a trail of sick, dead, and dying even when they did not engage the population in physical combat.[8] Recurrences of yellow fever and the resurgence of smallpox, which had been almost unheard of in recent decades, devastated residents, rural migrants, and especially Spanish soldiers unaccustomed to the climate. More significantly, the outbreaks also threatened the economic transactions forged between Cuba and the United States during the previous century. When the disease spread, ports in the U.S. South—especially New Orleans, but also ports in Texas and Alabama—made requests that ships arriving from Havana and Santiago de Cuba be quarantined as a result of conditions on the island, thus threatening not only to devastate Cuba's economy but also to adversely affect U.S. southern economies.[9]

The condition of the city and its new association with the wars did more than fuel Cubans' suspicion of the new administration. Reinforced by publications such as *Harper's Weekly* and the newspapers of William Randolph Hearst, this new image of Havana found its way into the minds of the U.S. public. No longer did writers laud the "exotic familiar" condition of Cuba. Instead, writers such as Stephen Bonsal and Frederic Remington noted only the devastatingly backward condition of the island and especially that of Havana.[10] For U.S. administrators, the city was elemental to any political mission in Cuba. Two things, at least, were certain. If U.S. interests were to be protected, the United States would need to figure out how to ensure and legitimate this relationship. Second, even if the administration managed to solidify a mutually beneficial relationship in Cuba, unless security and circulation in Havana could be secured, there would be little the island could offer as an economic and political partner.

As part of a larger political strategy meant to preempt a new government composed solely of Cubans, the media played a large role in portraying both the reconcentrados and the CLA's leadership as black after the war. Apart from the overt racism in U.S. media representations, the demographics of the city had also been altered by war such that Havana now registered vastly different demographic data. At least one scholar has speculated that a plausible explanation for the discrepancy between the high number of people of African descent listed on the last Spanish census and the lower number registered in the first census taken by the U.S. government as explained by the death toll of the reconcentrados rather than by perception or a simple error in counting.[11] If the population of reconcentrados was composed of people whom the colonial administration identified as African-descended, we can be reasonably assured that the U.S. administration would have classified them as black or Negro in accordance with U.S. law and custom. In fact, the 1899 census classified one-third of the island as African-descended.[12] The CLA had even higher numbers of African-descended in its rank and file and leadership—numbers somewhere between 40 and 60 percent, according to Louis A. Pérez Jr.—and given the displaced soldiers in the western provinces and in and around the capital city in the immediate aftermath of the war, the displaced populations who remained in and around Havana would have been easily identified as black by the incoming U.S. administration.[13]

The U.S. perception of the island as a result of the war extended to the members of the CLA. Given this, almost immediately after reorganizing the island, General Leonard Wood (by this time appointed the new military governor of the island) set about neutralizing the potential of a second guerrilla war that would mobilize disgruntled and disenfranchised former combatants. Five hundred thousand Cuban soldiers had emptied into the Cuban countryside once the occupation began, and those who chose to go back to the rural areas from which they came found ruined farms, scorched earth, and devastated cattle and crops, as well as a new government unwilling to share openly in the political process. The spike in banditry and the increase in crimes of opportunity and necessity during the war carried into the post-1899 period.[14] The association between the insurgency and a dangerous black Cuban constituency convinced Wood to disband the Cuban Liberation Army before a "misunderstanding" could lead to renewed military action. Fitzhugh Lee, in 1899, warned that "if by accident or bad management . . . an exchange of shots took place anywhere between the Cubans and American soldiers . . . the country might have a guerrilla war on its hands and our troubles [will] multiply."[15]

Part of these troubles, the administration was beginning to realize, was the history of the independence wars. The island had emerged from a thirty-year insurgent movement that was "explicitly anticolonial, antislavery, and antiracist."[16] However pervasive racism may have been under Spanish colonial rule, and however implicit its presence in the independence movement, Alejandro de la Fuente nonetheless illustrates the importance of Martí's discourse of racial inclusivity. Its significance lay not in its ability to become real through the struggle for independence but rather in the porous nature of the myths that it created; *mestizaje* was powerful not because it erased race in Cuba (indeed, it reinforced the idea of racial difference while doing away with the language necessary to deal with racism) but because it provided black Cubans with a legal and legitimate discursive means to demand racial inclusion as citizens of the nation. It similarly limited white elites' ability to legally exclude blacks from Cuba's emerging political structures on the basis of race.[17]

To bring Cuba under the purview of U.S. control was thus a two-pronged project at the end of the war. The occupying government had first to organize a police force capable of neutralizing the immediate threat of violence in the Cuban countryside. It also had to find a means of limiting the possibility of black inclusion in the new republic. To address the first problem the administration understood that many of the young American men serving in Cuba were unfit; language and cultural differences, not to mention the heat and geography of the island, left these men, or so General Wood believed, wary and susceptible to carrying out injustices with local residents from which the U.S. government might not so easily recover. Instead, General Wood organized a police force under the auspices of the government of occupation and quickly set about disarming members of the former insurgency.

The newly created Guardia Rural (Rural Guard) absorbed thousands of former CLA members into its ranks who were put to work patrolling crime on the city outskirts. Many of the former combatants, however, refused to relinquish their arms and disappeared instead into the Cuban *manigua* (the Cuban countryside, often associated with revolutionary fervor). To U.S. administrators of the Department of Havana as well as those in the Department of Santiago in the eastern side of the island, the population of guajiros constituted a threat similar to the one that Spanish administrators had been forced to contend with.[18] To complicate matters, guajiros were no longer isolated in the more remote areas of the island, as they had been years earlier. Lee recognized that if an altercation were to occur, the legitimacy of the U.S. administration on the island would come into question, as it would provide Cubans with visible evidence that U.S. administrators, like their Spanish predecessors, were unfit to govern. This should come as no surprise, since the administrative and governing challenges faced by the occupation were the same as those confronted by the former Spanish colonial government. The presence of the U.S. government of occupation on the island was an implicit promise of renewed stability and economic prosperity. In order to accomplish this ideal, however, it had to first deliver law, order, and stability to Cuba. More importantly, the emerging administrative basis of U.S. neocolonial rule required the establishment of policía by first and foremost securing the capital city from the population of now black and newly dangerous guajiros. If it could not accomplish this first task, then all other points were moot.

After disarming the remaining militias, the most important task before the U.S. government of occupation was setting up the political structures absent in 1899 but necessary for reestablishing a hegemonic relationship. The island was divided into administrative departments under which municipal bodies functioned much as they always had, albeit with different people now in charge. Despite the political rupture and the transition from Spanish colonial rule to a militarily occupied territory, the administrative organization of the city stayed much the same. In fact, the regulations previously approved by the colonial ayuntamiento in 1881 changed little under the new occupation government; the task facing General Wood was too great to worry about the internal organization of many of the city's already existing governing bodies.[19]

Scholars have assigned a pivotal role to the U.S. military occupation with regard to urban renewal and the new public works projects that it introduced, which were followed by massive urban growth and a period of architectural innovation in Havana's repartos that is visible in the city to this day. The trend to reproduce European styles such as the *bellas artes* movement and, later, the *movimiento moderno* is visibly present in the architectural design of buildings constructed from the mid-nineteenth century through the 1950s; the limits of Havana neighborhoods are thus visibly identifiable through the city's built environment. J. C. N. Forestier, Jose Luís Sert, and Le Corbusier were important influences even as urban planning reflected the ideas of Frederick Law Olmsted's Garden City neighborhoods, which became fashionable in Havana's newly developed outskirts in the early twentieth century.[20] In part because construction on the farms of Vedado and El Carmelo came to a standstill once the wars of independence started, the groundwork that allowed the modern and distinctive Havana neighborhoods to flourish is often credited to the U.S. government of occupation. In reality, however, Cuban urban planning guided this development.[21]

In 1861 the construction ordinances had been introduced, as well as the *Reglamento para los arquitectos municipales de La Habana*. With the professionalization of urban offices and the stakes in land development as high as they had ever been, the trend toward regulation only increased. When looking to regulate public works projects, the government of occupation therefore looked first toward Spanish law. As of 1882, there already existed in Cuba a General Law of Public Works, which itself emulated the 1877 general law on the peninsula, stipulating the conditions under which projects were to be carried out.[22] In 1899, the U.S. Department of War went to the trouble of translating the hundred-plus-page document and sending it through the government printing press. In the end, however, James H. Hitchman tells us that the U.S. Army Corps of Engineers, in charge of public works projects in Havana, relied instead on their own regulations because the Spanish laws were far too cumbersome. He further notes that when it came to public works projects, the corps often had to perform the contract work of engineers, since it was held that Cubans lacked expertise in this area.[23] The government of occupation, however, still had to contend with the greatest issue that it faced in Cuba: setting up the urban structures through which governing principles and hegemonic relationships would flow. The urban reorganization and public works projects of the North American government were part of the same process of legitimating the presence of the U.S. administration. Unlike many of the young servicemen in Cuba, the officers in charge of the occupation were seasoned veterans accustomed to U.S. foreign policy and expanding overseas influence. For General Wood, the importance of Havana in the process of making Cuba fit for self-government was clear. Of the $55 million allocated for Cuba, Wood spent approximately $23 million on public works efforts in and around Havana (see table 1 for breakdown).

The island was divided into two sectors for the purpose of administering public works. The U.S. Army Corps of Engineers would be in charge of Havana while a civilian department under Secretary of Public Works José Villalón would administer projects in the rest of the island. The occupation government's emphasis on the capital city was clear; Havana received a total of $100,000 a month for services, while projects in the other six provinces were allocated somewhere between $100,00 and $150,000, even when Villalón complained about lack of funds and the disproportionate amount of attention (and funds) spent on the capital city. Major General W. M. Black of the U.S. Army Corps of Engineers reported directly to General Wood, who was himself in charge of the

TABLE I   BREAKDOWN OF EXPENDITURES ON PUBLIC WORKS
IN CUBA, 1898–1902

	Total spent
Quarantine	$694,024.81
Public buildings, works, ports, and harbors	$5,833,607.90
Railroads	$57,338.51
Barracks and quarters	$2,525,483.78
Charities and hospitals	$4,124,986.60
Sanitation	$9,706,258.20
Maps and data collection	$408,820.00

SOURCE: Leonard Wood, *Civil Report*, 1902, 1:196, cited in James H. Hitchman, "Unfinished Business: Public Works in Cuba, 1898–1902" and *Informe sobre el censo de Cuba, 1899*, p. 759.

approval of all projects, contracts, materials, and accounting. The department employed no fewer than 3,800 men in Havana. It paid from one dollar a day for relatively unskilled labor up to four dollars a day for more specialized and skilled work. It had under its purview architects, mechanics, plumbers, and the like. Everyone, it seemed, with the exception of engineers (the creation of an engineering department under Chief Engineer and Major General W. M. Black successfully kept Cuban architects from playing prominent roles in urban organization). With a workforce of 800,000 people in the entire island, the 3,800 figure is significant. Much like the Spanish colonial government before it, the occupation government was the single largest employer in the city.[24]

The pressing concern that lay before General Wood and Major General Black was ensuring urban infrastructure in Havana. The presence of and access to urban services had also been an important aspect of Spanish rule in Cuba. Urbanism played a key role in Havana residents' willingness to support and legitimate the administration for as long as they did. In the final years of colonial rule, effective rule in Havana had hinged at least in part on the Spanish administration's ability (or lack thereof) to safeguard the city and provide residents with uninterrupted urban services such as trash collection and adequate police patrol. Once the war intensified and the insurgency gained control of larger areas of the island, the administration found itself with diminished funds for anything but the armed effort. It thus ceased making payments to many of its lower-ranking employees (such as members of the Havana police force), who in turn ceased providing residents with services. As urban services during the final years of colonial rule waned, so too did popular support for the Spanish government. The U.S. government of occupation would be held to the same expectations that, when unmet, had discredited the Spanish government in the eyes of local residents. This was a fact not lost on the military governor. The first order of business in the city may have been to disarm the insurgency, but the longest project that the occupation government engaged in was located in Havana and tied directly to the condition of the city in the aftermath of war.

The Corps of Engineers produced a series of maps that illustrate the areas of the city that were especially of interest. Published within Ludlow's annual report for the fiscal year 1899, the maps of the newly reorganized Department of Havana became part of the multiple ways in which the administration legitimized its presence. Far from being a unidirectional project, the maps they produced during this period are evidence of the multiple propositions that circulated within the city. Street cleaning, street paving, and improved sanitation were the bargaining chips of the new government, and these appeared to benefit everyone involved; by August 1899, the number of deaths in the municipality of Havana had decreased to 6,136 from the all-time high of 21,235, and deaths attributable to disease evidenced a similar decline, thus bringing the city closer to the promise of the modern and urbane ideal that Spanish colonial rule had been unable to fulfill and that the North American government seemed poised to achieve.[25] Streets were paved to avoid drainage problems and other potential health hazards, as well as to aid in productive transportation flows. It was estimated than an average of 3,402 vehicles of various sorts passed over city streets. There were roughly 180 kilometers of narrow streets that ran through Havana, many of these in varying degrees of disrepair and paved with compact, broken stone or, in areas by the port, with Belgian block (sett, or rectangular quarry stones used for paving). Many others were still dirt roads that remained unpaved.[26] Brick and asphalt were the desired materials for paving (brick for its ability to withstand the elements and asphalt to withstand the weight of traffic). In order to effectively pave streets, however, a renovated sewer system was necessary to prevent damage. The administration's efforts were hampered by the legal claims of a private company, Michael J. Dady and Co., to contracting rights in Cuba that dated to the colonial period and superseded those of the U.S. Army Corps of Engineers. Unable to settle the claims, the administration opted instead to repair city streets with macadam and to forgo the sewer system.

Public works projects to reinforce sanitation and hygiene measures soon followed. To avoid epidemics of yellow fever, public buildings were cleaned and disinfected. Thirty-five miles of sewers were cleaned out and renovated to allow for proper drainage, even if new sewers were not built.[27] Street-cleaning services that had been suspended during the war were once again reinstated, with services extended far beyond the limits of the core city.[28] A trash collection schedule was also reinstated (one can imagine the accumulation of trash and debris, especially after the peasant resettlement camps were left unattended), with service provided once a day in heavily congested areas of the city and twice to three times weekly elsewhere in the city.[29]

The new Office of the Municipal Architect—relying on the colonial office of the architect—was also created and staffed by eight employees. They were not only responsible for ensuring that new construction stayed within existing codes but were also tasked with being vigilant about existing structures. Homes that were deemed dangerous or unhygienic were immediately demolished.[30] This emphasis on hygiene extended to residents themselves. Soon after Ludlow's initial assessment of the city, routine censuses were conducted to monitor the health of local residents and the spread of disease. The local Sanitation Department of Havana and the national sanitation council investigated cases of typhoid, tuberculosis, meningitis, and yellow fever in the city and its surrounding areas, separating cases by demographics and age, race, and neighborhood district in order to more closely monitor and quarantine the sick.[31] By 1907, there were no reported cases of yellow fever in the municipality of Havana, and outbreaks of other diseases in the city and its outlying areas had been successfully contained as a result of the quarantines.[32] The city could at last be considered clean, and private contractors bid for the privilege—and the compensation—that public works now guaranteed.[33]

The United States aggressively focused its infrastructural efforts on sanitation and transportation. Central to the government's concern in Havana were the many parks, public buildings, roads, bridges, and wharves that needed attention. Cleaning, paving, repair, and renewal became the means of addressing urban issues. Public works projects thus became a panacea for the governing concerns of a new administration bent on securing political legitimacy.

One of the major legacies of the U.S. government of occupation's building projects was beginning construction of the seaside wall known as the malecón by the U.S. engineers Mead and Whitney in 1901. The malecón was built in six stages, ending in 1958 and extending for a full eight kilometers. The first stretch extended from the fort at La Punta to the street at Lealtad and began the transformation that would drastically alter the facade and orientation of the city by first and foremost providing a welcoming and aesthetically pleasing introduction.[34] Just as importantly, however, it also delineated the future direction of the Avenida del Golfo, which would unite the different areas of the city by creating a connective thread between them. The design and orientation of the malecón quite literally forced the city to face the sea and stressed the importance of mobility, including that which drew the visitors (or the viewer) away from the city center and toward the lush countryside. This marked one of the primary differences between the insular orientations of the colonial administration and those that followed Cuban independence. It was ostensibly a move to beautify the city, especially for the tourists that arrived by ship and passed through the bay.[35] Much like the improved sewer system, the move reinforced the importance not just of a modern and hygienic city, but one whose facade and built environmental features reflected its role in the emerging global capitalist economy.[36]

To ensure the efficacy of the new projects and the longevity of the urban design, a series of legislative measures approved by the U.S. Congress outlined the manner in which public works would be carried out. These mandated collaboration between Cuban and U.S. urban planners, prioritized projects, and made provisions for the manner in which projects would be contracted to different firms.[37] The military orders passed, on the other hand, turned the entire area of Havana, beginning at the bay and extending through the old city, into a military zone akin to that found only on La Fortaleza. The government of occupation enacted military power over the entirety of the city and effectively suspended civilian law. Although it promised not to affect private property, it also made clear that the orders of the chief military officer at La Fortaleza, including those that approved construction in the area, would not be superseded.[38]

Civil and military orders, however, were not enough to ensure the longevity or contours of the new republic. The Teller Amendment in April 1898 had been proposed in reaction to McKinley's declaration of war. McKinley's refusal to recognize an insurgent government in Cuba—itself the result of the suspicion that surrounded the CLA—aroused fears in members of the U.S. Congress that annexation was imminent. The racial and religious composition of the island was among the primary factors implicated in fears of annexation, as were economic concerns about what incorporation would mean for the economy of the U.S. South. The Teller Amendment restricted U.S. designs to end Spanish colonialism and propose a stable and sovereign government.[39]

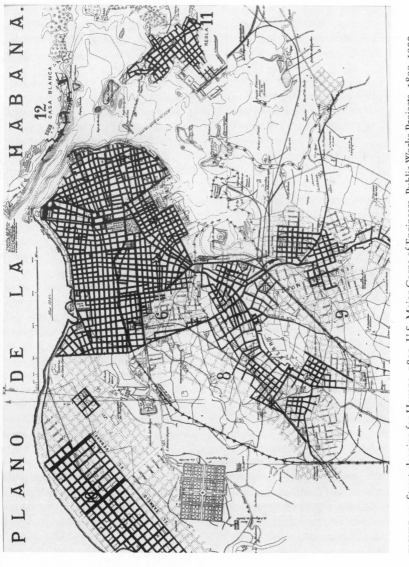

FIGURE 19. Street cleaning for Havana, 1899. U.S. Major Corps of Engineers, Public Works Projects, 1899–1900. Fifty-sixth Congress, First Session, House of Representatives, *Annual Reports of the War Department for the Fiscal Year Ended June 30, 1899* (Washington, DC: Government Printing Office, 1899).

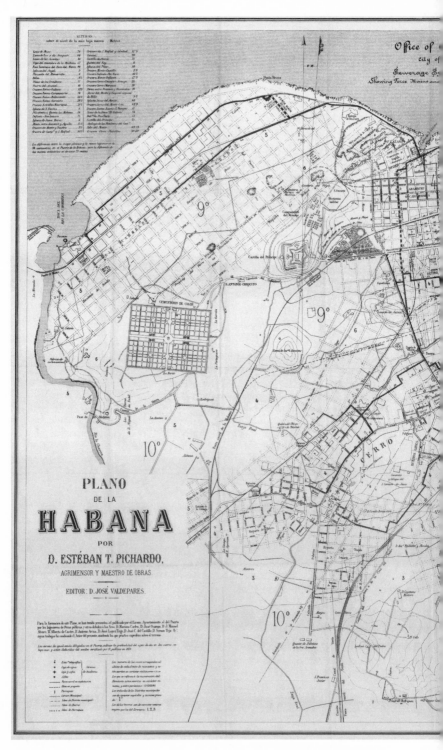

FIGURE 20. Proposed sewerage system, 1900. Office of Chief Engineer, Division of Cuba. Uncatalogued materials, courtesy of the Library of Congress, Geography and Map Division.

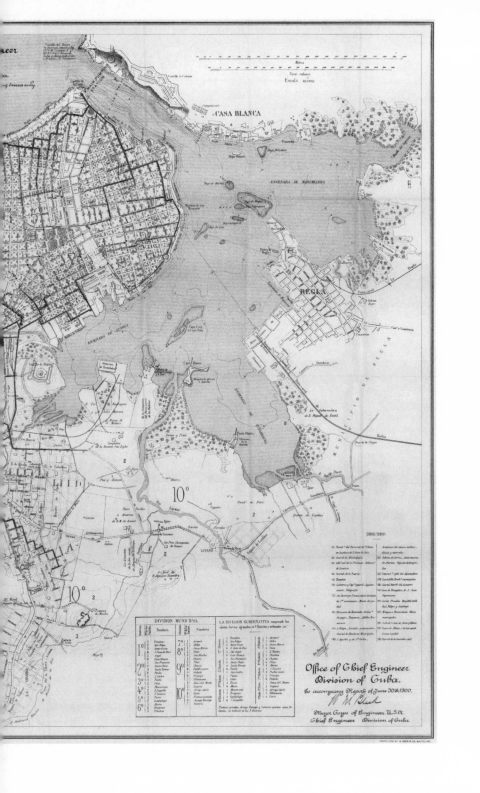

CASA BLANCA

ENSENADA DE MARIMELENA

REGLA

ENSENADA DE ATARES

10°

10°

10°

Escala 10.000

Office of Chief Engineer
Division of Cuba.

to accompany Report of June 30th 1900.

Major Corps of Engineers U.S.A.
Chief Engineer Division of Cuba.

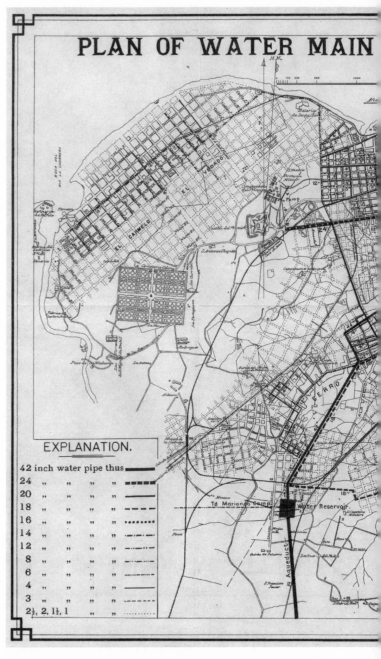

FIGURE 21. Plan of water main distribution of Havana, 1899. U.S. Major Corps of Engineers, Public Works Projects, 1899–1900. Fifty-sixth Congress, First Session, House of Representatives, *Annual Reports of the War Department for the Fiscal Year Ended June 30, 1899* (Washington, DC: Government Printing Office, 1899).

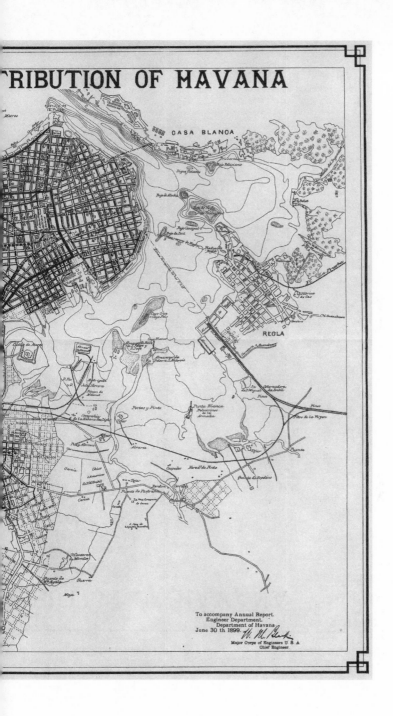

RIBUTION OF HAVANA

CASA BLANCA

REGLA

To accompany Annual Report.
Engineer Department.
Department of Havana
June 30 th 1899.

Major Corps of Engineers U S A
Chief Engineer.

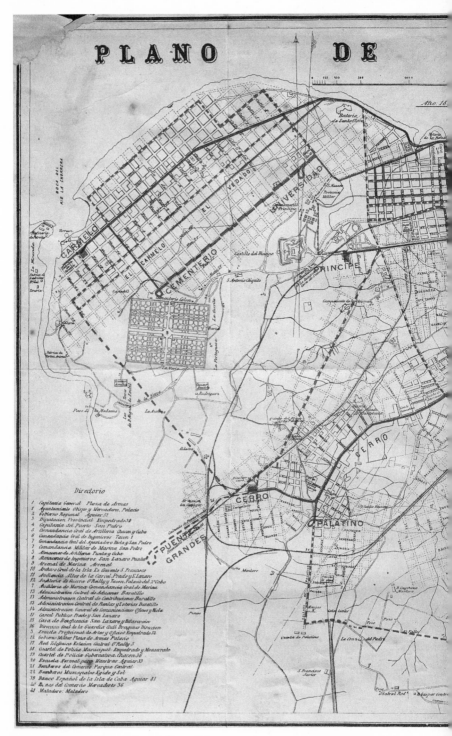

FIGURE 22. Proposed electric railway, 1894. U.S. Major Corps of Engineers. Mapoteca, M-485 005, Archivo Nacional de Cuba, Havana.

HABANA.

CASA BLANCA

REGLA

LUYANO

H.C.R.
CROSSING

AUTHORIZED SYSTEM
of the
HAVANA ELECTRIC RAILWAY CO.

Casas de Salud

34 Quinta Garcini: Carlos III
35 Quinta Integridad Nacional: Calzada Zapata.
36 Quinta La Benefica: Arango e J. del Monte.
37 Quinta del Rey: Calzada Cristina e. tes
38 Quinta Purisima Concepcion del Centro de
   Dependientes: Alejandro Ramirez. Jesus del
   Monte.

Paraderos

23 Paradero Concha FC de Marianao: Carlos III
24 Paradero Tulipan: Cerro FC de Marianao.
25 Paradero del Cerro FC de Marianao
26 Paradero de la Cienaga. FCU
27 Paradero de Jesus del Monte FCU Puente Agua Dulce
28 Paradero del Cerro FCU Calzada Palatino.
29 Estacion de Fesser FCU Regla
30 Paradero de Vapores de los FCU Muelle de Luz.
31 Administracion de los FCU Antigua Villanueva Dragones
32 Paradero del FC del Oeste Calzada de Cristina
33 Paradero y Administracion FCU Plaza S Juan de Dios

──────── Existing Single Track
════════ Existing Double Track
──────── Proposed Single Track
- - - - - Proposed Double Track
──────── Existing Single Track
         to be doubled.

FIGURE 23. Malecón, c. 1904. Photo courtesy of the Library of Congress.

To ensure advances toward a new government, the Cuban Constitutional Convention, from which the Platt Amendment emerged, was held
in Cuba in 1901. The amendment granted the United States decision-
making power over Cuban political affairs and assuaged U.S. concerns
over the nature of its future relationship with Cuba; the treaty is perhaps the single most frequently cited legislation when scholars look for
evidence of how Cuba's sovereign rights were curtailed immediately
after independence, but the importance of the convention is more far-
reaching than that. Alejandro de la Fuente writes that a little-noted
aspect of the convention was its importance in attempting to create the
political structures that would legally exclude the Cuban masses, many
of whom (indeed, one-third, according to the U.S. census figures at the
time) were African-descended. The ambivalence of this success was
reflected in the passage of an electoral law that did in fact exclude a portion of the population. This exclusion was based not on race—a growing legal improbability given the discourse of mestizaje that had long
defined the struggle for independence—but on literacy and property

stipulations, which also had the desired effects. As de la Fuente notes, however, this attempt was mediated by blacks' ability to use those same nonbiological and therefore attainable aspects of difference to limit legal and political exclusion.[40]

The ambivalent success of subsuming exclusion into the political structures of the country made legal and juridical directives singularly important. In this respect, the Platt Amendment had significant and lasting repercussions. It restricted Cuba's ability to enter into foreign treaties and to contract public debt. At the same time, the country ceded the right of intervention to the United States along with a portion of the island—the area where the U.S. Guantanamo Bay Naval Base is located—thereby relinquishing a significant aspect of its sovereignty. Another little-known aspect of the legislation dealt not just with the juridical obligations of the country but also with the terms by which Havana would be governed. Once the U.S. administration left the island the Platt Amendment stipulated that the Cuban government would need to execute and build upon the urban works projects introduced during the U.S. military occupation.[41] This clause was meant to correct the sanitation issues in Cuba's major port cities (Havana and Santiago de Cuba) that during the war had resulted in U.S. quarantines of Cuban vessels and a loss of profits for both countries. The measure was thus a telling reminder of the intricately linked economies that emerged during the period of Spanish colonial rule and the U.S. need to protect them once colonial structures were dismantled. It was also recognition of the importance that Cuba's capital city had acquired as the organizing and administrative base of government.

SURVEYING AND MAPPING THE CAPITAL CITY

Shortly after the end of the war with Spain the U.S. government of occupation began the largest urban mapping project that Cuba had undergone since the middle decades of the nineteenth century. Not since the Spanish colonial administration emphasized statistical mapping and census data collection had the city come under this type of close scrutiny.[42] Much as in the heyday of colonial rule, maps, census counts, data collection, and public works projects together comprised a larger project to survey, interpret, and plan. The importance of a U.S. perspective is articulated in the census data collected between 1899 and 1907. The 1899 Cuban census was closely modeled after U.S. census documents and published in both English and Spanish.[43] Victor H. Olmsted of the

U.S. census bureau arrived in Cuba to direct the Cuban undertaking. In its opening statement, Secretary of War Elihu Root noted that the census would be an essential component of an effective U.S. government in Cuba. Indispensable to this effort, he continued, was obtaining maps of the cities and provinces of the island, and thus the order was given by the census office to engage in mapmaking exercises. The result of the mapmaking exercise, again according to Root, was the division of the city and its surrounding areas.[44]

As tools and strategies of empire, maps and the mapmaking process rose to prominence with the introduction of capitalism and the rise of the early modern state.[45] Read as texts instead of objects, western maps can also be "a practice and discourse that names the world, categorizes people, bounds places, and territorializes socio-politico-economic regions," becoming integral components in the production of colonial and neocolonial subjects and spaces.[46] Transatlantic and sea voyages honed an imperial need for navigation tools, and once imperial forces were on the ground, the production of maps laid claim to newfound territories and disseminated information to residents and producers alike.[47] The process of forging twentieth-century neocolonial relationships was no different. Centuries later, when the importance of urban space was clear, the government of occupation relied on strategies similar to those used by the earlier colonial administration to legitimize claims to power. The maps produced were "not founded in some primal instinct 'to communicate a sense of place, some sense of *here* in relation to *there*,' but in the needs of the nascent state to take on form and organize its many interests." They transmit imperial desires via tangible propositions and function as tools in the violent act of birthing spaces that all colonial and neocolonial spaces go through.[48] The multitude of maps of Havana produced by the U.S. government of occupation serve as official, visual propositions that symbolically connected Cuba to the U.S. political body at a moment when the political possibilities associated with Cuban independence posed the most risk to the existing relationship between the two countries. Together with the Platt Amendment and the attempt to control the legal channels of inclusion, they were the foundation of a sovereign Cuban republic.

The literature on urbanization in Havana is deeply marked by the political transitions that occurred with the end of Spanish colonialism and the beginning of the Cuban republic.[49] It has tended to identify shifts in the city's urban trajectory that mirror the political processes of each era. The end result is a modern and urbane—if deeply unequal—metropolis.[50] Consider the series of maps created by the New York–

based firm Town Planning Associates that document the city's periods of expansion and growth. Created immediately before the political transition of 1959, the series of maps periodizes Havana's growth thus: 1750–1850, 1850–1899, and 1899–1924, with the most visible changes taking places in the 1899–1924 period.[51] The illustrations mark the 1899 military occupation as the start of the explosion in urban growth and ostensibly make the United States the harbinger of urban expansion while downplaying colonial urban change. Town Planning Associates created those maps, however, during an era in which Cuba stood as one of the most urbanized countries of world, with a large portion of the population residing in Havana. This period was also the height of the republican era, when Cuban ties to the United States had far surpassed those of the nineteenth century. The United States was a looming influence in twentieth-century Cuban affairs. It is not surprising, then, that its association with urban expansion is one that extends into and has been reinforced by the literature that surrounds the subject.

If, as Denis Wood suggests, maps reflect both the cultural values of a society and "the needs of the nascent state to take on form and organize its many interests,"[52] then the maps produced by the corps are notable for a number of reasons beyond the expansionist values that they convey. The maps that show the street-paving and street-cleaning projects implemented by the administration serve to "organize" the existing landscape into one that resonated with U.S. ideas of urbanism. Significantly, however, the urban plan that street cleaning and street paving reinforced was that of the former Spanish grid. Affluent neighborhoods had previously been established to the west of the core city under Spanish colonial rule, and these were the same neighborhoods that the U.S. public works projects now focused on. The "authority" that the maps convey was thus based on the earlier Spanish colonial urban model.

Viewing independence and the introduction of U.S. rule as a watershed moment in Havana's urban history results in a misleading emphasis on the impact of the U.S. administration in Havana. To be sure, the government of occupation set the tone for the urban development of the city well up to 1959, and the public works projects constructed during this period cannot be ignored. But the documents produced by the U.S. Army Corps of Engineers also reveal that the process of mapping the city lay at the center of a twentieth-century imperial project in which the use of space and the promise of urban renewal were as central as they had always been. The facades of the buildings may have changed as architectural currents from Europe and the United States were transferred to

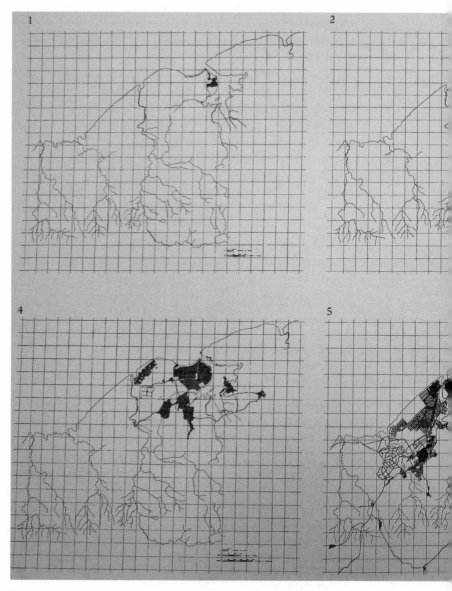

FIGURE 24. Town Planning Associates, *Plan piloto de La Habana, Directivos generales y diseños preliminarios,* 1959. Southeastern Architectural Archive, Tulane University Libraries, New Orleans.

3

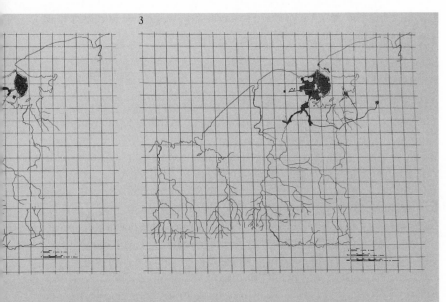

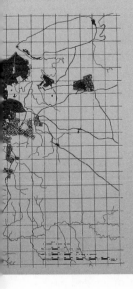

1	1519-1600	POBLACION	4000	HAB
		AREA	37	HA
		DENSIDAD	108	HAB/HA
2	1600-1750	POBLACION	62000	HAB
		AREA	151	HA
		DENSIDAD	330	HAB/HA
3	1750-1850	POBLACION	168000	HAB
		AREA	443	HA
		DENSIDAD	379	HAB/HA
4	1850-1899	POBLACION	242055	HAB
		AREA	560	HA
		DENSIDAD	241	HAB/HA
5	1899-1924	POBLACION	558000	HAB
		AREA	3000	HA
		DENSIDAD	186	HAB/HA

Havana, but the premise of the city as the administrative and legitimating force on the island remained much the same.

RESIDENT RESPONSES

At the start of the republican period, twenty-one men sat on the board of the Ayuntamiento. They were prepared to take on the direction of the city. Among the first things they did was pass an ordinance that left intact the military orders of the government of occupation. During the brief republican government before the 1906 intervention, as during the period of military occupation, North Americans and Cuban residents cleared vacant lots, urbanized repartos, and transformed vacant areas into public parks.[53] Between 1905 and 1907, the ayuntamiento approved at least eighty repartos for urbanization. These were to be employed in private use and public city use and for the widening of existing streets, among other purposes.[54]

Urban expansion was not a uni-directional project. The U.S. administration provided urban services for the same reasons that it mapped and surveyed the land around Havana. Local residents, for their part, recognized the contractual nature of the agreement. City residents aware of the political exchanges taking place made their complaints directly and publicly to the new administration. They lobbied not for the removal of the administration from Cuba but rather for its increased involvement in urban works. The residents of El Vedado and Príncipe, two of the more affluent neighborhoods developed during the latter part of the nineteenth century but which grew to prominence in the early part of the twentieth century, once again became vocal advocates of urban development. In a 1906 a petition to the provisional governor of the island, the new members of the old Asociación de Propietarios, Industriales y Vecinos del Vedado y Príncipe levied complaints against city officials and institutions in charge of urban development. The Sanitation Department, the Secretary of Public Works, the municipality of Havana, and the provisional council of Havana were among the associations they deemed deficient. The association specifically noted the neighborhood streets in El Vedado that were in disrepair or needed paving, the vacant lots that the city government had failed to fence, the lack of sufficient public lighting, and the improper labeling or mislabeling of city streets. They explained that together these things constituted examples of bad urban hygiene.[55] The provisional governor was sufficiently moved to forward the complaints of the association to the director of each newly formed department, Havana included.

The military occupation had officially ended in 1902, after the constitutional convention had ratified a new constitution and the Platt Amendment was written into the document.[56] Eleven of the sixteen Cuban delegates attending opposed ratifying the amendment, and of these, nine came from Oriente, including Juan Gualberto Gómez, one of the few black leaders of the independence wars to also emerge in the republican political arena. The existing government of occupation handed control of the country to Tomás Estrada Palma, who served as the first president of the republic and was re-elected again four years later, this time amid well-founded accusations of electoral fraud, open protests, arrests, and a call that members of the government step down and the opposition party be restored to power. In 1906, Estrada Palma called on President Theodore Roosevelt to interfere in Cuba and after a brief stint by Secretary of War William H. Taft, Roosevelt appointed Charles Magoon provisional governor of Cuba.

In this new republic, appeals first to the Cuban president and then to the provisional government from the association as well non-associated residents arrived with a renewed urgency. Residents sent letters and petitions directly addressed to the men in charge in which they explained the "unsanitary" and "unhygienic" condition of the city and made appeals for more or larger extensions of public works, and the administration responded.[57] Widows cited health reasons in their petitions asking that streets be repaired.[58] In 1907, over seventy local Havana residents, including merchants, business owners, and private citizens, sent a signed petition to Charles Magoon asking that Calle Teniente, located in the old part of the city and a main business area, be paved. They again referenced the positive effects for the hygiene of the city that paving would produce and again positioned their argument to resonate with the values of the new administration. From the working-class neighborhood of Jesús María, Ambrosio Suero, Pablo Haro, Carlos Martínez, Hortensio Gonzalez, Dionisio Gonzalez, and two hundred other residents similarly organized into committees that demanded that improvements be made in their barrio.[59] While it might appear that the Cuban administration bent to the will of the powerful association or that the association's members were exercising power that few residents or Cubans had access to, it should be noted that residents from across areas and suburbs of Havana also engaged in letter-writing campaigns. From Jesús del Monte and Víbora, for example, residents similarly and successfully initiated campaigns to repair their streets and install sewer systems in their neighborhoods.[60]

Local residents were actively engaged and deeply invested in the trajectory of urban growth, especially after experiencing the decline of urban services that went hand in hand with the end of Spanish colonial rule. Recognizing the processes though which legitimacy is maintained, they wrote letters and petitions addressed directly to the new administration (via the military governor of the island). Using the lessons learned from the colonial and urban Spanish administration, they held the United States responsible for the rebuilding of Havana. The physical changes taking place were indelibly marked by the city's colonial legacy. The colonial era had taught residents to redefine their urban positioning in accordance with the changes affecting the city. Therefore, in the midst of the military occupation and throughout the early years of the republican era, habaneros followed old methods of negotiating social and political change when they used the expectations of their new administration and its values to their own advantage. The flurry of personal correspondence directed at Cuba's provisional governors following 1899 illustrates residents' ability to manipulate strategies and affect the possibilities promised them with the end of colonial rule and into the new republic. When individuals such as Manuel Varona Suárez, president of the Asociación de Propietarios, Industriales y Vecinos del Vedado y Príncipe, complained to the provisional government and enumerated the shortcomings of each newly established urban department,[61] he was also revealing the expectations that habaneros had of the new administration and their willingness to hold it to the promise that it had implicitly made. Alongside the complaints of residents from Havana's affluent neighborhoods, residents of Jesús de Monte and Víbora—already writing letters—now formed a resident committee to lobby for urban works in their own neighborhoods.[62]

Cuban archival documents for the era following the 1899 political transition provide some evidence for the extent to which the strategies devised by residents worked. Time and again, provisional governors and republican administrators responded favorably to the petitions of neighborhood residents, escalating the number of urban works projects implemented and the number of offices opened to deal with urbanization.[63] Ultimately, however, the urban project imposed upon Havana was an unsustainable one. Only a few years into the republican era, there were visible signs of the breakdown of urban centralization. Residents held administrators responsible for these failures. While residents used the values of the republic as leverage to lobby for change, they also opposed attempted changes (even when these came under the rubric of urban modernization) when they threatened ideas of urban self-definition and restricted their own autonomy. When residents of Príncipe and Medina opposed the elongation of Calle 23 (one of the principal arteries that runs through Havana), they took on the full force of the Secretary of Public Works, again writing a flurry of letters to the president of the Cuban republic, Mario G. Menocal, to help them stop the construction project.[64]

The plan proposed by the Secretary of Public Works would have extended the street through the Colón Cemetery and expropriated properties by dissecting the neighborhoods in favor of the electric railway. The association realized that once the plan was carried out, similar projects would be implemented throughout Havana, such as the elongation of Calle 12, which would have united the affluent neighborhoods of Príncipe and El Vedado. The association once again employed the rhetoric of the new republic, focusing not on the expropriation of land, which would have spelled the end of any future neighborhood expansion, but rather on the limited gains of the railway compared to the detriment that it would cause to the sanitary conditions of the city.[65] Neither the Secretary of Public Works nor the central government chose to respond to any of the initial claims of the association. The increased pressure by the association did, however, manage to convince the government to suspend construction on the project to elongate Calle 23, which was deviated instead around the Colón Cemetery. The struggle between the association and the Secretary of Public Works reflected the pitfalls of the new urban project and was not the only one of its kind. As urbanization became increasingly centralized, the strategy first used by El Vedado residents of garnering the collective strength and resources of neighbors in order to oppose a central government flourished. In many Havana neighborhoods, residents established associations regardless of their economic or political standing. In lieu of these, they used the resources at their disposal to oppose the policies of the new administration and to lobby for desired changes. In Jesús María, for example, when urban departments showed no signs of acquiescing to resident demands for sanitary conditions, residents did not form into an urban association of the type visible in more affluent neighborhoods but instead came together as the Obreros del Barrio de Jesús María, making a social and class distinction between themselves and other habaneros. In a statement issued to neighborhood residents of a similar socioeconomic standing, the *obreros* (workers) called for collective action against the government until their demands for better working conditions and stable rent prices were met.[66] In Jesús del Monte and Víbora, the inability of the new administration to expediently renovate the neighborhood and keep up with the upward social mobility of its residents led the association to volunteer to absorb the costs of all public works projects if the administration would only allow them to enact the measures that they saw fit.[67] The moves of both neighborhood associations were reminiscent of those enacted by the first association of its kind: the Asociación de Propietarios, Industriales y Vecinos del Vedado y Príncipe. As in the colonial period, the associations were created as a collective effort to define the trajectory of urban change.

During the years of the U.S. military occupation, Havana lay at the interstices of mutually reinforcing projects. Once the seat of colonial rule, it had been transformed into a site of neocolonial and economic possibility. The process of forging a new relationship with a newly independent Cuba began, for U.S. administrators at least, through the reorganization and control of space that the military administration engaged in and that the public works projects facilitated. As much as 1899 might have been a watershed moment in terms of a political transition, then, the date did not bear witness to a transformation of the urban project in Havana, or even the imposition of a new form of urban rule. Instead, the decline of urban services followed by the immediate reinstatement of urban government was used in the same way that the racial constitution of the Cuban Liberation Army was used by U.S. politicians and media outlets: to portray Cubans as inferior and therefore incapable of self-government.[68] The three-year U.S. military occupation, the brief Cuban government, and the U.S. intervention that followed were meant to visually and materially restore law and order, legally codify the existing relationship between Cuba and the United States, and ensure U.S. economic interests on the island. The proliferation of public works projects in the aftermath of the final war of independence followed the same colonial trajectory of brokering political relationships and claiming territories by controlling the organization and use of physical space. Under the purview and then the orbit of the United States, the continued focus on Havana illustrates that claims to the island were inscribed in Havana and forged through different modes of urban representation.

Conclusion

Across the Atlantic and Back

A few years before the end of Spanish rule and before the city passed into U.S. hands, Havana residents had already begun to impress upon the crown the importance of maintaining political allegiances in Havana.[1] The certainty that their inclusion in the Spanish empire was not only necessary but also voluntary is what drove the events that surrounded Manuel M. Miranda's expulsion to the Spanish penal colony of Fernando Póo in western Africa.[2] Miranda was a *tabaquero* (cigar worker) employed in the Don Quijote de la Mancha cigar factory in Havana. A few weeks before his arrest by colonial authorities, he learned that a group of tabaqueros had decided to support the Spanish war effort. Tobacco workers had been active in political affairs and labor disputes at least since the middle of the nineteenth century, and by 1896 most were organizing in support of the separatist struggle, which explains the alarm that Miranda felt at the declaration.[3] This group was organizing a central effort to augment the waning forces of the Spanish voluntarios by conscripting Cuban workers. Miranda and a few other men from the Don Quijote factory protested the mandatory campaigns and set in motion the events that led to his expulsion from the city. His and the men's protest, he wrote, turned on the idea that no Cuban could be obligated *"a ser espanol"* (to be Spanish).[4]

The Spanish crown disagreed. Sovereignty over the island still rested on the crown's jurisdiction over territory and place, and the war was the visible manifestation of the formidable if contested nature of this claim.

Land (whether territory, property, or enclosure) has made up the constitutive basis of political sovereignty for centuries.[5] The *exercise* of dominion over lands and people beyond the initial ceremonial claims to space that Diego de Velázquez performed on Cuban shores centuries prior, however, was another matter altogether. In the case of Havana walled and regulated spaces were a material and territorial expression that spatially oriented an individual to the rule of law.[6] As in other towns and cities where the port oriented the economy, individuals looked outward toward the sea, where empire, economies, and possibilities abounded. In Havana, the confluence of law and order was made manifest through colonial urban form, and it was urban form—as manifested in the walled city—that facilitated the exercise of colonial sovereignty. The configuration of space that the walls and the extramuros demarcated figured prominently and brought into fruition the necessary components of empire to carve a space of civilization onto the whole of an uncivilized region while still allowing for the economic flows of the port.

Trade winds and ocean currents had made the city's location a propitious one worthy of the crown's attention, but enclosure had proven a costly and impractical venture over centuries of colonial rule. Amurallamiento had been an early and necessary step in protecting Havana from foreign and invading armies. Without the hinterland's ability to supply the city with corn, rice, plantains, and yucca, or without the interregional and often extralegal trade with colonial ports that brought flour into town, the continued scarcity of food might have otherwise proven insurmountable.[7] The eighteenth- and nineteenth-century penchant for reinforcing and extending construction of the walls in the face of multiple and failed attempts to secure the city from outside penetration, when the city's very existence had been premised on the circulation of Atlantic flows, reveals the power and the durability of urban empire. It also reveals the unsustainable and irreconcilable contradictions between colonialism in Cuba and the interdependence of Atlantic economies, politics, and social processes. Walls as material entities restrict and contain the very mobility and circulation that they are tasked with ensuring.[8] What this means is that the emphasis on the nineteenth century as an era of rupture that broke with earlier trajectories as a result of the economic reforms ushered in by the British occupation and the consequent growth of sugar and slavery is at best overly emphasized. In Havana, these factors exacerbated already existing urban patterns, but they did not create them anew. It was not, for example, a draconian and reactionary Spanish monarchy that made colonialism in Cuba and modern urban form irreconcilable.[9] Even within the struggles of the labor movement in which Miranda became embroiled (a labor movement made up of diverse ethnic, racial, and class interests but that coalesced around a largely white, urban, and male leadership) Spanish colonialism remained an attractive proposition for many well into the end of the nineteenth century, falling out of favor with creoles and immigrants only once internal factors provoked the turn toward separatism, something that is readily apparent in Miranda's tale.[10] Similarly, the U.S. occupation of Cuba based in Havana did not introduce new patterns of urban rule, nor did it rely on new technologies. The desire of historians to document change over time, which emphasizes political transitions as the key markers of historical transformation—something true of Cuban history—has led to a disregard for the layered history and multiple relationships embedded within Havana's urban topography.

Contemporary conservation efforts spearheaded by UNESCO, Cuban, and international coalitions, for example, target the "colonial core" of Havana's perimeter and represent its colonial history in a way that erases Guanabacoa from the original area that the city occupied. With its neoclassical architecture, the neighborhood of Jesús María has also been assigned a place in the late nineteenth-century and early twentieth-century history of the country instead of being historicized as the extramuro living spaces of the first black and free colonial vecinos. Both areas were constitutive components of the civilized space that the walls enclosed, yet the commodification of patrimonio, with its emphasis on architecture, architectural facades, and conservation, reinforces the idea of distinct urban periods adjacent to one another. Architectural historian Timothy Hyde, however, has noted in his examination of the confluence of law and architecture in Havana that in its physical fabric "the modern city co-existed with its predecessors."[11] This implies not the side-by-side growth of the city that the conservation blueprint would soon bring into being but rather the shifting and layered geographies that colonial residents traversed.

Instead of creating an impregnable boundary, enclosure produced a political order through spatial orientation that consisted of everything within its own bounds (i.e., the intramuros), including subjects and citizens.[12] The relationships engendered by enclosure thus established the first correlation between bodies, territories, and sovereignty, which extended the crown's dominion not only over space and territories but also over the bodies of its subjects. This was an extension of dominion that intimately affected colonial subjects like Manuel M. Miranda. As a vassal of the Spanish crown, Miranda was also subject to enclosure, though his refusal to "be Spanish" while still residing within the very locus of Hispanic civilization in the Americas—the town—is evidence of the tenuous nature of this claim. When, for example, Miranda returned to the Don Quijote factory to find that the celador was looking for him, he considered his options carefully. He thought about turning himself in or even appealing directly to the governor, since he believed that he had done nothing to warrant arrest. Perhaps his friends convinced him otherwise, or perhaps the bodies overflowing the holding cells of El Morro, once used to hold pirates, corsairs, and the troops of invading armies, convinced him that was not a good idea. Whatever the reason, and now believing that he would be conscripted into the Spanish army should the authorities find him, Miranda fled from Havana and away from the purview of Spanish authority. In the end, Miranda wrote in his memoir, "Me escondí en Guanabacoa" (I hid in Guanabacoa).[13] The physical limits of the empire, it seemed, were still located outside the city and in the once-Amerindian and black village across the bay, but despite Miranda's attempt to circumvent Spanish authority, the crown's dominion not only reached into Guanabacoa but also extended over his own body, and he was unable to flee its reach.

Miranda's movement through the geographies of empire and his eventual return to Havana (after Cuba's independence) illustrate colonial subjects' abilities to straddle distinct spaces and territories. While Havana's walls proved the permeability of its borders through the mobility of colonial subjects, the port did the same for the Atlantic processes between and across imperial geographies. The port and the constant flow of information, goods, and people facilitated movement to and from the city and created "spatially overlapping sovereignties."[14] These were the ever-present and contested terrains of the city akin to those found in border towns.[15] Ironically, Havana is contained within a Cuban geography with the most natural of borders: Cuba is surrounded by water, and the sea constitutes the northern and eastern boundaries of the city. Its liminality was a product of geography and subjectivity produced by the port on the one hand and the walls on the other. Enclosure announced a secure perimeter while it signaled the acute vulnerability of the crown, made all the more so by the city's position at the interstices of empires and exchanges on the sea.

As in all border spaces, the social relations implicit in space also mapped onto the bodies and restricted the movement of individuals.

Soon after his arrival at a friend's home in Guanabacoa, for example, Miranda was intercepted by the colonial authorities. He was put on a ship headed across the Atlantic in a journey that would deliver him directly to the Iberian peninsula. The *deportación* (deportation) that Miranda was subjected to was part of the crown's strategy to ensure the longevity of colonial rule. It was the mirror process of reconcentración, but unlike the nineteenth-century wartime strategy, it had long been used as a colonial means to rid the island of political threats, black and white alike. The crown had exercised its ability to deport individuals, particularly those living in Havana, since its early preoccupation with the religious and ethnic origins of new settlers in the sixteenth and early seventeenth centuries. By the nineteenth century, numbers of *deportados* (deportees) increased due to the growing concern over slave and separatist revolts. After the Aponte slave rebellion in 1812, for example, sixty-three prisoners were spared death sentences but were deported to the Spanish colony of St. Augustine, Florida.[16] Their expulsion into outlying territories calls attention to John TePaske's emphasis on the importance of the periphery to the constitution and practice of empire.[17] Instead of solidifying the limits of empire, the walls contributed to "the existence of a corrupted divide between internal and external policing," which suggests "an increasingly blurred distinction between the inside and outside of the nation itself, and not only between criminals within and enemies without."[18] Deportation to outlying areas *beyond* the city but *within* the empire recognized the rights of royal subjects at the same time that it produced criminals for the empire.

By the end of the nineteenth century, empire and colonialism were also geographic propositions, and the presence of walls alternately marked and claimed territory in the New World while it produced and separated individuals. The inversion of the intramuros and extramuros can be explained through this production of space and subjects. In his discussion of the Berlin Wall and East and West German subjectivities, historian Greg Eghigian notes that the image of the East German subject as theocratic and de-individuated popular in West Germany is itself a subjectivity produced by the presence of the Berlin Wall. Walls there have thus paradoxically produced the very subjects whom the state aims to protect its citizens from and whom it categorically denounces as at odds with the idea of nation.[19] In Havana, it was this production of colonial subjectivity and the necessarily permeable border (to allow for commercial and other trade between town and hinterland and colony and empire, as well as with other imperial locales) that facilitated the inversion of nineteenth-century city space. The area of land that ringed the city and created a border between intramuros and extramuros also produced the metaphorical condition that Cirilo Villaverde described as the city's existence between *"luz y sombra."*[20] The liminality that Villaverde attributed to Havana's physical spaces also marked its temporal existence. Mario Coyula, for example, wrote that economic and political success in Havana was achieved not despite the conflicting interests present in the city but rather *because* Havana was able to contain these within different but simultaneously occurring temporalities. These were the result of the city's ability to produce space and meanings that have endured in its topography.

The contested terrains produced by the colonial process discussed here are still visible in the contemporary city, reinforced by the fact that its crumbling facades are visible to even the casual observer. Havana's architectural and built environment have produced the link between colonial Havana and the contemporary Cuban city, constructing in the process Fidel Castro's Cuba as an integral part of the exhibition of colonial Havana and incorporating the revolutionary government of 1959 as the essential element of the post–Special Period urban landscape.[21] The draw for foreign visitors and tourists thus lies in the dis/articulation of the city from the politics of Cuban history, where revolution is "an image that is merely part of the city's landscape void of politics that can exist in the contemporary world" and that might challenge Western modernity.[22] This is an enduring concern as the cities of Latin America and the Caribbean become commodities in the sale and purchase of "third-world" authenticity in ways that implicate colonial and colonized subjects. Miranda's expulsion from Havana and his incarceration on the penal colony of Fernando Póo over a century ago, for example, should be a reminder that patrimonio as a sovereign right bleeds onto the physical bodies of individuals. In a modern-day example elsewhere in the Americas, John F. Collins notes that in Brazilian cities, cultural heritage has turned into a new type of state property that is created by cataloguing "social forms configured as essential to community identity" in places such as archives.[23] Quoting anthropologist Richard Handler, he goes on to write that the colonial subject is linked to territories as a quasi-natural extension of the physical landscape, as "property open to enclosure under capitalism."[24]

In twenty-first-century Havana, the struggle between state and subject over access to city space is ongoing. The lyrics of the musical duo Obsesión, one of the hip-hop groups born in post–Special Period Havana despite an austere U.S. embargo and the Cuban government's taboo against North American cultural forms, serve as yet another illustration that circulation flows and exchanges continue to permeate borders of various sorts. The duo has taken Calle G, the seven-hundred-meter green-area pedestrian artery that delineates the northwest border of El Vedado, as the subject of one of their compositions. Calle G is an alternative to the leisure space of the Malecón and the waterfront congregating space that it offers youth from the nearby neighborhoods of Centro Habana. Instead, Calle G is lined with commemorative busts of the prominent leaders of the Americas. The likenesses of José Martí, Benito Juárez, and Martin Luther King Jr. mark contemporary Cuba's link to a history of social justice. Interrupting this discourse on the boulevard, however, is the image of José Miguel Gómez, president of Cuba during the race war of 1912. The aberration of the image has been consistently defended as "patrimonio," prompting Obsesión to respond with "abajo! / Y no me digan que eso es patrimonio / Que no se pu' tumbar porque es de Eusebio! / No entiendo que hace ese tipo 'allá' / Después de una revolución que se hiso 'aquí' . . . tumbelo!"[25] The reference is to Eusebio Leal, the city historian and director of what is arguably one of the most powerful and independent government offices in Havana that oversee the urban changes taking place. The rejection of patrimonio as an organizing element of urban space is one born from the dissonance caused by the state's discourse on Cuban history and the built environment of the city. The organization of the city and access to urban space, it seems, remains a contested terrain.

Notes

1. Documentos sobre el derribo de las murallas, 1863, Archivo Nacional de Cuba, Havana (hereafter cited as ANC), Fondo Obras Públicas, legajo 42, no. 479; Carlos Venegas Fornias, *La urbanización de las murallas: Dependencia y modernidad* (Havana: Editorial Letras Cubanas, 1990), 44.

2. *Vecino* was a legal distinction for Spanish subjects and heads of household. The origin of the term is rooted in early modern Spanish understandings of local citizenship. It held the promise of legal rights for vassals of the king considered *naturales* (native of) who could satisfy both local and Spanish ideas of communal belonging. In the early modern Caribbean, it was possible for free blacks and women to hold this title, something that would change as the parameters of the category shifted under colonial rule. See Tamar Herzog, *Defining Nations: Immigrants and Citizens in Early Modern Spain and Spanish America* (New Haven, CT: Yale University Press, 2003).

3. By the nineteenth century, colonial officials were especially concerned with slave and separatist revolts among the free black population of Cuba. See Michele Reid-Vazquez, *The Year of the Lash: Free People of Color in Cuba and the Nineteenth-Century Atlantic World* (Athens: University of Georgia Press, 2011), and Matt D. Childs, *The 1812 Aponte Rebellion in Cuba and the Struggle against Atlantic Slavery* (Chapel Hill: University of North Carolina Press, 2006).

4. Individual and corporate interests and identities cut across various categories. Ethnic and racial affiliation, for example, as well as class and occupation, often defined political and economic interests. See Joan Casanovas, *Bread, or Bullets! Urban Labor and Spanish Colonialism in Cuba, 1850–1898* (Pittsburgh: University of Pittsburgh Press, 1998).

5. Alejandro de la Fuente, *Havana and the Atlantic in the Sixteenth Century* (Chapel Hill: University of North Carolina Press, 2008).

6. The first plan to wall the city appeared in 1603. A version of Juan Cristóbal de Roda's plan was set in motion in 1640, and the walls, in fits and starts of construction, would not be considered complete until 1760. Even then, additions and debates around their extension continued to circulate in Havana well into the end of the nineteenth century.

7. Valerie Fraser, *The Architecture of Conquest: Building in the Viceroyalty of Peru, 1535–1635*, 2nd ed. (Cambridge: Cambridge University Press, 2009); Richard L. Kagan, "A World without Walls: City and Town in Colonial Spanish America," in *City Walls: The Urban Enceinte in Global Perspective*, ed. James D. Tracy (Cambridge: Cambridge University Press, 2000), 117–52.

8. De la Fuente, *Havana and the Atlantic*, 1–3.

9. Ibid., 10.

10. Francisco Bedoya Pereda, *La Habana desaparecida* (Havana: Ediciones Boloña, 2008).

11. *Ordenanzas de construcción para la ciudad de La Habana, y pueblos de su termino municipal* (Havana: Imprenta del Gobierno y Capitanía General por S.M., 1866), 10–11.

12. I suggest here that the city walls serve as metaphors for how the city develops and that exclusion was a central component of the process. For an excellent discussion of how the relationship between racism, excluded inclusion, and blackness produces populations that reify the boundaries of normative space, see Lisa B. Y. Calvente, "'This Is One Line You Won't Have to Worry about Crossing': Crossing Borders and Becoming," in *Latina/o Discourse in Vernacular Spaces: Somos de Una Voz?*, edited by Michelle A. Holling and Bernadette M. Calafell (Lanham, MD: Lexington Books 2010). For a more general and theoretical discussion of included/excluded, see Lisa B. Y. Calvente, "Keep on Keepin' on: Performing and Imag(in)ing Leadership and Homespace within the Black Diaspora" (PhD diss., University of North Carolina at Chapel Hill, 2008). I would especially like to thank Lisa B. Y. Calvente for her help with included/excluded as organizing concepts of urban space.

13. United Nations Educational, Scientific, and Cultural Organization (UNESCO), "Convention Concerning the Protection of the World Cultural and Natural Heritage," November 16, 1972, http://whc.unesco.org/en/conventiontext/; UNESCO, "Committee Decisions, CONF 015 VIII.20: Nominations to the World Heritage List (inscribed sites)," December 13–17, 1982, http://whc.unesco.org/en/decisions/5276.

14. Guadalupe García, "Inventing a Caribbean Paris: Imperial Inroads, Public Works, and the Invention of Republican Havana," unpublished manuscript, 2015, Microsoft Word File.

15. Joseph L. Scarpaci, Roberto Segre, and Mario Coyula, *Havana: Two Faces of the Antillean Metropolis*, rev. ed. (Chapel Hill: University of North Carolina Press, 2002).

16. See John F. Collins, "Culture, Content, and the Enclosure of Human Being: UNESCO's 'Intangible' Heritage in the New Millennium," *Radical History Review*, no. 109 (2011): 121–35.

17. Wendy Brown, *Walled States, Waning Sovereignty* (Brooklyn: Zone Books, 2010).

18. In the 1982 designation of Havana as a World Heritage Site, all 143 hectares of the original walled city were included, as well as outlying military and colonial structures. However, over 2,000 hectares actually encompassed historically relevant colonial sites and buildings.

19. Trade winds and ocean currents reinforced the navigational choices that Columbus and his contemporaries made by sailing not only west but also *south* to locate lands where scientific belief held that the intemperate climate would produce residents with childlike or monstrous constitutions suitable for colonization. Nicolás Wey Gómez, *The Tropics of Empire: Why Columbus Sailed South to the Indies* (Cambridge, MA: MIT Press, 2008).

20. L. Antonio Curet and Mark W. Hauser, eds., *Islands at the Crossroads: Migration, Seafaring, and Interaction in the Caribbean* (Tuscaloosa: University of Alabama Press, 2011); Franklin W. Knight, *The Caribbean: The Genesis of a Fragmented Nationalism,* 2nd ed. (New York: Oxford University Press, 1990).

21. J. H. Elliott, *Empires of the Atlantic World: Britain and Spain in America, 1492–1830* (New Haven, CT: Yale University Press, 2006); Richard L. Kagan and Geoffrey Parker, eds., *Spain, Europe, and the Atlantic World: Essays in Honour of John H. Elliott* (Cambridge: Cambridge University Press, 1995); Kris E. Lane, *Pillaging the Empire: Piracy in the Americas, 1500–1750* (New York: Routledge, 1998); Franklin W. Knight and Peggy K. Liss, eds., *Atlantic Port Cities: Economy, Culture, and Society in the Atlantic World, 1650–1850* (Knoxville: University of Tennessee Press, 1991).

22. See Peter A. Coclanis, ed., *The Atlantic Economy during the Seventeenth and Eighteenth Centuries: Organization, Operation, Practice, and Personnel* (Columbia: University of South Carolina Press, 2005); Patrick O'Flanagan, *Port Cities of Atlantic Iberia, c. 1500–1900* (Burlington, VT: Ashgate, 2008).

23. The English-language literature on the subject is extensive. For a representative sample, see Charlotte Cosner, *The Golden Leaf: How Tobacco Shaped Cuba and the Atlantic World* (Nashville: Vanderbilt University Press, 2015); Sherry Johnson, *The Social Transformation of Eighteenth-Century Cuba* (Gainesville: University Press of Florida, 2001); Knight, *Caribbean;* Allan J. Kuethe, *Cuba, 1753–1815: Crown, Military, and Society* (Knoxville: University of Tennessee Press, 1986); Rebecca J. Scott, *Slave Emancipation in Cuba: The Transition to Free Labor, 1860–1899* (Princeton, NJ: Princeton University Press, 1985); William C. Van Norman, *Shade-Grown Slavery: The Lives of Slaves on Coffee Plantations in Cuba* (Nashville: Vanderbilt University Press, 2013). See also Fernando Ortiz, *Contrapunteo cubano del tabaco y el azúcar* (Caracas, Venezuela: Biblioteca Ayacucho, 1987).

24. Patricia L. Price, "At the Crossroads: Critical Race Theory and Critical Geographies of Race," *Progress in Human Geography* 34, no. 2 (2010): 149.

25. Teresa P. R. Caldeira, *City of Walls: Crime, Segregation, and Citizenship in São Paolo* (Berkeley: University of California Press, 2001); Brown, *Walled States;* João Biehl, *Vita: Life in a Zone of Social Abandonment,* rev. ed. (Berkeley: University of California Press, 2013); Brodwyn Fischer, *A Poverty of Rights: Citizenship and Inequality in Twentieth-Century Rio de Janeiro* (Stanford, CA: Stanford University Press, 2010); Brodwyn Fischer, Bryan M. Cann, and Javier

Auyero, eds., *Cities from Scratch: Poverty and Informality in Urban Latin America* (Durham: Duke University Press, 2014).

26. See Porfirio Sanz Camañes, *La ciudades en la América Hispana: Siglos XV al XVIII* (Madrid: Sílex Ediciones, 2004).

27. Knight and Liss, *Atlantic Port Cities;* Paul E. Hoffman, *The Spanish Crown and the Defense of the Caribbean, 1535–1585: Precedent, Patrimonialism, and Royal Parsimony* (Baton Rouge: Louisiana State University Press, 1980); Bibiano Torres Ramírez, *La Armada de Barlovento* (Seville: Escuela de Estudios Hispano-Americanos, 1981); O'Flanagan, *Port Cities.*

28. See De la Fuente, *Havana and the Atlantic;* Alison Games, "Atlantic History: Definitions, Challenges, and Opportunities," *American Historical Review* 111, no. 3 (2006): 741–57; David Armitage and Michael J. Braddick, eds., *The British Atlantic World, 1500–1800* (New York: Palgrave Macmillan, 2002); Sherwin K. Bryant, Rachel Sarah O'Toole, and Ben Vinson III, eds., *Africans to Spanish America: Expanding the Diaspora* (Urbana: University of Illinois Press, 2014).

29. Jan de Vries, *European Urbanization, 1500–1800* (Cambridge, MA: Harvard University Press, 1984); Jan de Vries, *The Economy of Europe in an Age of Crisis, 1600–1750* (Cambridge: Cambridge University Press, 1976); Robert S. Duplessis, *Transitions to Capitalism in Early Modern Europe* (Cambridge: Cambridge University Press, 1997).

30. See Sherwin K. Bryant, *Rivers of Gold, Lives of Bondage: Governing through Slavery in Colonial Quito* (Chapel Hill: University of North Carolina Press, 2014).

31. Frank Broeze, "Introduction," in *Brides of the Sea: Port Cities of Asia from the 16th–20th Centuries,* ed. Frank Broeze (Honolulu: University of Hawaii Press, 1989), 9.

32. See Scarpaci, Segre, and Coyula, *Havana;* Carlos Venegas Fornias, "La Habana entre dos siglos," in *Arquitectura cubana: Metamorfosis, pensamiento y crítica: Selección de textos,* ed. Elvia Rosa Castro and Concepción Otero (Havana: Artecubano Ediciones, 2002), 23.

33. See Childs, *1812 Aponte Rebellion;* Camillia Cowling, *Conceiving Freedom: Women of Color, Gender, and the Abolition of Slavery in Havana and Rio de Janeiro* (Chapel Hill: University of North Carolina Press, 2013); Manuel Barcia, *The Great African Slave Revolt of 1825: Cuba and the Fight for Freedom in Matanzas* (Baton Rouge: Louisiana State University Press, 2012); Van Norman, *Shade-Grown Slavery.* Fernando Ortiz was an early pioneer in studies that placed black subjects—free and enslaved—in urban areas of the island. Fernando Ortiz, *Los negros curros* (Havana: Editorial de Ciencias Sociales, 1995). The publication of Jorge Cañizares-Esguerra, Matt D. Childs, and James Sidbury, eds., *The Black Urban Atlantic in the Age of the Slave Trade* (Philadelphia: University of Pennsylvania Press, 2013), is a promising start in new directions of research.

34. See Mary Jo Deegan, *Jane Addams and the Men of the Chicago School, 1892–1918* (New Brunswick, NJ: Transaction, 1988); Dennis Smith, *The Chicago School: A Liberal Critique of Capitalism* (London: Palgrave Macmillan, 1988); Manuel Castells, *Imperialismo y urbanización en América Latina* (Barcelona: G.

Gili, 1973); Alfred W. McCoy and Ed C. de Jesus, eds., *Philippine Social History: Global Trade and Local Transformations* (Honolulu: University of Hawaii Press, 1982); Terence G. McGee, *The Urbanization Process in the Third World: Explorations in Search of a Theory* (London: G. Bell and Sons, 1975). For alternative work in this area, see Peter Reeves, Frank Broeze, and Kenneth McPherson, "Studying the Asian Port City," in *Brides of Sea: Port Cities of Asia from the 16th–20th Centuries*, ed. Frank Broeze (Honolulu: University of Hawaii Press, 1989), 29–53.

35. U.S. studies of cities are rooted in the field of urban sociology. Its philosophical foundations derive from Karl Marx, Émile Durkheim, Max Weber, and Georg Simmel. U.S. urban studies built upon urban sociology's philosophical foundations to create the framework for modern studies of urbanization. See, for example, Georg Simmel, "The Metropolis and Mental Life," in *The Nineteenth-Century Visual Culture Reader*, ed. Vanessa R. Schwartz and Jeannene M. Przyblyski (New York: Routledge, 2004), 51–55; Max Weber, *The City*, ed. and trans. Don Martindale and Gertrud Neuwirth (Glencoe, IL: Free Press, 1958); Louis Wirth, "Urbanism as a Way of Life," *American Journal of Sociology* 44, no. 1 (1938): 1–24.

36. See Oscar Lewis, *The Children of Sánchez: Autobiography of a Mexican Family*, rev. ed. (New York: Vintage Books, 2011); William T. Sanders and David Webster, "The Mesoamerican Urban Tradition," *American Anthropologist*, n.s., 90, no. 3 (1988), 521–46.

37. Scholars have negotiated the region's seemingly differing urban trajectories with conceptual nuance. Susan M. Socolow and Lyman L. Johnson discourage describing a "prototypical" city in Latin America, instead focusing on the idea of the city and its governing practices and the practical advantages of a regular urban plan. Angel Rama similarly posits a framework for approaching the city that might be found in the various ways in which founders and residents imagined the city and its spaces; Angel Rama, *The Lettered City*, trans. John Charles Chasteen (Durham, NC: Duke University Press, 1996). See Jorge E. Hardoy, "Two Thousand Years of Latin American Urbanization," in *Urbanization in Latin America: Approaches and Issues*, ed. Jorge E. Hardoy, 3–55 (Garden City, NY: Anchor Books, 1975), 29; Susan Migden Socolow and Lyman L. Johnson, "Urbanization in Colonial Latin America," *Journal of Urban History* 8, no. 1 (1981): 27–59; Rama, *Lettered City*.

38. Kagan, "World without Walls"; Richard L. Kagan, *Urban Images of the Hispanic World, 1493–1793* (New Haven, CT: Yale University Press, 2000); Richard M. Morse, "Cities as People," in *Rethinking the Latin American City*, ed. Jorge E. Hardoy and Richard M. Morse (Baltimore: Johns Hopkins University Press, 1992), 3–19.

39. Morse, "Cities as People," 3.

40. Kagan, "World without Walls."

41. Kagan, *Urban Images*, 10; *Siete Partidas,* Ley 52.

42. R. Douglas Cope, *The Limits of Racial Domination: Plebeian Society in Colonial Mexico City, 1660–1720* (Madison: University of Wisconsin Press, 1994). See Cope for a discussion of race mixture in early colonial Mexico.

43. The similarity between American port cities and European cities does not end here. Iberian experiences in Europe contributed to American developments. Spain's experience with revolt in the Low Countries and the failed siege of Leiden (as well as of Antwerp, where the city walls were higher than those of Leiden) all affected attempts to plan and regulate Spanish American port cities.

44. For a discussion of the city as a European idea, see Socolow and Johnson, "Urbanization in Colonial Latin America"; Rama, *Lettered City*. For alternative interpretations, see Néstor García Canclini, *Hybrid Cultures: Strategies for Entering and Leaving Modernity*, rev. ed., trans. Christopher L. Chiappari and Silvia L. López (Minneapolis: University of Minnesota Press, 2005); Néstor García Canclini, *Consumers and Citizens: Globalization and Multicultural Conflicts*, trans. George Yúdice (Minneapolis: University of Minnesota Press, 2001); Joanne Rappaport and Tom Cummins, *Beyond the Lettered City: Indigenous Literacies in the Andes* (Durham, NC: Duke University Press, 2012).

45. See, for example, Ulrike Freitag et al., eds., *The City in the Ottoman Empire: Migration and the Making of Urban Modernity* (New York: Routledge, 2011); Biray Kolluoğlu and Meltem Toksöz, eds., *Cities of the Mediterranean: From the Ottomans to the Present Day* (New York: I. B. Tauris, 2010); Edhem Eldem, Daniel Goffman, and Bruce Masters, *The Ottoman City between East and West: Aleppo, Izmir, and Istanbul* (Cambridge: Cambridge University Press, 2005). Special thanks to I. Kaya Sahin for his patience and help with the literature on Mediterranean and Ottoman cities.

46. Broeze, *Brides of the Sea*, 26. Also see Haneda Masashi, ed., *Asian Port Cities, 1600–1800: Local and Foreign Cultural Interactions* (Singapore: National University of Singapore Press, 2009); McCoy and de Jesus, *Philippine Social History*; McGee, *Urbanization Process*. For new work in this area, see Reeves, Broeze, and McPherson, "Studying the Asian Port City."

47. I should note that this is not an Atlantic history of Havana. I attempt to situate the city within the axis of imperial trajectories that crossed the Atlantic, converged around the circum-Caribbean, and were responsible for producing a specific set of local conditions. For excellent discussions on the state of Atlantic history as a field, see Games, "Atlantic History"; Armitage and Braddick, *British Atlantic World*.

48. For a discussion of the differences between "urbanization," "urbanism," and "urban growth," see Morse, "Cities as People."

49. Quoted in Ada Ferrer, *Insurgent Cuba: Race, Nation, and Revolution, 1868–1898* (Chapel Hill: University of North Carolina Press, 1999), 148. See also Guadalupe García, "Urban *Guajiros*: Colonial *Reconcentración*, Rural Displacement, and Criminalisation in Western Cuba, 1895–1902," *Journal of Latin American Studies* 43, no. 2 (2011): 209–35.

50. Kuethe, *Cuba, 1753–1815*.

CHAPTER I. PRODUCING PLACE

1. Juan de la Cosa, 1504, Museo Naval de Madrid (hereafter cited as MNM), Colección Antigua. The claim that La Cosa's *carta* (map) is the oldest depiction of the Americas is not undisputed. The Vinland Map, acquired by Yale in 1964,

depicts fifteenth-century Norse exploration that includes portions of the Americas. The age of the map, however, has never been definitively authenticated.

2. See Henri Lefebvre, *The Production of Space*, trans. Donald Nicholson-Smith (Oxford: Blackwell, 1992), 68–168. On maps and mapping, see J. B. Harley, *The New Nature of Maps: Essays in the History of Cartography*, edited by Paul Laxton (Baltimore: Johns Hopkins University Press, 2002); Dennis Wood, *Rethinking the Power of Maps* (New York: Guilford Press, 2010); and John Pickles, *A History of Spaces: Cartographic Reason, Mapping, and the Geo-Coded World* (New York: Routledge, 2004). The terms by which Europeans visually imagined the region mirror the discourse found in Columbus's *Diario*, which similarly excludes the Amerindian peoples of the Caribbean vis-à-vis European ideas of governance and religion.

3. Ricardo Cerezo Martínez, *La cartografía náutica española en los siglos XIV, XV y XVI* (Madrid: Consejo Superior de Investigaciones Científicas, 1994); Alida C. Metcalf, "Amerigo Vespucci and the Four Finger (Kunstmann II) World Map," *e-Perimetron* 7, no. 1 (2012): 36–44.

4. Nicolás Wey Gómez, *The Tropics of Empire: Why Columbus Sailed South to the Indies* (Cambridge, MA: MIT Press, 2008), xiv.

5. The term refers to grants that gave early European settlers access to land and the labor of Amerindian people as an incentive to remain in the Americas.

6. G. Douglas Inglis, "Historical Demography of Colonial Cuba, 1492–1780" (PhD diss., Texas Christian University, 1979).

7. Levi Marrero, *Cuba: Economía y sociedad*, vol. 1 (Río Piedras, Puerto Rico: Editorial San Juan, 1972), 106.

8. Karl Offen and Jordana Dym, "Introduction," in *Mapping Latin America: A Cartographic Reader*, ed. Jordana Dym and Karl Offen (Chicago: University of Chicago Press, 2011), 7. Where space emphasizes the many possibilities inherent in an area, place attributes its success to the relationships embedded therein. See Lefebvre, *Production of Space*.

9. J. H. Elliott, *Empires of the Atlantic World: Britain and Spain in America, 1492–1830* (New Haven, CT: Yale University Press, 2006), 41.

10. Julio Le Riverend Brusone, *La Habana, espacio y vida* (Havana: Editorial MAPFRE, 1992); Manuel Pérez Beato, *Habana antigua* (Havana: Imprenta Seoane, Fernández y ca., 1936); Esteban Pichardo y Tapia, *Diccionario provincial casi razonado de vozes y frases cubanas*, ed. Gladys Alonso González and Ángel L. Fernández Guerra (Havana: Editorial de Ciencias Sociales, 1985).

11. "Transcripción de las Ordenanzas de descubrimiento, nueva población y pacificación de las Indias dadas por Felipe II, el 13 de julio de 1573, en el bosque de Segovia, según el original que se conserva en el Archivo General de Indias," reprinted in *Colección de documentos inéditos relativos al descubrimiento, conquista, y colonización de las posesiones españolas en América y Oceanía*, 42 vols. (Madrid, 1864–84), 1:8, 1:497–531. (Hereafter cited as CODOI.)

12. Christopher Columbus, *Diario del primer viaje*, and Bartolomé de las Casas, *Historia de la Indias*, book 3, in Marrero, *Cuba*, 12.

13. Alejandro De la Fuente, *Havana and the Atlantic in the Sixteenth Century* (Chapel Hill: University of North Carolina Press, 2008), 225.

14. Marrero, *Cuba*, 215–17.

15. Sherwin K. Bryant, *Rivers of Gold, Lives of Bondage: Governing through Slavery in Colonial Quito* (Chapel Hill: University of North Carolina Press, 2014).

16. See De la Fuente, *Havana and the Atlantic*.

17. Quoted in Le Riverend Brusone, *La Habana*, 45.

18. The need to ensure the safety of Havana drove the 1552 decision that restricted the felling of trees in the dense forests that surrounded the city. Potential residents, the cabildo argued, would be discouraged from settling in Havana for want of natural resources if deforestation continued. See Emilio Roig de Leuchsenring, *Historia de La Habana*, vol. 1, *Desde sus primeros días hasta 1565* (Havana: Municipio de La Habana, 1938), 130.

19. Inglis, "Historical Demography," 60–61.

20. Francisco Bedoya Pereda, *La Habana desaparecida* (Havana: Ediciones Boloña, 2008), 54.

21. Bedoya Pereda, *La Habana desaparecida*; Maria Luisa Lobo Montalvo, *Havana: History and Architecture of a Romantic City*, trans. Lorna Scott Fox (New York: Monacelli Press, 2000), 51–52; Juan de las Cuevas Toraya, *500 años de construcciones en Cuba* (Havana: Chavin, Servicios Gráficos y Editoriales, 2001), 8–9. The new Fuerza effectively replaced the damaged Fuerza Vieja, which had weathered an attack by the French corsair Robert Baal and prevented at least one other. The attack by Sores, however, rendered the structure obsolete and illustrated the need for a larger and more strategic system of defense.

22. Bedoya Pereda, *La Habana desaparecida*, 58.

23. Marrero, *Cuba*, 409; Bedoya Pereda, *La Habana desaparecida*. The project was completed under Cristóbal de Roda, Antonelli's nephew.

24. Torreones located at La Chorrera (built 1634–1636), Cojímar (built 1646–1649), and Bacuranao (built 1689–1695) promised an early system of alert and detection.

25. Roberto A. Hernández Suárez, *Cuba en la estrategia político militar del imperio español: 1561–1725* (Havana: Editoria Historia, 2007), 88.

26. Franklin W. Knight, *The Caribbean: The Genesis of a Fragmented Nationalism*, 2nd ed. (New York: Oxford University Press, 1990); Hernández Suárez, *Cuba en la estrategia político militar*, 17.

27. Inglis, "Historical Demography," 59.

28. De la Fuente, *Havana and the Atlantic*.

29. Bedoya Pereda, *La Habana desaparecida*, 82–84.

30. Ibid., 84, 145.

31. Joaquín E. Weiss, *La arquitectura colonial cubana* (Havana: Letras Cubanas, 1979), 145.

32. Plan de La Habana, 1576, Archivo General de Indias, Seville (hereafter AGI).

33. De la Fuente's *Havana and the Atlantic* is a monumental feat of archival research, and it is to date the only English-language study of early colonial Havana, along with Irene Wright's comprehensive study of the early city, which remains among the best references for research on early Havana. Irene A.

Wright, *The Early History of Cuba, 1492–1586: Written from Original Sources* (New York: Macmillan, 1916).

34. Irene A. Wright, "Rescates with Special Attention to Cuba, 1599–1610," *Hispanic American Historical Review* 3, no. 3 (1920): 358.

35. "Relación de las ciudades de América española a las que se concedieron escudos de armas," Biblioteca Nacional de España, Madrid (hereafter cited as BNE), Papeles Varios de Indias, Manuscript Division, MSS/3046.

36. Colectivo de Autores de Plan Maestro para la Revitalización Integral de La Habana Vieja y Dirección Provincial de Planificación Física Ciudad de La Habana, *Regulaciones urbanísticas: Ciudad de La Habana: La Habana Vieja: Centro histórico* (Havana: Ediciones Boloña, 2008), 38.

37. Paul Hiltpold, "Noble Status and Urban Privilege: Burgos, 1572," *Sixteenth Century Journal* 12, no. 4 (1981): 21–44.

38. C. H. Haring, "The Genesis of Royal Government in the Spanish Indies," *Hispanic American Historical Review* 7, no. 2 (1927): 141–91; Inglis, "Historical Demography," 42.

39. See Alejandro Cañeque, *The King's Living Image: The Culture and Politics of Viceregal Power in Colonial Mexico* (New York: Routledge, 2004).

40. Ramiro Guerra, *Manual de historia de Cuba desde su descubrimiento hasta 1868* (Havana: Editorial de Ciencias Sociales, 1971), 124.

41. *Actas capitulares del Ayuntamiento de La Habana*, ed. Emilio Roig de Leuchsenring, 3 vols. (Havana: Municipio de La Habana, 1937–46), 1:9. (Hereafter cited as ACAH.)

42. François Soyer, "Faith, Culture, and Fear: Comparing Islamophobia in Early Modern Spain and Twenty-First-Century Europe," *Ethnic and Racial Studies* 36, no. 3 (2013): 399–416.

43. María Sandra García Pérez, "El padrón municipal de habitantes: Origen, evolución y significado." *Hispania Nova: Revista de Historia Contemporánea*, no. 7 (2007): http://hispanianoa.rediris.es/7/articulos/7a005.pdf.

44. John Preston Moore, *The Cabildo in Peru under the Hapsburgs: A Study in the Origins and Powers of the Town Council in the Viceroyalty of Peru, 1530–1700* (Durham, NC: Duke University Press, 1954).

45. Leo J. Garofalo, "The Shape of a Diaspora: The Movement of Afro-Iberians to Colonial Spanish America," in *Africans to Spanish America: Expanding the Diaspora*, ed. Sherwin K. Bryant, Rachel Sarah O'Toole, and Ben Vinson III, 2nd ed. (Urbana-Champaign: University of Illinois Press, 2014), 27–49.

46. Manuel M. Miranda, *Memorias de un deportado* (Havana: Imprenta La Luz, 1903).

47. Quoted in De la Fuente, *Havana and the Atlantic*, 97.

48. Ibid., 87.

49. 22 August 1550; 22 August 1565, ACAH, 3–5, 283–294.

50. Irene A. Wright, *Historia documentada de San Cristobal de la Habana en el siglo XVI*, vol. 1 (Havana: Imprenta "El Siglo XX," 1927), 73.

51. "Testamento otorgado por Francisco de Rojas, negro horro, natural de Terranova y vecino de la Habana," 10 June 1579, in *Índices y extractos del Archivo de Protocolos de La Habana, 1578–1585*, vol. 1, ed. María Teresa de Rojas (Havana, 1947), 772r–773r.

52. De la Fuente, *Havana and the Atlantic.*

53. American exemptions from categories marked by abjection were not dissimilar from those occurring in sixteenth-century Seville, where Christian identity and vecino status could both be negotiated. See Garofalo, "Shape of a Diaspora."

54. Joseph L. Scarpaci, Roberto Segre, and Mario Coyula, *Havana: Two Faces of the Antillean Metropolis,* rev. ed. (Chapel Hill: University of North Carolina Press, 2002).

55. The *barrio* designation for the two areas did not officially appear until 1603 with Cristóbal de Roda's plan. Though the barrios would eventually be broken up and subdivided, their limits would remain intact into the twentieth century.

56. Street nomenclature in Havana has a long, complicated, and highly politicized history. Most intramuro streets have been known by various names, with incoming political administrations often changing them. I refer to intramuro and extramuro streets by their commonly accepted (and often early colonial) names, some of which are still in colloquial use in contemporary Havana. For an excellent compilation, see Manuel Fernández Santalices, *Las calles de La Habana intramuros: Arte, historia y tradiciones en las calles y plazas de La Habana vieja* (Miami: Saeta Ediciones, 1989).

57. José M. Bens Arrarte, "Apuntes sobre La Habana del siglo XVIII: La urbanización del extramuro," in *Cuba: Arquitectura y urbanismo,* edited by Felipe J. Préstamo y Hernández (Miami: Ediciones Universal, 1995); Fernández Santalices, *Las calles de La Habana intramuros,* 23–25.

58. César García del Pino, *La Habana bajo el reinado de los Austria* (Havana: Ediciones Boloña, 2008), 149.

59. The casa capitular housed the governors until their residence was relocated to the Castillo de la Real Fuerza in 1718. They were relocated again in 1777 to the Palacio de los Capitanes Generales.

60. García del Pino, *La Habana bajo,* 149.

61. De la Fuente, *Havana and the Atlantic,* 116.

62. ACAH, 1:49.

63. Francisco Calvillo, "Plan of La Habana," 1576 (AGI), Mapas y Planos (hereafter cited as MP) Santo Domingo (hereafter cited as SD), 41091, AGI/26.23//MP SD, 4.

64. Julio Le Riverend Brusone, *Síntesis histórico de la cubanidad en el siglo XVIII* (Havana: Molina, 1940), 50.

65. "Transcripción de las Ordenanzas de descubrimiento, nueva población y pacificación de las Indias dadas por Felipe II, el 13 de julio de 1573, en el bosque de Segovia, según el original que se conserva en el Archivo General de Indias," reprinted in CODOI, 1:8, 1:497–531.

66. Angel Rama, *The Lettered City,* trans. John Charles Chasteen (Durham, NC: Duke University Press, 1996), 5; Yi-Fu Tuan, *Space and Place: The Perspective of Experience* (Minneapolis: University of Minnesota Press, 2003); Weiss, *La arquitectura colonial cubana.*

67. The Cáceres ordinances were drafted at approximately the same time as King Philip II's *Ordenanzas de descubrimiento,* but they would not be ratified

until the cabildo meeting of 1640. The articles dealing with land issues, however, went into effect immediately as a result of an *auto*.

68. Leuchsenring, *Historia de La Habana*, 128.

69. "Ordenanzas de Cáceres," reprinted in Hortensia Pichardo Viñals, *Documentos para la historia de Cuba*, vol. 1, 5th ed. (Havana: Editorial Pueblo y Educación, 1984), 115; Colectivo de Autores, *Regulaciones urbanísticas*, 37. See also Francisco Domínguez Compañy, "Ordenanzas municipales hispano-americanas," *Revista de Historia de América*, no. 86 (1978): 9–60.

70. 11 January 1566, ACAH, vol. 2.

71. Wright, *Early History of Cuba*; Duvon C. Corbitt, "Mercedes and Realengos: A Survey of the Public Land System in Cuba," *Hispanic American Historical Review* 19, no. 3 (1939): 262–85.

72. Mariano Peset and Margarita Menegus, "Rey propietario o rey soberano," *Historia Mexicana* 43, no. 4 (1994): 563–99. Monarchic claims to land were not unchallenged; on the peninsula, the jurist Juan López de Palacios Rubio, among others, acknowledged the crown's just right over the tribute and labor obligations of indigenous populations, though ownership of land was another matter altogether.

73. Corbitt, "Mercedes and Realengos."

74. Rebecca Earle, *The Body of the Conquistador: Food, Race, and the Colonial Experience in Spanish America, 1492–1700* (Cambridge: Cambridge University Press, 2012), 21–22; Rebecca Earle, "'Temples diversos o contrarios a su salud, complexión y naturaleza': Spanish Health and the Colonial City in Early Modern Spanish America," paper presented at "Urban Empire: A Symposium on Cities of the Early Modern Hispanic World," Tulane University, New Orleans, LA, March 20, 2010. See as well Daniela Bleichmar et al., eds., *Science in the Spanish and Portuguese Empires, 1500–1800* (Stanford, CA: Stanford University Press, 2009); Bryant, *Rivers of Gold, Lives of Bondage*; Wey Gómez, *Tropics of Empire*.

75. Concern with climate and geography was not specific to Spaniards but was characteristic of Europeans in general who encountered and tried to control the geographies of the circum-Caribbean. See Christopher Morris, *The Big Muddy: An Environmental History of the Mississippi and Its Peoples from Hernando de Soto to Hurricane Katrina* (Oxford: Oxford University Press, 2012).

76. CODOI, vols. 1 and 7.

77. Quoted in Richard L. Kagan, "A World without Walls: City and Town in Colonial Spanish America," in *City Walls: The Urban Enceinte in Global Perspective*, ed. James D. Tracy (Cambridge: Cambridge University Press, 2000), 136.

78. CODOI, vols. 1 and 7.

79. Inglis, "Historical Demography," 48.

80. Le Riverend Brusone, *La Habana*, 64–74.

81. Jorge Le-Roy y Cassá, *Estudios sobre la mortalidad de La Habana durante el siglo XIX y los comienzos del actual* (Havana: Imprenta Lloredo y Cia., 1913); Pedro A. Herrera López, *Tres personajes de la noble Habana* (Havana: Editorial Letras Cubanas, 2005), 152–62. Between 1646 and 1650, the average number of deaths per 1,000 inhabitants was 45. The hardest-hit year was 1649, when death tolls reached 120 per 1,000 inhabitants.

82. Herrera López, *Tres personajes,* 153.

83. Reprinted in ibid., 154.

84. Quoted in ibid.

85. Karl W. Butzer, "From Columbus to Acosta: Science, Geography, and the New World," *Annals of the Association of American Geographers* 82, no. 3 (1992): 543–65.

86. López de Velasco worked with (and, one might say, through) his patron, the jurist Juan de Ovando y Godoy, especially once the latter was appointed by the crown to bring new life to the Council of the Indies in 1569. Ibid.

87. See Ada Ferrer, *Freedom's Mirror: Cuba and Haiti in the Age of Revolution* (Cambridge: Cambridge University Press, 2014), and Jane Landers, *Atlantic Creoles in the Age of Revolution* (Cambridge: Cambridge University Press, 2011).

88. Mario González, *Sobre planos, esquemas y planes directores de la ciudad de La Habana* (Havana: Grupo para el Desarrollo Integral de la Capital, 1993).

89. Ibid.; Le Riverend Brusone, *La Habana;* Colectivo de Autores, *Regulaciones urbanísticas.*

90. Francisco Pérez Guzmán, *La Habana: Clave de un imperio* (Havana: Editorial de Ciencias Sociales, 1997), 23–24.

91. Lefebvre, *Production of Space,* 68–168.

92. Patricia L. Price, "At the Crossroads: Critical Race Theory and Critical Geographies of Race," *Progress in Human Geography* 34, no. 2 (2010): 153. Emphasis mine.

93. Ibid., 149.

94. Cristóbal de Roda, "Plan de Roda, 1603," in *Cien planos de La Habana en los archivos españoles* (Madrid: Servicio de Publicaciones del MOPU, Secretaría General Técnica, 1985), 99.

95. I am referring here to Michel Foucault's notion of biopower, or the birth of a system that distinguishes between populations on the basis of biology. Security, according to Foucault, is about establishing optimal "averages" of life and loss among a population, as well as a bandwidth of acceptable behaviors, that effectively ensure a society's survival at the necessary expense of those defined as outsiders and therefore expendable. See the lectures of January 11 and 18, 1978, in Michel Foucault, *Security, Territory, Population: Lectures at the Collège de France, 1977–1978,* ed. Michel Senellart, trans. Graham Burchell (London: Picador, 2009), 1–54. See also Lisa B. Y. Calvente for a discussion of the importance of racism, blackness, and life improvement over survival within biopolitical life; Calvente describes the urban terrain as the foreground for the state to intervene and transform the social landscape. Lisa B. Y. Calvente, "Keep on Keepin' on: Performing and Imag(in)ing Leadership and Homespace within the Black Diaspora" (PhD diss., University of North Carolina Chapel Hill, 2008).

96. Price, "At the Crossroads," 153.

97. Lefebvre, *Production of Space,* 118.

98. "Solares de Manuel Martínez Correa," 27 March 1753, AGI, MP SD, 290; "Habana: Recinto, bahia, paseo nuevo y cercanías," 26 November 1776, AGI, MP SD, 431; "Planta de la muralla de la ciudad de la Habana," 22 July

1675, AGI, MP SD, 69; "Plano de parte de la plaza de La Habana contigua al arsenal de la marina," 5 May 1774, AGI, MP SD, 395.

99. William Childers, "'Granada': Race and Place in Early Modern Spain," in *Spectacle and Topophilia: Reading Early Modern and Postmodern Hispanic Cultures,* ed. David R. Castillo and Bradley J. Nelson (Nashville: Vanderbilt University Press, 2011), 19–42.

100. Le Riverend Brusone, *La Habana,* 50.

101. Jorge E. Hardoy, "Two Thousand Years of Latin American Urbanization," in *Urbanization in Latin America: Approaches and Issues,* ed. Jorge E. Hardoy (Garden City, NY: Anchor Books, 1975), 17.

102. Butzer, "From Columbus to Acosta."

103. Letter from Hernan Cortés, Manuscript 27, Tulane University, Howard-Tilton Memorial Library, Latin American Library, Cortés, Hernando (1485–1547) Collection.

104. De la Fuente, *Havana and the Atlantic,* 224.

105. Ibid.

CHAPTER 2. PLACE

Epigraph: In the original Spanish, the excerpt reads, "No solamente Castilla . . . viene a ser la obligada y la interesada, sino los demás Reynos y Provincias de esta Corona y Monarquía, que . . . fuera justo que se ofrecieran, y aun se les pidiera ayudáran con algun socorro . . . si no se pone presto eficaz remedio, está a pique de dar en tierra . . . pues las casas se caen, y ninguna se vuelve a reedificar: los Lugares se yerman: los vecinos se huyen y se ausentan, y dexan los campos desiertos. . . . Y así será conveniente buscar otros medios con que V. M. alivie su Real Hacienda."

1. Respuesta a cartas del capitán general de Cuba, 20–12–1608, AGI, Santo Domingo, 869, L. 5, F. 196R–197V.

2. Magdalena de Cobrera, viuda y heredera de Gaspar de Arteaga, 1691, AGI, Escribanía, Pleitos de La Habana, 52A.

3. Petronila Medrano y Cobrera, vecina de La Habana, hija y heredera de Magdalena de Cobrera, 1725, AGI, Escribanía, Pleitos de La Habana, 58A.

4. Sebastián Calvo de la Puerta, AGI, Escribanía, Pleitos de La Habana, 56B.

5. Magdalena Cobrera, viuda de Gaspar de Arteaga y vecina de la Habana, 1864, AGI, Escribanía, Pleitos de La Habana, Ministerio de Ultramar 62/1744–1745.

6. Francisco Pérez Guzmán, *La Habana: Clave de un imperio* (Havana: Editorial de Ciencias Sociales, 1997), 25.

7. Fábrica de la muralla de la ciudad de La Habana, 1681–1704, AGI, Fondo Santo Domingo, legajo 458; Cuentas de la fábrica de la muralla de La Habana, 1685, AGI, Fondo Santo Domingo, legajo 459.

8. A Cuban vara measured approximately 33.38 inches. According to Joaquín Weiss, the walls measured 16,053.10 feet (4,893 meters), while according to José Manuel Fernandez-Nuñez, they were 4,892 meters, with a discrepancy in their estimates of .984 meters. Joaquín E. Weiss, *La arquitectura colonial cubana* (Havana: Letras Cubanas, 1979); José Manuel Fernandez Nuñez, *Colonial*

Havana: A Fortress of the Americas, trans. Fernando Nápoles Tapia (Havana: Editorial José Martí, 1998). There is also some discrepancy as to the height of the walls. Discrepancies are likely the result of the place where the walls were measured as well as the exclusion of the bricks that lay on top of the stone walls.

9. Juan de Síscara, "Planta de la muralla de la ciudad de la Habana," 22 July 1675, AGI, Mapoteca Santo Domingo, 69, 70; Planta y fortificación de la ciudad de la Habana (muralla), 7 August 1679, AGI, Mapoteca Santo Domingo, 81.

10. Juan de Síscara, "Planta y discreción de toda la circunvalación echa y por hacer de la ciudad de la Habana," 28 August 1677, AGI, Mapoteca Santo Domingo, 73; Planta de la muralla de la ciudad de la Habana, 23 August 1676, AGI, Mapoteca Santo Domingo, 71.

11. Respuesta a cartas del Capitán General de Cuba, 20 December 1680, AGI, Santo Domingo, 869, legajo 5, fols. 196r–197v.

12. Pago de cierta cantidad a Gaspar Ruiz de Pereda, 16 April 1608, AGI, Santo Domingo, 869, legajo 5, fols. 166r–168r.

13. Carta a S. M. sobre la muralla, 4 August 1678, Cartas del Virrey Payo Enriquez de Rivera (1673–1680), AGI, México, 50, no. 55; Carta del Virrey a Francisco de Salazar, 15 August 1684, Cartas del Virrey Marques de la Laguna (1680–1686), AGI, México, 54, R.2, no. 49.

14. Correspondencia de Diego de Córdoba, 18 February 1697, 15 March 1697, AGI, Santo Domingo, 113, R.4, no. 25.

15. Real cédula, 1674, AGI, Escribania, Pleitos de La Habana, 1674–1676, 46A.

16. Cartas de gobernadores, 20 March 1674, AGI, Santo Domingo, R.1, no. 12; Envío de esclavos de las obras d a la Habana a Cartagena, 17 December 1607, AGI, Santo Domingo, 869, legajo 5, fols. 149v–150r; Pago de cierta cantidad a Gaspar Ruiz de Pereda, 16 April 1608, AGI, Santo Domingo, 869, legajo 5, fols. 166r–168r; Carta de Gobernadores, 20 March 1674, AGI, Santo Domingo, 105, R.1, no. 12; Julio Le Riverend Brusone, *Síntesis histórico de la cubanidad del siglo XVIII* (Havana: Molina, 1940); Fernandez Nuñez, *Colonial Havana.*

17. Carta de Gobernadores, 20 March 1674, AGI, Santo Domingo, 105, R.1, no. 12.

18. María Elena Díaz, *The Virgin, the King, and the Royal Slaves of El Cobre: Negotiating Freedom in Colonial Cuba, 1670–1780* (Stanford, CA: Stanford University Press, 2000).

19. Petición José Pardio, Nicolás Antonio de Ponte, Francisco Fernández de Leon, and Felipe Lezcano, 1681, AGI, Escribanía, Pleitos de La Habana, 1679–1681, 46B.

20. Correspondencia de Diego Antonio de Viana, 1688, Cartas de valores y distribución de Hacienda de Gobierno, etc., 1610–1697, AGI, Contaduría, 1160.

21. Weiss, *La arquitectura colonial cubana.*

22. John Jay TePaske, "La política española en el Caribe durante los siglos XVII y XVIII," in *La influencia de España en el Caribe, la Florida, y la Luisiana, 1500–1800,* ed. Antonio Acosta and Juan Marchena (Madrid: Instituto de Cooperación Iberoamericana, 1983), 83.

23. John Robert McNeill, *Atlantic Empires of France and Spain: Louisbourg and Havana, 1700–1763* (Chapel Hill: University of North Carolina Press, 1985), 85–88.

24. Paga sobre una armadillo que se pretende hacer en la Habana, 1626 and 1630, BNE, Manuscritos, R17270/31.

25. McNeill, *Atlantic Empires of France and Spain*, 98.

26. Reinaldo Funes Monzote, *From Rainforest to Cane Field: An Environmental History since 1492*, translated by Alex Martin (Chapel Hill: University of North Carolina Press, 2008), 21–37.

27. Town Planning and Associates (Paul Lester Weiner, Jose Luis Sert, Paul Schulz, Seelye Stevenson Value, and Knecht, consulting engineers), *Plan Piloto de La Habana*, March 1959, University of Miami Libraries, Cuban Heritage Collection (hereafter cited as CHC).

28. While the meaning of this term varied over time and region, at this juncture it likely referred to someone not a vecino of Havana.

29. Francisco de Barreda, "Puntual, verídica, topográfica descripción del famoso puerto, y ciudad de San Christoval de La Habana en la isla de Cuba," 1719, BNE, VE/321/21.

30. Alejandro de la Fuente, "Su 'único derecho': Los esclavos y la ley," *Debate y Perspectivas: Cuadernos de Historia y Ciencias Sociales*, no. 4 (2004): 7–22.

31. Sherry Johnson, *The Social Transformation of Eighteenth-Century Cuba* (Gainesville: University Press of Florida, 2001).

32. Funes Monzote, *From Rainforest to Cane Field*, 28–30.

33. Manuel Moreno Fraginals describes the process of sugar expansion and the meaning of the term "cinturón azucarero" in *El ingenio: Complejo económico social cubano del azúcar* (Havana: Editorial de Ciencias Sociales, 1978); Funes Monzote, *From Rainforest to Cane Field*, 29.

34. Funes Monzote, *From Rainforest to Cane Field*, 32.

35. Sherry Johnson, "'La guerra contra los habitantes de los Arrabales': Changing Patterns of Land Use and Land Tenancy in and around Havana, 1763–1800," *Hispanic American Historical Review* 77, no. 2 (1997): 184.

36. Moreno Fraginals, *El ingenio*; Julio Le Riverend Brusone, *La Habana, espacio y vida* (Havana: Editorial MAPFRE, 1992), 74. The limits of the city in this case were fixed by the presence of the walls in such a way that the lack of space created "suburbs" in extramuro barrios that were an unwavering—if excluded—part of the urban landscape and whose economic, social, and political orientation looked to Havana and not toward the cinturón azucarero described by Moreno Fraginals. The division of "urban" and "rural," while tenuous in modern definitions of the terms, was one clear in the minds of most Cuban residents, especially those living in Havana and in the extramuros. See Johnson, "La guerra contra los habitantes," 184.

37. Al derecho de la sisa dedicado a la fábrica de la muralla, 1 April 1728, ANC, Reales Ordenes y Cédulas, legajo 47, no. 1; Derecho de sisa para muralla, 15 July 1729, ANC, Reales Ordenes y Cédulas, legajo 56, no. 1.

38. Pleito entre Sebastián Calvo de la Puerta y Petronilla Medrano y Cobrera, 1722, AGI, Escribanía, Pleitos de La Habana, 56B; Petronila Medrano y Corbera, 1725, AGI, Escribanía, Pleitos de La Habana, 58A.

39. RC, 24 November 1735, in Acto y RC sobre venta y consejo composición de tierras realengas, 1755, ANC, Realengos, legajo 91, no. 15.

40. Le Riverend Brusone, *Síntesis histórico*, 104; Johnson, "La guerra contra los habitantes," 183–84.

41. RC, 24 November 1735, in Acto y RC sobre venta y consejo composición de tierras realengas, 1755, ANC, Realengos, legajo 91, no. 15.

42. Arthur Scott Aiton, "Real Hacienda in New Spain under the First Viceroy," *Hispanic American Historical Review* 6, no. 4 (1926): 232.

43. RC, 24 November 1735, in Acto y Real Cédula sobre venta y consejo composición de tierras realengas, 1755, ANC, Realengos, legajo 91, no. 15.

44. Real cédula, 24 November 1735, in Acto y Real Cédula sobre venta y consejo composición de tierras realengas, 1755, ANC, Realengos, legajo 91, no. 15. See as well Tania Murray Li, *The Will to Improve: Governmentality, Development, and the Practice of Politics* (Durham, NC: Duke University Press, 2007).

45. Plano de unos solares situados en el barrio de Nuestra Señora de Guadalupe, 1738, AGI, Mapoteca Santo Domingo, 238, fol. 5.

46. Abel Fernández y Símón, *Plano de la ciudad de la Habana, 1955, in Habana: Desarrollo urbano* (Havana: Ediciones GEO, 2002).

47. Mapa y diseño de la estancia que fue del ayudante Marcelo de Carmona, 7 July 1747, AGI, Mapoteca Santo Domingo, 229; Croquis de los solares situados frente a la muralla, cerca de la Puerta de Tierra, 27 March 1753, AGI, Mapoteca Santo Domingo, 290.

48. Juan M. Chailloux Cardona, "Síntesis histórica de la vivienda popular: Los horrores del solar habanero" (PhD diss., Universidad de La Habana, 1945). The copy that I consulted is housed at the University of Miami Libraries, CHC. The author notes that land scarcity kept the resolution from passing.

49. Spain's conflict with Britain began in the Guerra del Asiento (1739), also referred to as the War of Jenkins's Ear in Britain and the English-speaking territories. The war was the result of land claim disputes as both empires vied for power in the Americas. It not only encompassed the North American mainland but also spread into the Caribbean theater, where it became largely a naval affair. After 1742, the conflict was subsumed into the larger struggles that followed in the War of the Austrian Succession, which ended in 1748. European conflict in 1754 soon gave way to the Seven Years' War (1756–1763) and involved almost all the European superpowers in a conflict over disputed claims to territory and extra-territorial supremacy. The Battle of Havana occurred as a result of the Seven Years' War and ended after three months (June 6, 1762–August 13, 1762).

50. Juan de Prado, "Diarios de las operaciones del sitio de La Habana en 1762," 31 October 1762, BNE, R/39723.

51. Guillermo Calleja Leal, *1762, La Habana Inglesa: La toma de La Habana por los ingleses* (Madrid: Agencia Española de Cooperación Internacional, 1999); Celia María Parcero Torre, *La pérdida de La Habana y las reformas borbónicas en Cuba, 1760–1773* (Valladolid, Spain: Junta de Castilla y León, 1998).

52. Patrick Mackellar, *A Correct Journal of the Landing His Majesty's Forces on the Island of Cuba; and of the Siege and Surrender of Havannah,*

August 13, 1762, 2nd ed. (London, Green and Russell, 1762), 3, Early American Imprints, Series 1: Evans 1639–1800, no. 9165.

53. Reglamento para la guarnicion de La Habana,"1700 and 1746, BNE, VE/1463/22.

54. Parcero Torre, *La pérdida de La Habana*.

55. Juan de Prado, "Diarios de las operaciones del sitio de La Habana en 1762," 31 October 1762, BNE, R/39723.

56. Escuadra del cargo del Marques del Real Transporte, y de las embarcaciones apresadas por los ingleses dentro del Puerto de la Habana, 2 August 1762, BNE, Manuscript Division, MSS/18766/21.

57. Allan J. Kuethe, *Cuba, 1753–1815: Crown, Military, and Society* (Knoxville: University of Tennessee Press, 1986), 3.

58. See Juan Florencio García, *Pepe Antonio: Biografía del héroe popular cubano Don José Antonio Gómez de Bullones* (Havana: Cultural, 1928); Alvaro de la Iglesia, *Pepe Antonio* (Havana: Editorial Letras Cubanas, 1979).

59. Florencio García, *Pepe Antonio*, 83. At the height of battle, Gómez's forces never surpassed three hundred men, a small force when compared to the militiamen and troops stationed in Havana.

60. Ibid., 102–4.

61. *Milicias de color* had been active on the island since the early 1600s and extended social and economic benefits to African-descended men and their families. See David Sartorius, *Ever Faithful: Race, Loyalty, and the Ends of Empire in Spanish Cuba* (Durham, NC: Duke University Press, 2014); David Sartorius, "My Vassals: Free-Colored Militias in Cuba and the Ends of Spanish Empire," *Journal of Colonialism and Colonial History* 5, no. 2 (2004): 1–25; Ben Vinson III, *Bearing Arms for His Majesty: The Free-Colored Militia in Colonial Mexico* (Stanford, CA: Stanford University Press, 2001); Ben Vinson III, "Free Colored Voices: Issues of Representation and Racial Identity in the Colonial Mexican Militia," *Journal of Negro History* 80, no. 4 (1995): 170–82.

62. David Sartorius, *Ever Faithful*, 4–8.

63. Sherwin K. Bryant, *Rivers of Gold, Lives of Bondage*.

64. Juan de Prado, "Diarios de las operaciones del sitio de La Habana en 1762," 31 October 1762, BNE, R/39723.

65. Conde de Ricla, "Sobre la libertad de los negros esclavos que se distinguieron durante el sitio de La Habana por los ingleses en 1762," reprinted in Archivo Nacional de Cuba, *Papeles sobre la toma de La Habana por los ingleses en 1762* (Havana: Archivo Nacional de Cuba, 1948), 181.

66. Sherry Johnson, *"Señoras en sus clases no ordinarias"*: Enemy Collaborators or Courageous Defenders of the Family?" *Cuban Studies* 34 (2003): 11–37.

67. Guadalupe García, "'Nuestra patria La Habana': Reading the 1762 British Occupation of the City." *Nuevo Mundo / Mundos Nuevos*, Debáts (March 31, 2011): doi: 10.4000/nuevomundo.61119.

68. Florencio García, *Pepe Antonio*, 95.

69. Conde de Aranda, "Votos de la Junta de Generales nombrada por Carlos III para el conocimiento del procesos sobre la Pérdida de La Habana," 1719–1798, Cartas al Marqués de Grimaldi, BNE, Manuscript Division; Carta y

consulta al Rey por el Conde de Aranda Presidente de la junta, 1764, BNE, Manuscript Division.

70. Copia de la Resolución de Carlos III, sobre la sentencia contra el Mariscal de Campo Juan de Prado y otros, por haber entregado La Habana a los ingleses, 1759–1788, BNE, Manuscript Division; Decreto de Carlos III, aprobando la sentencia contra Don Juan de Prado, Gobernador de La Habana y otros, por haberse entregado a los ingleses, 1759–1788, BNE, Manuscript Division; Proceso y sentencia dada al Gobernador de La Habana, Don Juan de Prado, BNE, Manuscript Division.

71. Roberto A. Hernández Suárez, *Cuba en la estrategia político militar del imperio español: 1561–1725* (Havana: Editoria Historia, 2007), 24.

72. Pérez Guzmán, *La Habana*, 28–29.

73. Papeles relativos a la expedición de Alejandro O'Reilly a Nueva Orleans, y otros documentos sobre América Central, 1769–1784, BNE, Manuscript Division, Mss/17616.

74. Allan J. Kuethe, "The Development of the Cuban Military as a Sociopolitical Elite, 1763–83," *Hispanic American Historical Review* 61, no. 4 (1981): 695–704.

75. Johnson, "Señoras en sus clases no ordinarias," 14.

76. Johnson, "La guerra contra los habitantes."

77. Cuestionario de la diligencias hechas por el padre procurador de San Juan de Dios, 4 August 1841, ANC, Fondo Realengos, legajo 22, no. 16.

78. Johnson, "La guerra contra los habitantes," 13.

79. Ibid., 11; Le Riverend Brusone, *La Habana*.

80. Instrucción que se formó para la leva de dos compañías de fusileros que S.M. mandó formar en Cataluña, 1 June 1768, BNE, Manuscript Division, MSS/18745/40.

81. Sherry Johnson, "'Honor is Life': Military Reform and the Transformation of Cuban Society: 1753–1796" (PhD diss., University of Florida, 1995), 96–122.

82. Population increase in and around Havana coincided with demographic growth throughout Spanish America, where the population also increased between 1742 and 1810.

83. Plano de parte de la plaza de la Habana contigua al arsenal de marina, 5 October 1774, AGI, Mapoteca Santo Domingo, 395.

84. Ibid., 204.

85. Kuethe, "Development of the Cuban Military," 701.

86. Ibid., 698.

87. Le Riverend Brusone, *La Habana*, 124; Carlos Venegas Fornias, *La urbanización de las murallas: Dependencia y modernidad* (Havana: Editorial Letras Cubanas, 1990), 12.

88. Carlos Venegas Fornias, *Cuba y sus pueblos: Censos y mapas de los siglos XVIII y XIX* (Havana: Centro de Investigación y Desarrollo de la Cultura Cubana Juan Marinello, 2002), 43.

89. Ibid., 42–43.

90. Joseph L. Scarpaci, Roberto Segre, and Mario Coyula, *Havana: Two Faces of the Antillean Metropolis,* rev. ed. (Chapel Hill: University of North

Carolina Press, 2002), 3; Antoni Kapcia, *Havana: The Making of Cuban Culture* (Oxford: Berg, 2005), 33, 60; Le Riverend Brusone, *La Habana*.

91. Humboldt, *Ensayo político*, 23.

92. Of the seven extramuro neighborhoods, by 1810 Jesús María and La Salud were the most racially diverse. In La Salud, black residents outnumbered whites 16,729 to 11,690, and in Jesús María, 8,242 to 3,363. Ibid.

93. Instrucción que observar los Capitanes de Partido de la jurisdicción de la Havana responsables al Capitán General, Havana, 1765, University of Florida, Gainsville, George A. Smathers Library, Harold and Mary Jean Hanson Rare Book Collection.

94. Ibid.

95. Ibid.

96. Ibid., 205.

97. Le Riverend Brusone, *La Habana*.

98. Venegas Fornias, *La urbanización de las murallas*, 9–12.

99. Humboldt, *Ensayo político*, 105.

100. Today it is the site of the Cathedral of Havana.

101. Le Riverend Brusone, *La Habana*, 88.

102. The Alameda de Extramuros would later be called the Paseo de Isabel II, the Paseo del Prado, and today, the Paseo de Martí. The gates were strategically placed in two locations; the gate at La Punta was located in the northern side of the city in order to communicate with the fort bearing the same name, while the Puerta de Tierra was located next to the city center, at the site where the paths that lead from the city center to "el monte" (rural areas) converged. These paths would eventually become the major calzadas of greater Havana.

103. The print is housed in the Permanent Collection of the Museo de Bellas Artes, Havana.

104. The spaces of the intramuros most commonly depicted in this light were the city squares, which became increasingly associated with either the Spanish elite or the new, poverty-ridden arrivals to the city. Negative portrayals extended to include many of the spaces associated with Spanish colonialism. The *valla de gallos* (cockfighting ring), for example, would be removed from the repertoire of "decent" recreational activities open to the general populace with the advent of independence, as this would become a distinctly Spanish and barbaric pastime.

105. This work is housed in the Permanent Collection of the Museo de Bellas Artes, Havana.

106. For young Spanish women of upper-class status, the "symbiosis of social classes" that habaneros were privy to was limited by the custom of having family honor intrinsically connected to the bodies of women, resulting in a more limited mobility for women of this class.

107. For more on the literature on women, gender, and public space, see Kathryn Burns, *Colonial Habits: Convents and the Spiritual Economy of Cuzco, Peru* (Durham: Duke University Press, 1999); Sandra Lauderdale Graham, *House and Street: The Domestic World of Servants and Masters in Nineteenth-Century Rio de Janeiro* (Austin: University of Texas Press, 1992); Lyman L. Johnson and Sonya Lipsett-Rivera, eds., *The Faces of Honor: Sex, Shame, and Violence in Colonial Latin America* (Albuquerque: University of New Mexico

Press, 1998); Susan Migden Socolow, *The Women of Colonial Latin America* (Cambridge: Cambridge University Press, 2000); Ann Twinam, *Public Lives, Private Secrets: Gender, Honor, Sexuality, and Illegitimacy in Colonial Spanish America* (Stanford, CA: Stanford University Press, 1999).

108. Outbreaks of yellow fever were a constant source of concern for both colonial officials and residents of the city during the nineteenth century. Ironically, the city layout and the architecture of the intramuros actually facilitated its spread, as the narrow streets and the upward-stretching buildings blocked the sun and created a damp, dark environment in which the virus could thrive. Urban density only made the problem worse.

109. Reglamento de la casa de salud establecida en el muelle de porras, 1820, ANC, Junta Superior de Sanidad, legajo 11, no. 122; Charles Belot, *The Yellow Fever at Havana: Its Nature and Its Treatment* (Savannah, GA: Morning News Steam Printing House, 1878).

110. Humboldt, *Ensayo político*, 10.

111. Ibid., 13.

112. Approximately 4,489,030 pesos in commerce entered the walled city on a weekly basis through the gates at Tierra. This figure includes goods for consumption such as raw materials, foodstuffs, and manufactured goods but excludes any goods marked for export. Alberto Parreño, *Guía del comercio de La Habana para el año de 1823* (Havana: Oficina de D. Pedro Nolasco Palmer é Hijo, 1822), 248–49. The edition that I consulted is housed at University of Florida, Gainesville, George A. Smathers Library, Harold and Mary Jean Hanson Rare Book Collection.

113. "Bando sobre que se destechen las casas de guano, o yaguas que estén dentro de la ciudad," ANC, Boletín del Archivo Nacional, 28, 83–84.

114. Of the 3,497 homes counted in Havana in 1756, 3,024 were made of *teja*, while 181 were made *de alto*. The remainder would presumably have been made of a combination of guano and other inexpensive building materials. "Indicadores urbanos tomados de la visita pastoral de Morell de Santa Cruz, 1756–1757," reprinted in Venegas Fornias, *Cuba y sus pueblos*, 135.

115. Copia de RC impresa del rey relacionado con la venta de solares en la isla y fraude del Real derecho de alcabala, 21 August 1777, ANC, Fondo Donativos y Remisiones, legajo 572, no. 16.

116. Havana, Diputación de Policía, *Informe de la diputación de policía al excelentísimo señor presidente, gobernador y capitán general del estado de sus tareas y providencias que deben adoptarse para conserver la pública tranquilidad* (Havana: Oficina de Arazoza y Soler, 1816). The edition I consulted is housed at the University of Miami Libraries, CHC.

117. Parreño, *Guía del comercio de La Habana*, 26–47.

118. The resulting report to the captain general went on to specifically note that existing regulations should be tightened for criollos throughout the island, and not just in Havana, where these concerns seemed to be the greatest.

119. Cirilo Villaverde, *Cecilia Valdés; ó, La loma del angel* (Havana: Imprente Literaria, 1839); Cirilo Villaverde, *Cecilia Valdés, o, La loma del angel: Novela de costumbres cubanas publicada en New York en 1882*, ed. Esteban Rodríguez Herrera (Havana: Editorial Lex, 1953).

120. Le Riverend Brusone, *La Habana;* Venegas Fornias, *Cuba y sus pueblos,* 66–68. In the census of 1817, however, new categories of differentiation emerged to take the place of what had existed between the intramuros and extramuros.

CHAPTER 3. MODERN SPACE

Epigraph: *Incendio acaecido en el barrio de Jesús María el día 11 de febrero de este año* (Havana: Oficina del Gobierno y Capitanía General por S. M., 1828), 4. The edition that I consulted is housed at the University of Florida, Gainesville, George A. Smathers Library, Harold and Mary Jean Hanson Rare Book Collection.

1. *Incendio acaecido en el barrio de Jesús María.*
2. Alexander von Humboldt, *Ensayo político sobre la isla de Cuba,* trans. D. J. B. de V. Y. M., 2nd ed. (Paris: Librería de Lecointe), 15.
3. "Moreno/a" was one of several colonial racial designations. In Cuba as in much of Spanish America, the designations served to classify populations to maintain a social order. As in most of Spanish America, however, though racial hierarchies existed, relationships were just as likely to be forged outside of these castes as they were within them.
4. Incendio en La Habana, 28 April 1802, AGI, Fondo Estado, 2, no. 32. Planos de población, 1825, Biblioteca Nacional de España, MR 42, 414; José del Rio, *Plano del puerto y de la ciudad de La Habana, 1798* (Havana: Ediciones GEO, 2002); Alexander Humboldt, *Plano del puerto y de la villa de la Habana, 1820* (Havana: Ediciones GEO, 2002). By the mid-nineteenth century, the barrio of San Lázaro would become especially prominent as housing grew and filled the area.
5. El Intendente de la Habana Luis Viguri, 3 August 1815, AGI, Fondo Ultramar, 121, no. 21; Fermín Hernández, escribano del tribunal de Cuentas de La Habana, 3 August 1815, AGI, Fondo Ultramar, 121, no. 21.
6. Julio Le Riverend Brusone, *Síntesis histórico de la cubanidad del siglo XVIII* (Havana: Molina, 1940), 17–18.
7. *Incendio acaecido en el barrio de Jesús María,* 4.
8. Juan M. Chailloux Cardona, *Los horrores del solar habanero: Síntesis histórica de la vivienda popular,* 2nd ed. (Havana: Editorial de Ciencias Sociales, 2008).
9. Juan M. Chailloux Cardona, "Síntesis histórica de la vivienda popular: Los horrores del solar habanero" (PhD diss., Universidad de La Habana, 1945).
10. Carlos Venegas Fornias, *La urbanización de las murallas: Dependencia y modernidad* (Havana: Editorial Letras Cubanas, 1990). As part of this organization campaign, the island was itself divided into eleven districts. Ibid., 93.
11. Carlos Venegas Fornias, *Cuba y sus pueblos: Censos y mapas de los siglos XVIII y XIX* (Havana: Centro de Investigación y Desarrollo de la Cultura Cubana Juan Marinello, 2002), 86.
12. See Ada Ferrer, *Freedom's Mirror: Cuba and Haiti in the Age of Revolution* (Cambridge: Cambridge University Press, 2014).
13. Prior to 1763, sugar exports leaving out of the port of Havana that were recorded by the customs house had not yet reached even thirty-one thousand

arrobas. Alberto Parreño, *Guía del comercio de La Habana para el año de 1823* (Havana: Oficina de D. Pedro Nolasco Palmer é Hijo, 1822), 250.

14. Humboldt, *Ensayo político,* 17–18.

15. For a representative sample, see Francisco Calvillo, "Ciudad y bahía de La Habana," 1576, AGI, MP Santo Domingo, 4; Cristóbal de Roda, "Descripción y planta de la ciudad de La Habana, 1603," in *Cien planos de La Habana en los archivos españoles* (Madrid: Dirección General de Arquitectura y Vivienda, Ministerio de Obras Públicas y Urbanismo, EPES Industrias Gráfica, 1985), 99; Juan de Síscara, 1691, "Habana," AGI; Bruno Caballero, "Planta de La Habana," 1730, AGI, MP SD 160; Habana, 1741, ANC, M-494-1; Anónimo, *Plano topográfico de La Habana,* 1744; Fuertes en el Puerto, 1762, BNE 1557318; Inscripción idiográfica de el gran puerto y ciudad de la Habana, 1743, BNE, MR 43 225; Silvestre Abarca, *Plan de Abarca,* 1763; Mariano La Roque, *Plano de la ciudad de San Cristóbal,* 1777; Anónimo, *Plano de la ciudad de La Habana y entrada a su puerto,* 1780; José del Rio, Plano del Puerto y ciudad de la Havana, 1798, ANC, M-474; Alejo Helvecio Lanier, *Plano de la Habana,* 1823; Anónimo, *Plano de La Habana y sus barrios extramuros,* 1829; Anónimo, *Plano de La Habana,* 1831; Rafael Rodríguez, *Plano topográfico, histórico, y artístico de la ciudad y puerto de La Habana;* Rafael Rodríguez, *Plano topográfico, histórico, y estadístico de la ciudad y puerto de La Habana,* 1841, in *Atlas cubano* (Havana: Biblioteca Nacional José Martí, 2000); Rafael Rodríguez, *Plano topográfico de los barrios extramuros de la ciudad de La Habana,* 1841; Antonio María de la Torre, "Plano pintoresco de La Habana con los números de las casas, 1841," in *Album pintoresco de la isla de Cuba* (Havana: C. B. May, 1853); "Plano topográfico de los barrios extramuros de La Habana, 1845," in *Planos de bolsillo de la isla de Cuba, la ciudad de La Habana y sus barios extramuros* (Havana: Imprenta del Gobierno y Capitanía General, 1844); Anónimo, "Plano de la plaza de La Habana, 1846," in *Planos de bolsillo de la isla de Cuba, la ciudad de La Habana y sus barios extramuros* (Havana: Imprenta del Gobierno y Capitanía General, 1844); Plano pintoresco de La Habana con los números de las casas, 1853, ANC M-521; Antonio María de la Torre, *Plano pintoresco de La Habana,* 1857; José María de la Torre, *Plano de La Habana,* 1857; José María de la Torre, *Plano de La Habana,* 1866, Biblioteca Nacional de España, MA 00072588; Francisco de Albear, Plano de la ciudad de La Habana (Havana Master Plan), 1874, ANC M-540. The number of military architects working on surveying, planning, and fortification efforts in Cuba—and Havana specifically—spiked dramatically after 1763. Of these, Ignacio Yoldi, Agustin Crame, Silvestre Abarca, Luis Huet, and Mariano de la Rocque (also Mariano Larroque), were especially prolific between 1764 and 1784. This would have been the height of Spanish militarization efforts following the British siege of Havana. After the 1840s, topographic plans of both intramuros and extramuros increased markedly, as did plans and maps that depicted a unified city. Francisco de Albear's plan in 1874 marks a culminating point in land surveying and planning, embodied in his cartographic depiction of the city. The representative sample of plans and maps was culled from hundreds of plans and drawings I consulted in rare book collections, archival holdings, and digital repositories. Citations without a call number are found in the author's personal digital collections.

16. Carlos Venegas Fornias, *Cuba y sus pueblos: Censos y mapas de los siglos XVIII y XIX* (Havana: Centro de Investigación y Desarrollo de la Cultura Cubana Juan Marinello, 2002), 86.

17. Miguel Tacón, *Relación del gobierno superior y capitanía general de la Isla de Cuba, estendida por el teniente general D. Miguel Tacón* . . . (Havana: Imprenta del Gobierno y Capitanía General, 1838), 20. The edition that I consulted is housed at the University of Florida, Gainesville, George A. Smathers Library, Harold and Mary Jean Hanson Rare Book Collection.

18. Even mule parking lots were created so that vendors traveling into the city to sell their wares would have a safe place to lodge their animals for a small fee.

19. Tacón, *Relación del gobierno superior y capitanía general*, 13–14.

20. Ibid., 20–21.

21. Ibid., 10–13.

22. Omar Felipe Mauri, *La primera de Cuba: La estación ferroviaria de Bejucal* (Havana: Editorial Unicornio, 2002). The first railroad lines were used primarily for the transport of sugar, but the development of urban rail lines soon facilitated travel within Havana province and then later, with the expansion of the railroad, into Matanzas.

23. Venegas Fornias, *Cuba y sus pueblos*, 94–98.

24. Ibid., 95–96.

25. Ibid., 6–8.

26. Miguel Tacón, *Correspondencia reservada del Capitán General don Miguel Tacón, con el gobierno de Madrid, 1834–1836: El General Tacón y su época, 1834–1838* (Havana: Consejo Nacional de Cultura, Biblioteca Nacional José Martí, Dept. de Colección Cubana, 1963).

27. Tacón, *Relación del gobierno superior y capitanía general*, 4.

28. José Antonio Saco, *La vagancia en Cuba* (Havana: Ministerio de Educación, Dirección de Cultura, 1946).

29. Ibid., 57.

30. Ibid., 58.

31. Saco publicly denounced the illegal slave trade and gave his support to the Academia Cubana de Literatura. The literary organization was largely criollo and antislavery, and Saco was forced into exile in 1834.

32. Public works expenses were kept at a minimum because of the use of forced labor, such as from convicts as well as *cimarrones* and the enslaved. Also, Tacón instituted a series of fifty-peso fines for violating the new public order ordinances, such as by bathing in the sea or having loose animals in the Havana streets. Those who could not pay the fine were forced to labor on the public works projects.

33. *Bando de gobernación y policía de la Isla de Cuba, espedido por el escmo. Sr. Don Gerónimo Valdés, gobernador y capitán general; y Apéndice al bando de gobernación y policía de la Isla de Cuba* (Havana: Imprenta del Gobierno y Capitanía General por S.M., 1842), 30. The edition that I consulted is housed at the University of Florida, Gainesville, George A. Smathers Library, Harold and Mary Jean Hanson Rare Book Collection. While the new hospitals would now be located in the extramuros, those being built would also be

subject to increased regulation, including the monitoring of physical spaces. Thus, while the measure was meant to control pollution within and outside the walls, it also reinforced the association between poor hygiene and the intramuros and the growing correlation between modernity and the extramuros.

34. Ibid., 7.

35. María de las Mercedes Santa Cruz y Montalvo, *La Havane par madame la Comtesse Merlin*, vol. 1 (Paris: Librairie d'Amyot, 1844), 349.

36. Ibid., ii, 351.

37. Ibid., 284–85.

38. Ibid., 312.

39. Cirilo Villaverde, *Cecilia Valdés ó la Loma del angel* (Caracas, Venezuela: Biblioteca Ayacucho, 1981). The novel, written in 1839 and revised in 1882, is set in the Havana of the 1830s.

40. See Loló de la Torriente, *La Habana de Cecilia Valdes* (Havana: J. Montero, 1946); Luz M. Mena, "Raza, género y espacio: Las mujeres negras y mulatas negocian su lugar en la Habana durante la década de 1830," *Revista de Estudios Sociales* 26 (April 2007): 73–85; and Jorge Romero León, *Retórica de imaginación urbana: La ciudad y sus sujetos en Cecilia Valdés y Quincas Borba* (Caracas, Venezuela: Fundación Centro de Estudios Latinoamericanos Rómulo Gallegos, 1997).

41. Miguel Tacón, *Relación del gobierno superior y capitanía general*.

42. According to the numbers cited by Alexander von Humboldt, the number of slaves who passed through the port of Havana more than doubled between the first and second decades of the nineteenth century, surpassing the 1 million mark for the first time in Cuba. Alexander von Humboldt, *The Island of Cuba*, trans. J. S. Thrasher (New York: Derby and Jackson, 1856), 218–23.

43. Kenneth F. Kiple, *Blacks in Colonial Cuba, 1774–1899* (Gainesville: University Press of Florida, 1976), 121. The population of free blacks remained in steady flux throughout these decades, alternately increasing and decreasing in percentage.

44. Rafael Duharte Jiménez, *El negro en la sociedad colonial* (Santiago de Cuba: Editorial Oriente, 1988), 13.

45. Jorge Castellanos and Isabel Castellanos, *Cultura afrocubana*, vol. 1, *El negro en Cuba, 1492–1844* (Miami: Ediciones Universal, 1988), 153–54.

46. Ibid., 154. This also affected the free African-descended population by raising the price that slaves were forced to pay in order to purchase their own freedom, thereby increasing the time that it took slaves to do so and limiting the number of slaves able to go through the process.

47. Humboldt, *Ensayo político;* Duharte Jiménez, *El negro en la sociedad colonial*, 11.

48. Duharte Jiménez, *El negro en la sociedad colonial*, 11.

49. Vera M. Kutzinski, *Sugar's Secrets: Race and the Erotics of Cuban Nationalism* (Charlottesville: University Press of Virginia, 1993).

50. *Bando de gobernación*.

51. Under Article 12 of the new legislation, for example, profanity was strictly prohibited, as were any behaviors not befitting *"las buenas costumbres,"* a definition that was left to the discretion of the neighborhood watchmen and security guards in each district.

52. Ibid., 8.

53. Ibid., 12.

54. Ibid., 29.

55. Ibid., 30.

56. *Ordenanzas municipales de la ciudad de La Habana* (Havana: Imprenta del Gobierno y Capitanía General, 1855), 23. The edition that I consulted is housed at the University of Miami Libraries, CHC.

57. Ibid., 18, 32.

58. Ibid., 57.

59. *Incendio acaecido en el barrio de Jesús María.*

60. *Ordenanzas municipales de la ciudad de La Habana,* 12.

61. Ibid., 26.

62. Ibid., 24.

63. These were the two-wheeled carriages drawn by a horse, with the volante being the smaller and more manageable of the two.

64. *Bando de gobernación,* 17.

65. Ibid., 25.

66. Ibid., 11, 23 (Articles 23 and 79).

67. Ibid., 22.

68. Ibid., 26.

69. See Matt Childs, *The 1812 Aponte Rebellion in Cuba and the Struggle against Atlantic Slavery* (Chapel Hill: University of North Carolina Press, 2006); Phillip A. Howard, *Changing History: Afro-Cuban Cabildos and Societies of Color in the Nineteenth Century* (Baton Rouge: Louisiana State University Press, 1998); William C. van Norman, "The Process of Cultural Change among Cuban Bozales during the Nineteenth Century," *The Americas* 62, no. 2 (October 2005): 177–207.

70. *Bando de gobernación,* 25. The restriction on dress, however, did not apply on days of celebration.

71. For a discussion of black representation in nineteenth-century Cuba, see Vera M. Kutzinski, *Sugar's Secrets: Race and the Erotics of Cuban Nationalism* (Charlottesville: University Press of Virginia, 1993), and Jill Lane, *Blackface Cuba: 1840–1895* (Philadelphia: University of Pennsylvania Press, 2005).

72. District 1 was Catedral, District 2 was Espíritu Santo, District 3 was Salud, District 4 was Factoria, District 5 was Horcón, and District 6 was Regla.

73. *Ordenanzas municipales de la ciudad de La Habana,* 22.

74. Ibid., 24.

75. Castellanos and Castellanos, *Cultura afrocubana,* 156; *Bando de gobernación,* 9.

76. *Ordenanzas de construcción para la ciudad de La Habana, y pueblos de su termino municipal* (Havana: Imprenta del Gobierno y Capitanía General por S.M., 1866), 19.

77. Ibid., 10.

78. Ibid., 14–15.

79. *Reglamento para los arquitectos municipales de La Habana* (Havana: Imprenta del Gobierno y Capitanía General por S.M., 1861). The edition that I

consulted is housed at the Library of Congress, Washington, DC, Hispanic Reading Room.

80. Gwendolyn Midlo Hall, *Social Control in Slave Plantation Societies: A Comparison of St. Domingue and Cuba* (Baltimore: Johns Hopkins University Press, 1971), 131.

81. José de la Concha, *Memoria dirigida al Excmo. Sr. Don Francisco Serrano y Domínguez, capitan general de la isla de Cuba* (Madrid: Imprenta de La Reforma, 1867).

82. Fernando Ortiz, *Los negros curros* (Havana: Editorial de Ciencias Sociales, 1995).

83. Fernando Ortiz, *Los negros brujos* (Miami: Ediciones Universal, 1973).

84. See, for example, Víctor Patricio Landaluze's *Los negros curros*, housed in the Permanent Collection of the Museo de Bellas Artes, Havana.

85. The bufo was a genre of theatre that flourished in the mid-nineteenth century and was associated with the independence movement in Cuba. It served as a criollo foil to "high-culture" entertainment popularized by Tacón and dominated by peninsulares. Under Tacón, opera became the entertainment of choice for elite habaneros. The Teatro Tacón was inaugurated in 1838 specifically to house the opera troupes visiting from Europe.

86. Matías Montes Huidobro, "La reacción antijerárquica en el teatro cubano colonial," *Cuadernos Hispanoamericanos*, no. 334 (1978): 5–19.

87. Eric Lott, *Love and Theft: Blackface Minstrelsy and the American Working Class* (New York: Oxford University Press, 1993).

88. See Jill Lane, *Blackface Cuba, 1840–1895* (Philadelphia: University of Pennsylvania Press, 2005); Mary Cruz, *Creto Gangá* (Havana: Contemporáneos, 1974); Montes Huidobro, "La reacción antijerárquica."

89. The importance of race in the process of state formation has been addressed by significant works in Cuban studies. See Lane, *Blackface Cuba;* Ada Ferrer, *Insurgent Cuba: Race, Nation, and Revolution, 1868–1898* (Chapel Hill: University of North Carolina Press, 1999). Discourses of racial equality were familiar components of nineteenth-century society. They served as a mobilizing strategy and held the promise of social parity for all who supported "Cuba libre." Following independence, discourse and rhetoric would similarly become an important tool in the ability of Cubans of color to mobilize the idea of a racially inclusive nation and demand equality. See Alejandro De la Fuente, *A Nation for All: Race, Inequality, and Politics in Twentieth-Century Cuba* (Chapel Hill: University of North Carolina Press, 2001).

90. Esteban Pichardo y Tapia, *Diccionario provincial casi razonado de vozes y frases cubanas*, quoted in Sergio Valdés Bernal, *Lengua nacional e identidad cultural del cubano* (Havana: Editorial de Ciencias Sociales, 1998). Pichardo was a prominent Cuban scholar whose work on the Spanish language in Cuba was published throughout the nineteenth century.

91. Esteban Pichardo y Tapia, *Diccionario provincial casi razonado de vozes y frases cubanas*, edited by Gladys Alonso González and Ángel L. Fernández Guerra (Havana: Editorial de Ciencias Sociales, 1985).

92. Cruz, *Creto Gangá.*

93. Jorge Castellanos and Isabel Castellanos, "The Geographic, Ethnologic, and Linguistic Roots of Cuban Blacks," *Cuban Studies* 17 (1987): 95–110.

94. Cruz, *Creto Gangá*, 94. Crespo's blackvoice contributions were so regular that in 1848, *La Prensa* (where the "real" Crespo was working) gave Creto Gangá an official position as a writer.

95. Lane, *Blackface Cuba*, 41.

96. In colonial Cuba, the slave trade continued at a significant rate well into the middle of the nineteenth century, accounting for the large number of new arrivals. For a breakdown of the numbers, see Rebecca J. Scott, *Slave Emancipation in Cuba: The Transition to Free Labor, 1860–1899* (Princeton, NJ: Princeton University Press, 1985). See also Louis A. Pérez Jr., *Cuba: Between Reform and Revolution*, 2nd ed. (New York: Oxford University Press, 1995).

97. Vera Kutzinski, *Sugar's Secrets: Race and the Erotics of Cuban Nationalism* (Charlottesville: University Press of Virginia, 1993).

98. Arrom, cited in Lane, *Blackface Cuba*, 171.

99. Cruz, *Creto Gangá*, 49.

100. "Canto de bodas," reprinted in Jorge Luis Morales, ed., *Poesía afroantillana y negrista (Puerto Rico, República Dominicana, Cuba)*, 2nd ed. (Río Piedras: Editorial Universitaria, Universidad de Puerto Rico, 1981).

101. Fernando Ortiz, *Ensayos etnográficos*, edited by Miguel Barnet and Angel L. Fernández (Havana: Editorial de Ciencias Sociales, 1984).

102. Castellanos and Castellanos, *Cultura afrocubana*, 56.

103. Plácido, "Que se lo cuente a su abuela," reprinted in Kutzinski, *Sugar's Secrets*, 86.

104. Castellanos and Castellanos, *Cultura afrocubana* 332. Among the exiled was José Antonio Saco. For an analysis of the colonial backlash, see Michele Reid-Vazquez, *The Year of the Lash: Free People of Color in Cuba and the Nineteenth-Century Atlantic World* (Athens: University of Georgia Press, 2011).

105. Castellanos and Castellanos, *Cultura afrocubana*, 332–33.

106. Rine Leal, ed., *Teatro bufo, siglo XIX: Antología* (Havana: Editorial Arte y Literatura, 1975), 345.

107. Ibid., 248.

108. Matthias Perl, "Cultura y lengua gallegas en Cuba: Acerca de la caracterización lingüística del gallego en el teatro bufo del siglo XIX," *Santiago: Revista de la Universidad de Oriente* 70 (1988): 189–96.

109. Pichardo y Tapia, *Diccionario provincial casi razonado*, 155.

110. See, for example, Joseph L. Scarpaci, Roberto Segre, and Mario Coyula, *Havana: Two Faces of the Antillean Metropolis*, rev. ed. (Chapel Hill: University of North Carolina Press, 2002); Venegas Fornias, *Cuba y sus pueblos*.

CHAPTER 4. CITY

1. *Ordenanzas de construcción para la ciudad de La Habana, y pueblos de su termino municipal* (Havana: Imprenta del Gobierno y Capitanía General por S.M., 1866), 7.

2. Ibid., 7–8.

3. Nicolás José Gutiérrez, "Moción sobre los mercados habaneros, 25 March 1860," *Cuadernos de Historia de la Salud Pública* 67 (1984): 68.

4. Dr. Charles Belot, like many of his medical contemporaries, also fixated on the lack of government foresight in preventing disease. He blamed the administration for perpetuating the conditions that led to yearly outbreaks, yet the yearly death rates as a result of disease actually declined for the period in question. The number of disease cases began its decline under Tacón, with infections never again reaching their pre-1834 levels in Havana until the wars of independence, at which time the rate of infection would far surpass anything ever before seen in the city. Mortality rates as a result of disease similarly continued to decline well into the mid-nineteenth century, when the work of professionals such as Gutiérrez and Belot helped to focus public attention on the issue. Charles Belot, *The Yellow Fever at Havana: Its Nature and Its Treatment* (Savannah, GA: Morning News Steam Printing House, 1878); Jorge Le-Roy y Cassá, *Estudios sobre la mortalidad en La Habana durante el siglo XIX y los comienzos del actual* (Havana: Imprenta Lloredo y Cia., 1913). The mid-nineteenth-century fixation on the health and hygiene of the city was therefore not the result of deteriorating conditions in Havana. Rather, it stemmed from a growing concern with the disconnect between a specific vision of Havana and the preponderance of urban pockets that failed to meet these standards.

5. *Ordenanzas de construcción para la ciudad de La Habana*, 9.

6. Samuel Hazard, *Cuba with Pen and Pencil* (Hartford, CT: Hartford Publishing, 1871), 84.

7. Ibid., 68.

8. See Louis A. Pérez Jr., ed., *Impressions of Cuba in the Nineteenth Century: The Travel Diary of Joseph J. Dimock* (Wilmington, DE: Scholarly Resources, 1998); Hazard, *Cuba with Pen and Pencil*; Rachel Wilson Moore, John Wilson Moore, and George Truman, *Journal of Rachel Wilson Moore, Kept during a Tour to the West Indies and South America, in 1863–64* (Philadelphia: T.E. Zell, 1867).

9. Moore, Moore, and Truman, *Journal of Rachel Wilson Moore*, 24.

10. Benjamín Vallín, *Las reformas en la isla de Cuba* (Madrid: Imprenta de M. Minuesa, 1862), 3. The edition that I consulted is housed at the University of Florida, Gainesville, George A. Smathers Library, Harold and Mary Jean Hanson Rare Books Collection.

11. See Carlos Venegas Fornias, *La urbanización de las murallas: Dependencia y modernidad* (Havana: Editorial Letras Cubanas, 1990).

12. See Louis A. Pérez Jr., *On Becoming Cuban: Identity, Nationality, and Culture* (Chapel Hill: University of North Carolina Press, 1999), 22–23.

13. Ibid., 22.

14. Carlos Venegas Fornias, *Cuba y sus pueblos: Censos y mapas de los siglos XVIII y XIX* (Havana: Centro de Investigación y Desarrollo de la Cultura Cubana Juan Marinello, 2002), 98–101.

15. Venegas Fornias, *La urbanización de las murallas*, 38.

16. See Roberto Segre, "Havana, from Tacón to Forestier," in *Planning Latin America's Capital Cities, 1850–1950*, ed. Arturo Almandoz (London: Routledge, 2002), 197.

17. Ibid., 194. The significance of the new arrivals is illustrated in the previous chapter, which mentioned many recent immigrants, such as the writer Bartolomé Crespo, who did not share in the economic status or political allegiances of the Spanish vanguard.

18. See Anthony Pagden, *Lords of All the World: Ideologies of Empire in Spain, Britain, and France, c. 1500–c. 1800* (New Haven, CT: Yale University Press, 1995).

19. Miguel Tacón, *Relación del gobierno superior y capitanía general de la Isla de Cuba, estendida por el teniente general D. Miguel Tacón* . . . (Havana: Imprenta del Gobierno y Capitanía General, 1838).

20. John G. Wurdemann, *Notes on Cuba, Containing an Account of Its Discovery and Early History* . . . (Boston: J. Munroe, 1844).

21. Segre, "Havana, from Tacón to Forestier," 197–98.

22. Ibid., 197.

23. Alexander von Humboldt, *Ensayo político sobre la isla de Cuba*, trans. D. J. B. de V. Y. M., 2nd ed. (Paris: Libreria de Lecointe, 1836), 15.

24. Julio Le Riverend Brusone, *La Habana, espacio y vida* (Havana: Editorial MAPFRE, 1992).

25. Segre, "Havana, from Tacón to Forestier," 200.

26. Asociación de Propietarios, Industriales y Vecinos del Vedado y Príncipe, *Discusión pronunciado en al acto de descubrir el retrato del Dr. Manuel Varela Suárez* (Havana: Imprenta Seone y Fernández, 1928), 6.

27. Ibid., 7.

28. Ibid.

29. Zenaida Iglesias Sánchez, "El Parque Central," *Habana radio*, August 8, 2005.

30. Ibid.

31. Segre, "Havana, from Tacón to Forestier," 200.

32. Solicitud de Juan García para limpiar la Bahía de La Habana, 1882, ANC, Fondo Junta Superior de Sanidad, legajo 8, no. 1.

33. El brote de cólera publicado en los periódicos de La Habana, 1867–1878, 1890, ANC, Fondo Junta Superior de Sanidad, legajo 5, no. 230; Cólera asiático en La Habana, 1890, ANC, Fondo Junta Superior de Sanidad, legajo 9, no. 41; Cordón sanitario en La Habana para prevenir la propagación del cólera, 1890, ANC, Fondo Junta Superior de Sanidad, legajo 9, no. 41.

34. Orden vigente sobre la cuarentena de barcos, ANC, Fondo Junta Superior de Sanidad, legajo 11, no. 181; Traslación de establos a los afueras de la ciudad, 1890, ANC, Fondo Junta Superior de Sanidad, legajo 9, no. 29; Traslación de trenes funerarios a las afueras de la ciudad, 1890, ANC, Fondo Junta Superior de Sanidad, legajo 9, no. 32; Orden de fumigación de pasajeros y equipaje llegados de La Habana, 1894, ANC, Fondo Junta Superior de Sanidad, legajo 18, no. 72.

35. Le-Roy y Cassá, *Estudios sobre la mortalidad*, 6.

36. Fernando Inclán Lavastida, *Historia de Marianao de la época indígena a los tiempos actuales* (Marianao: Editorial "El Sol," 1943).

37. Segre, "Havana, from Tacón to Forestier," 199.

38. Louis A. Pérez Jr., *Cuba: Between Reform and Revolution,* 2nd ed. (New York: Oxford University Press, 1995), 132.

39. Ibid., 131.

40. Francisco de Paula Gelabert, *Cuadros de costumbres cubanas* (Havana: Imprenta de la Botica de Santo Domingo, 1875). The edition that I consulted is housed at the University of Florida, Gainesville, George A. Smathers Library, Harold and Mary Jean Hanson Rare Book Collection.

41. Ibid., 133.

42. Ibid., 131–47.

43. Ibid., 123–31.

44. Eduardo Varela Zequeira, *La policía de La Habana (Cuebas y Sabaté)* (Havana: Imprenta y Papelería "La Universal," 1894).

45. Francisco García Morales, *Guía de gobierno y policía de la Isla de Cuba, compendio de las atribuciones gubernativas de los alcaldes, tenientes de alcalde y alcaldes de barrio, con un prontuario alfabético de la legislación vigente sobre policía y orden público* (Havana: La Propaganda Literaria, 1881). The edition that I consulted is housed at the University of Florida, Gainesville, George A. Smathers Library, Harold and Mary Jean Hanson Rare Book Collection.

46. Ibid.

47. Ibid., 19.

48. Ibid., 20, 25.

49. Quoted in María del Carmen Barcia, *Una sociedad en crisis: La Habana a finales del siglo XIX* (Havana: Editorial de Ciencias Sociales, 2000), 110.

50. Ibid., 40–41.

51. Kinet Francisco Lorenzo, vecino de La Habana, por el crímen de falsificación de papeles durante la Guerra de Independencia, 1875, ANC, Fondo Cárceles y Presidios, legajo 70, no. 22.

52. "Resolución del Gobierno General," 23 February 1880, in García Morales, *Guía de gobierno y policía de la Isla de Cuba,* 29.

53. Yolanda Díaz Martínez, "Sociedad, violencia y criminalidad masculina en La Habana de finales del siglo XIX: Aproximaciones a una realidad," in *La sociedad cubana en los albores de la República,* ed. Mildred de la Torre Molina et al. (Havana: Editorial de Ciencias Sociales, 2002), 49–89.

54. ANC, Fondo Cárceles y Presidios, legajos 69–76.

55. See Díaz Martínez, "Sociedad, violencia y criminalidad masculina."

56. G. G. Y. F., *Los criminales de Cuba y el inspector Trujillo* (Havana: La Propaganda Literaria, 1881).

57. Ibid., 16.

58. Varela Zequeira, *La policía de La Habana.*

59. G. G. Y. F., *Los criminales de Cuba,* 24–32.

60. Ibid., 5.

61. Ibid., 37.

62. José Antonio Saco, *La vagancia en Cuba* (Havana: Ministerio de Educación, Dirección de Cultura, 1946).

63. Diego Alcántara, 1877, ANC, Fondo Cárceles y Presidios, legajo 69, no. 3; Bernabé Alcántara, ANC, 1857, Fondo Cárceles y Presidios, legajo 69, no. 4; José Angel Labarde, 1874, ANC, Fondo Cárceles y Presidios, legajo 70, no. 28;

Juan de Armas, 1859, ANC, Fondo Cárceles y Presidios, legajo 70, no. 15; Jorge Fernández, 1869, ANC, Fondo Cárceles y Presidios, legajo 70, no. 8.

64. Varela Zequeira, *La policía de La Habana.*

CHAPTER 5. EMPIRE'S END

Epigraph: Quoted in María del Carmen Barcia, *Una sociedad en crisis: La Habana a finales del siglo XIX* (Havana: Editorial de Ciencias Sociales, 2000), 110.

1. John Lawrence Tone, *War and Genocide in Cuba, 1895–1898* (Chapel Hill: University of North Carolina Press, 2006), 191. While there is a general consensus on the number of people who perished or were displaced as a direct result of the reconcentración, the numbers still vary from conservative estimates of 60,000 to those approaching 200,000. Early estimates were even higher and in the range of 400,000 to 500,000 people. I consulted Cuban and U.S. census records taken before and after the war as well as figures provided by the U.S. military administration in Havana, and I relied on Tone's interpretation of census data.

2. Guadalupe García, "Urban *Guajiros:* Colonial *Reconcentración,* Rural Displacement, and Criminalisation in Western Cuba, 1895–1902," *Journal of Latin American Studies* 43, no. 2 (2011): 209–35.

3. This was the first bando to affect western Cuba, but the first order had been issued on February 16, 1896, and affected only the eastern provinces of Sancti Spíritus, Puerto Príncipe, and Santiago de Cuba. The reason that the policy was not unilaterally implemented had to do with the importance of agriculture and the colonial government's uncertainty over its ability to meet the needs of the reconcentrados. Senate Comm. on Foreign Affairs, *Concentration and Other Proclamations of General Weyler,* 55th Cong., 2nd Sess. (11 April 1898), 549–51.

4. See Félix de Echauz y Guinart, *Lo que se ha hecho y lo que se hay que hacer en Cuba: Breves indicaciones sobre la campaña* (Barcelona: Imprenta del Diario de Barcelona, 1872).

5. Ibid., 13.

6. Presidente del Consejo de Ministros, "Carta confidencial al Excmo. Sr. D. Antonio Cánovas del Castillo," reprinted in Valeriano Weyler, *Mi mando en Cuba* (Havana: Imprenta, Litografía y Casa Editorial de Felipe González Rojas, 1910), 30–31.

7. "Circular del cuartel general del ejército," 1 July 1895, in Weyler, *Mi mando en Cuba,* 34.

8. Weyler, *Mi mando en Cuba,* 427. Large rural enterprises were allowed to continue production if they were able to show a clear allegiance to the colonial administration.

9. Ibid., 41. The bandos were not all the same, and there were certainly exceptions to who was subject to the relocation orders. Planters not behind on their taxes, for example, were allowed to maintain production during the war.

10. Tone, *War and Genocide in Cuba,* 198.

11. Ibid.

12. See Stephen Bonsal, *The Real Condition of Cuba To-day* (New York: Harper and Brothers Publishers, 1897); Frederic Remington, *The Collected Writings of Frederic Remington*, ed. Peggy Samuels and Harold Samuels (Garden City, NY: Doubleday, 1979).

13. Senate Comm. on Foreign Affairs, *Correspondence, United States Consulate-General Fitzhugh Lee to Mr. Day, November 23, 1897*, S. Rep. No. 710, 55th Cong., 2nd Sess. (11 April 1898), 8–9.

14. Ibid., 97.

15. Ibid; Tone, *War and Genocide in Cuba*, 211–12. Reconcentración and mortality in the two eastern provinces of Puerto Príncipe and Santiago de Cuba were comparatively low.

16. Senate Comm. on Foreign Affairs, *Correspondence, United States Consulate-General Fitzhugh Lee to Mr. Day, December 14, 1897*, S. Rep. No. 727, 55th Cong., 2nd Sess. (11 April 1898), 14.

17. Matthew Smallman-Raynor and Andrew D. Cliff, "The Spatial Dynamics of Epidemic Diseases in War and Peace: Cuba and the Insurrection against Spain, 1895–98," *Transaction of the Institute of British Geographers*, n.s., 24, no. 3 (1999): 331–52.

18. Senate Comm. on Foreign Affairs, *Correspondence, United States Consulate-General Fitzhugh Lee to Mr. Day, November 23, 1897*, S. Rep. No. 712, 55th Cong., 2nd Sess. (11 April 1898), 9–11.

19. Blanco revised this stipulation in November 1897 and did away with the legal distinctions that criminalized reconcentrados with family members suspected of supporting the insurgency.

20. In a bando dated November 10 and a communication issued November 13, Blanco agreed to the end of the reconcentración. The order, however, did not apply to all reconcentrados; Blanco cited the high number of women and children who would perish without the daily rations that the administration was attempting to provide. *Juntas protectoras* were also created to oversee the care of those who remained in towns and cities after the order. Funding, which was not nearly sufficient to cover the expense, was provided based on the number of reconcentrados living in each municipality. See Francisco Pérez Guzmán, *La Habana: Clave de un imperio* (Havana: Editorial de Ciencias Sociales, 1997), 115–21.

21. "Blanco's Measures in Cuba," *New York Times*, 11 November 1897.

22. "Blanco's Relief Measures," *New York Times*, 1 April 1898.

23. National Institutes of Health, *Public Health Reports* vo11, no. 50 (11 December 1897): 1154–1155; http://www. pubmedcenter.nih.gov.

24. National Institutes of Health, *Public Health Reports* 12, no. 49 (3 December 1897): 1330; http://www.ncbi.nlm.nih.gov/pmc/articles/PMC1998902/.

25. Pérez Guzmán, *La Habana*, 114.

26. Smallman-Raynor and Cliff, "Spatial Dynamics of Epidemic Disease," 331.

27. Mariola Espinosa, "A Fever for Empire: U.S. Disease Eradication in Cuba as Colonial Public Health," in *Colonial Crucible: Empire in the Making of the Modern American State*, ed. Alfred W. McCoy and Francisco A. Scarano (Madison: University of Wisconsin Press, 2009), 288–96.

28. "Actas de las sesiones celebradas por la Junta Superior de Sanidad de La Habana," 1896–1898, ANC, Fondo Junta Superior de Sanidad, legajo 6, no. 6.

29. For a discussion of the relationship between disease, criminality, and urban disorder, see Julia Kirk Blackwelder and Lyman L. Johnson, "Changing Criminal Patterns in Buenos Aires, 1890 to 1914," *Journal of Latin American Studies* 14, no. 2 (1982): 359–79.

30. Jorge Le-Roy y Cassá, *Estudios sobre la mortalidad en La Habana durante el siglo XIX y los comienzos del actual* (Havana: Imprenta Loredo y Cia., 1913).

31. Smallman-Raynor and Cliff, "Spatial Dynamics of Epidemic Disease," 342.

32. Quoted in ibid., 341.

33. See Yolanda Díaz Martínez, "Sociedad, violencia y criminalidad masculina en La Habana de finales del siglo XIX: Aproximaciones a una realidad," in *La sociedad cubana en los albores de la República*, ed. Mildred de la Torre Molina et al. (Havana: Editorial de Ciencias Sociales, 2002), 49–89.

34. "Position of the Junta," *New York Times*, 8 April 1898.

35. "Four Reconcentrados Assassinated," *New York Times*, 7 April 1898.

36. "Blanco's Relief Measures," *New York Times*, 1 April 1898.

37. "Reconcentrados Sent Home," *New York Times*, 21 September 1898.

38. Quoted in Smallman-Raynor and Cliff, "Spatial Dynamics of Epidemic Disease," 342.

39. "Blanco's Relief Measures," *New York Times*, 1 April 1898.

40. Senate Comm. on Foreign Affairs, *Translation of the Articles of General Blanco's Proclamation of the 30th March, 1898, Suspending the Reconcentración*, Enclosure No. 1, S. Rep. No. 809, 55th Cong., 2nd Sess. (11 April 1898), 28.

41. Clara Barton, *The Red Cross: A History of This Remarkable International Movement in the Interest of Humanity* (Washington, DC: American National Red Cross 1898), 519.

42. "Blanco's Relief Measures," *New York Times*, 1 April 1898; Barton, *Red Cross*, 363.

43. See William E. Barton, *The Life of Clara Barton, Founder of the American Red Cross*, vol. 2 (New York: Houghton Mifflin, 1922).

44. Senate Comm. on Foreign Affairs, *Statement Made by Mr. Stephen Bonsal on the 11th Day of June, 1897*, 55th Cong., 2nd Sess. (11 April 1898), 397–417.

45. Barton, *Red Cross*, 528.

46. Pérez Guzmán, *La Habana*, 25.

47. Hortensia Pichardo Viñals, *Documentos para la historia de Cuba*, vol. 1, 5th ed. (Havana: Editorial Pueblo y Educación, 1984), 364.

48. José Manuel Fernández Nuñez, *Colonial Havana: A Fortress of the Americas*, trans. Fernando Nápoles Tapia (Havana: Editorial José Martí, 1998), 64–69.

49. Plan de Albear (1874); Fernández Nuñez, *Colonial Havana*, 65.

50. Fernández Nuñez, *Colonial Havana*, 66–67.

51. Antoni Kapcia, *Cuba in Revolution: A History since the Fifties* (London: Reaktion Books, 2008), 11. Such associations referenced the fear and popularity

of leaders such as Antonio Maceo and his insurgent forces as they moved beyond Oriente and toward the significantly "whiter" areas of the western provinces.

52. Smallman-Raynor and Cliff, "Spatial Dynamics of Epidemic Disease."

53. Ada Ferrer, "Rustic Men, Civilized Nation: Race, Culture, and Contention on the Eve of Cuban Independence," *Hispanic American Historical Review* 78, no. 4 (1998): 663–86.

54. Ibid., 674.

55. Miguel Barnet, *Biography of a Runaway Slave*, trans. W. Nick Hill, rev. ed. (Willimantic, CT: Curbstone Press, 1995), 162–63.

56. Matt D. Childs, *The 1812 Aponte Rebellion in Cuba and the Struggle against Atlantic Slavery* (Chapel Hill: University of North Carolina Press, 2006); Michele Reid-Vazquez, *The Year of the Lash: Free People of Color in Cuba and the Nineteenth-Century Atlantic World* (Athens: University of Georgia Press, 2011).

57. Gonzalo de Quesada and Henry Davenport Northrop, *Cuba's Great Struggle for Freedom* (Washington, DC, 1898).

58. William Ludlow, *Annual Report for Fiscal Year Ended June 30, 1899, from Dec. 22, 1898* (Havana: U.S. Army Department of Havana, 1899).

CHAPTER 6. NORTH AMERICANS IN HAVANA

1. "Discurso del Dr. Carlos Miguel de Céspedes," Forum del Colegio de Arquitectos sobre La Plaza de República y el Monumento a Martí, 11 May 1953, and Francisco Gómez Díaz, *De Forestier a Sert: Ciudad y arquitectura en La Habana, 1925–1969* (Madrid: Abada Editores, 2008).

2. See Louis A. Pérez Jr., *The War of 1898: The United States and Cuba in History and Historiography* (Chapel Hill: University of North Carolina Press, 1999), and Jules R. Benjamin, *The United States and the Origins of the Cuban Revolution: An Empire of Liberty in an Age of National Liberation* (Princeton, NJ: Princeton University Press, 1990).

3. See Ada Ferrer, *Insurgent Cuba: Race, Nation, and Revolution, 1868–1898* (Chapel Hill: University of North Carolina Press, 1999).

4. Condición del Puerto, 1903, ANC, Secretaría de la Presidencia, legajo 73, no. 25; ANC, Secretaría de la Presidencia, 1907, legajo 106, no. 64.

5. William Ludlow, *Annual Report for Fiscal Year Ended June 30, 1899, from Dec. 22, 1898* (Havana: U.S. Army, Department of Havana, 1899).

6. The Spanish colonial administration set up relief boards staffed by residents and allocated funding to help with the effort, including providing small plots of land for subsistence agriculture.

7. Ludlow, *Annual Report*, 25.

8. Matthew Smallman-Raynor and Andrew D. Cliff, "The Spatial Dynamics of Epidemic Diseases in War and Peace: Cuba and the Insurrection against Spain, 1895–98," *Transactions of the Institute of British Geographers*, n.s., 24, no. 3 (1999): 331–52.

9. Expediente memorandum concerniente a las deplorables condiciones sanitarias de los puertos de Cuba, 23 July 1903, ANC, Secretaría de la Presidencia, caja 73, no. 25. See also Mariola Espinosa, "The Threat from Havana: South-

ern Public Health, Yellow Fever, and the U.S. Intervention in the Cuban Struggle for Independence, 1878–1898," *Journal of Southern History* 72, no. 3 (2006): 541–68.

10. See Stephen Bonsal, *The Real Condition of Cuba To-day* (New York: Harper and Brothers, 1897); Frederic Remington, *The Collected Writings of Frederic Remington,* ed. Peggy Samuels and Harold Samuels (Garden City, NY: Doubleday, 1979).

11. Kenneth F. Kiple, *Blacks in Colonial Cuba, 1774–1899* (Gainesville: University Press of Florida, 1976).

12. Director General, República de Cuba, *Censo de la República de Cuba, año de 1899* (Havana: Maza, Arroyo y Caso, S. and C., 1901). Two census reports appeared in 1899, one in English and the other in Spanish. The figures here rely on both reports.

13. Louis A. Pérez Jr., "The Pursuit of Pacification: Banditry and the United States' Occupation of Cuba, 1899–1902," *Journal of Latin American Studies* 18, no. 2 (1986): 313–32.

14. Ibid.

15. Quoted in Pérez, "The Pursuit of Pacification," 324.

16. Ferrer, *Insurgent Cuba,* 196.

17. Alejandro de la Fuente, "Myths of Racial Democracy: Cuba, 1900–1912," *Latin American Research Review* 34, no. 3 (1999): 39–73.

18. Ludlow, *Annual Report,* 15.

19. *Reglamento para el régimen interior del Ayuntamiento de La Habana* (Havana: Imprenta P. Fernández y Cía., 1900). The edition that I consulted is housed at the Library of Congress, Washington, DC, Geography and Map Division.

20. Mario Coyula, "La arquitectura del movimiento moderno en Cuba: Luces y sombras," paper presented at "Relaciones entre la arquitectura moderna del Caribe y América Latina," Centro Cultural León, Santiago de los Caballeros, Dominican Republic, September 18, 2009.

21. Joseph L. Scarpaci, Roberto Segre, and Mario Coyula, *Havana: Two Faces of the Antillean Metropolis,* rev. ed. (Chapel Hill: University of North Carolina Press, 2002).

22. *Translation of the General Law of Public Works of the Island of Cuba, and Regulations for Its Execution: With the Addition of All Subsequent Provisions Published to Date (1891)* (Washington, DC: War Department, 1899).

23. James H. Hitchman, "Unfinished Business: Public Works in Cuba, 1898–1902," *The Americas* 31, no. 3 (1975): 355–59.

24. Ibid.

25. Ludlow, *Annual Report,* 52–53.

26. Hitchman, "Unfinished Business."

27. Ibid., 186–87, 191–92.

28. Ludlow, *Annual Report,* 12.

29. Ibid., 187–88. Luis M. Cowley, "Recogida de basuras en las calles: Depósitos destinados a contener esos residuos domésticos," *Revista de Medicina y Cirugía de La Habana* 14 (1909): 631–39.

30. Ludlow, *Annual Report,* 193–96.

31. Informe demógrafo, estado de defunciones ocurridos en La Habana durante la decena terminada 10 de agosto de 1903, Departamento de Sanidad de La Habana, 1903, ANC, Fondo Secretaría de la Presidencia, legajo 115, no. 10; Fiebre amarilla en los distritos de La Habana, 1906, and Letter from Chief Sanitary Officer to William H. Taft recommending quarantine of the harbor and districts of Las Cruces, Lajas, Ranchuelo, and Palmira, 10 and 27 October 1906, ANC, Fondo Secretaría de la Presidencia, legajo 106, no. 78.

32. Carlos J. Finlay, Jefe de Sanidad de la República, Departamento Nacional de Sanidad, "Informe anual sanitario y demográfico de la República de Cuba bajo la administración provisional de los Estados Unidos," Havana, 1908.

33. Comunicación sobre el contracto para la compra del abono de los establos y la limpieza de La Habana, 1909, ANC, Fondo Secretaría de la Presidencia, legajo 101, no. 90.

34. Gómez Díaz, *De Forestier a Sert*.

35. K. Edge, J. Scarpaci, and H. Woofter, "Mapping and Designing Havana: Republican, Socialist, and Global Spaces," *Cities* 23, no. 2 (2006): 85–98.

36. Rosalie Schwartz, *Pleasure Island: Tourism and Temptation in Cuba* (Lincoln: University of Nebraska Press, 1999).

37. Civil Order 29, 19 January 1900; Civil Order 220, 28 May 1900; Civil Order 155, 14 April 1900; Civil Order 24, 28 June 1900; Civil Order 159, 1902.

38. Military order no. 31, military order no. 64, military order no. 176, reprinted in Francisco M. Duque and Julio G. Bellver, eds., *Jurisprudencia en material de policía urbana: Decretos, acuerdos, y otras resoluciones sobre dicha materia, dictados para el municipio de La Habana* (Havana: Imprenta y Librería La Moderna Poesía, 1924), 110–11.

39. Sovereignty in the amendment implied a nation free from physical occupation or rule by a foreign power—i.e., colonialism. What emerged instead was the system anew under neocolonial rule in Cuba.

40. De la Fuente, "Myths of Racial Democracy."

41. Victor H. Olmsted and Henry Gannett, eds., *Cuba: Population, History, and Resources, 1907* (Washington, DC: United States Bureau of the Census, 1909), 41.

42. Carlos Venegas Fornias, *Cuba y sus pueblos: Censos y mapas de los siglos XVIII y XIX* (Havana: Centro de Investigación y Desarrollo de la Cultura Cubana Juan Marinello, 2002).

43. *Informe sobre el censo de Cuba, 1899* (Washington, DC: Imprenta del Gobierno, 1900); Olmsted and Gannett, *Cuba*.

44. *Informe sobre el censo de Cuba*, 10.

45. John Pickles, *A History of Spaces: Cartographic Reason, Mapping, and the Geo-Coded World* (New York: Routledge, 2004), and Denis Wood, *Rethinking the Power of Maps* (New York: Guilford Press, 2010).

46. John Pickles, *A History of Spaces*, 20–21.

47. This discussion is not meant to dismiss precolonial and non-European uses of the "maps" that were often used as notation systems; however, indige-

nous conceptions of time, space, property, and ownership differed markedly from European ideas of these same concepts. Because of this, indigenous societies and empires produced devices with significantly different purposes than their European counterparts.

48. Wood, *Rethinking the Power of Maps*, 38–39.

49. Scarpaci, Segre, and Coyula, *Havana;* Julio Le Riverend, *La Habana, espacio y vida* (Havana: Editorial MAPFRE, 1992). While the literature on urbanization has tended to view independence as a watershed event, recent scholarship is deemphasizing the colonial transition. See Mildred de la Torre Molina et al., eds., *La sociedad cubana en los albores de la República* (Havana: Editorial de Ciencias Sociales, 2002). Those who do mark the transition as a difficult one for certain sectors of habaneros, for example, do so by emphasizing not U.S. policies affecting Havana (and the rest of Cuba) but rather the social changes that took place in the city prior to independence and that were subsequently intensified by the policies that followed with the U.S. occupation. See María Poumier, *Apuntes sobre la vida cotidiana en Cuba en 1898* (Havana: Editorial de Ciencias Sociales, 1975).

50. See Jorge E. Hardoy, "Two Thousand Years of Latin American Urbanization," in *Urbanization in Latin America: Approaches and Issues,* ed. Jorge E. Hardoy (Garden City, NY: Anchor Books, 1975), 51. I should note that I am using Morse's definitions of urbanism ("elegant public buildings and improved public services, street-paving, flood control, cultural and educational centers") and urbanization (relative population growth) to argue that Havana's urbanization in the early twentieth century was mistaken for the introduction of urbanism, hence the ease with which a "new urbanism" is attributed to the U.S. government of occupation. See Richard M. Morse, "Cities as People," 7.

51. Town Planning Associates, *Plan piloto de La Habana*, 1959, Southeastern Architectural Archive, Tulane University.

52. Wood, *Rethinking the Power of Maps*, 38–39.

53. Solicitud de parque público, 1909, ANC, Fondo Secretaría de la Presidencia, legajo 18, no. 13. Contract approved by William H. Taft to build in the arsenal, 1906, ANC, Secretaría de la Presidencia, caja 96, no. 29; Paving and lighting plan, 1905–1906, ANC, Secretaría de la Presidencia, caja 87, no. 49; General plan to improve barrios, 1909, ANC, Secretaría de la Presidencia, legajo 78, no. 75.

54. Duque and Bellver, *Jurisprudencia en material de policía urbana,* 18–99.

55. Letter to Charles Magoon from Asociación de Propietarios, Industriales y Vecinos del Vedado y Príncipe, 25 October 1906, ANC, Fondo Secretaría de la Presidencia, legajo 101, no. 95.

56. The Platt Amendment took effect in 1903 and was the necessary condition for withdrawal of the remaining U.S. troops in Cuba.

57. Paving and lighting plan, 1905–1906, ANC, Secretaría de la Presidencia, caja 87, no. 49; General plan to improve barrios, 1909, ANC, Secretaría de la Presidencia, legajo 78, no. 75.

58. Correspondence, 1907, ANC, Secretaría de la Presidencia, caja 27, no. 17.

59. Correspondence to Charles Magoon, W.M. Black, U.S. Army Corps of Engineers, 1907, ANC, Fondo Secretaría de la Presidencia, legajo 24, no. 17. Declaración por los obreros del barrio de Jesús María, 1908, ANC, Fondo Secretaría de la Presidencia, legajo 96, no. 67, expediente 2. For a discussion of class in one Havana neighborhood, see Mario Coyula, "La lección de Alamar," *Espacio Laical* 4 (2011): 54–61.

60. Letter to Provisional Governor Charles Magoon, January 1907, ANC, Fondo Secretaría de la Presidencia, legajo 67, no. 38.

61. Quejas por la Asociación de Propietarios, Industriales y Vecinos del Vedado y Príncipe, enviada al Gobernador Provisional Charles Magoon, 1906, ANC, Fondo Secretaría de la Presidencia, legajo 101, no. 95.

62. Correspondencia al Gobernador Provisional Charles Magoon, 1908, ANC, Fondo Secretaría de la Presidencia, legajo 67, no. 38.

63. Estadística detallada que contiene relación de los empleados de planificación y temporreros, en los distintos cargos que ocupan, en la Jefatura de Obras Públicas de la Ciudad de La Habana, 1906–1907, ANC, Fondo Secretaría de la Presidencia, legajo 66, no. 8.64.

64. Memo e instancia de la Asociación de Propietarios, Industriales y Vecinos de los Barrios de Medina Príncipe sobre la prolongación de la Calle 23 en El Vedado, 1914, ANC, Fondo Secretaría de la Presidencia, legajo 49, no. 38, expediente 1.

65. Ibid.

66. Declaración por los obreros del barrio de Jesús María, 1908, ANC, Fondo Secretaría de la Presidencia, legajo 96, no. 67, expediente 2. After the 1906 occupation, class would become an important distinction around which neighborhoods were organized. In 1911, Pogolotti, Marianao, the "Barrio Obrero Rendención," was one of the first to introduce this trend, with almost 1,100 small homes built in "typical" Cuban fashion. Coyula, "La lección de Alamar."

67. Correspondencia al Gobernador Provisional Charles Magoon, 1908, ANC, Fondo Secretaría de la Presidencia, legajo 67, no. 38.

68. See Benjamin, *United States and the Origins of the Cuban Revolution.*

CONCLUSION

1. David Sartorius, *Ever Faithful: Race, Loyalty, and the Ends of Empire in Spanish Cuba* (Durham, NC: Duke University Press, 2013).

2. Manuel M. Miranda, *Memorias de un deportado* (Havana: Imprenta La Luz, 1903).

3. Joan Casanovas, *Bread, or Bullets! Urban Labor and Spanish Colonialism in Cuba, 1850–1898* (Pittsburgh: University of Pittsburgh Press, 1998).

4. Miranda, *Memorias de un deportado,* 6.

5. Wendy Brown, *Walled States, Waning Sovereignty* (Brooklyn: Zone Books, 2010). From the classical writings of John Locke and Carl Schmitt to contemporary scholars writing on nations and borders, the theme of dominion and territory has been central to formulations about the exercise of political power. For classical writers, dominion over space and territory premised sover-

eignty rather than constituted it, and thus when Christopher Columbus and Pedrarias D'ávila sailed west under the Spanish flag and arrived on the unsettled lands that would later contain the towns and cities of the empire, Spanish dominion was already assumed. When they consecrated towns and cities immediately upon arrival, the practice was a performative one that codified for other European sovereigns and claimed for the empire a power that they already believed they possessed.

6. Ibid.

7. Francisco de Barreda, "Puntual, verídica, topográfica descripción del famoso puerto, y ciudad de La Habana," 1719, BNE, VE321/21.

8. Brown, *Walled States,* 21.

9. Juan B. Amores, *Cuba y España, 1868–1898: El final de un sueño* (Pamplona: Eunsa, 1998); Philip S. Foner, *A History of Cuba and Its Relations with the United States,* vol. 1, *1492–1845: From the Conquest of Cuba to La Escalera* (New York: International Publishers, 1962).

10. Casanovas, *Bread, or Bullets!,* 12–13; Sartorius, *Ever Faithful.*

11. Timothy Hyde, *Constitutional Modernism: Architecture and Civil Society in Cuba, 1933–1959* (Minneapolis: University of Minnesota Press, 2012), 5.

12. Brown, *Walled States,* 45.

13. Miranda, *Memorias de un deportado,* 6.

14. Brown, *Walled States,* 28. See Kelly Lytle Hernández, *Migra! A History of the U.S. Border Patrol* (Berkeley: University of California Press, 2010); Peter Andreas, *Border Games: Policing the U.S.-Mexico Divide,* 2nd ed. (Ithaca, NY: Cornell University Press, 2009); Elana Zilberg, *Space of Detention: The Making of a Transnational Gang Crisis between Los Angeles and San Salvador* (Durham, NC: Duke University Press, 2011).

15. Gloria Anzaldúa, *Borderlands / La Frontera: The New Mestiza,* 4thed. (San Francisco: Aunt Lute Books, 2012); Cherríe Moraga and Gloria Anzaldúa, eds., *This Bridge Called My Back: Writings by Radical Women of Color,* 2nd ed. (New York: Persephone Press, 1983).

16. Matt D. Childs, *The 1812 Aponte Rebellion in Cuba and the Struggle against Atlantic Slavery* (Chapel Hill: University of North Carolina Press, 2006), 2.

17. John Jay TePaske, "Integral to Empire: The Vital Peripheries of Colonial Spanish America," in *Negotiated Empires: Center and Peripheries in the Americas, 1500–1820,* ed. Christine Daniels and Michael V. Kennedy (New York: Routledge, 2002), 29–41.

18. Brown, *Walled States,* 25.

19. Greg Eghigian, "Homo Munitus: The East German Observed," in *Socialist Modern: East German Everyday Culture and Politics,* ed. Katherine Pence and Paul Betts (Ann Arbor: University of Michigan Press, 2008), 43–44.

20. Cirilo Villaverde, *Cecilia Valdés ó La loma del angel* (Caracas, Venezuela: Biblioteca Ayacucho, 1981).

21. Lisa B. Y. Calvente and Guadalupe García, "The City Speaks: Dis/articulating Revolutionary Havana, Cuba, and Global Belonging," *Cultural Studies* 28, no. 3, (2014): 438–62.

22. Ibid., 442.

23. John F. Collins, "Culture, Content, and the Enclosure of Human Being: UNESCO's 'Intangible' Heritage in the New Millennium," *Radical History Review*, no. 109 (2011): 121–35.

24. Ibid., 128.

25. "Down! / And don't tell me that it is patrimonio / That it can't be torn down because it belongs to Eusebio! / I don't understand what that guy is doing 'there' / After the revolution that was had 'here' . . . tear it down!"

Bibliography

ARCHIVAL COLLECTIONS
Havana, Cuba
　Archivo Nacional de Cuba (ANC)
Boletín del Archivo Nacional
Cárceles y Presidios
Donativos y Remisiones
Junta Superior de Sanidad
Mapoteca
Obras Públicas
Realengos
Reales Ordenes y Cédulas
Secretaría de la Presidencia

Seville, Spain
　Archivo General de Indias, Seville (AGI)
Contaduría
Escribanía de Cámara
Estado
Santo Domingo
Mapas y Planos
Ultramar

SPECIAL COLLECTIONS AND LIBRARIES
Chicago, Illinois
  Newberry Library
Manuscripts and Archives
Maps, Travel, and Exploration

Gainesville, Florida
University of Florida, George A. Smathers Library, Harold and Mary Jean
  Hanson Rare Book Collection

Havana, Cuba
Biblioteca Nacional José Martí (BNJM), Colección Cubana
Instituto de Historia de Cuba

Madrid, Spain
Biblioteca Nacional de España (BNE), Manuscript Division
Museo Naval de Madrid (MNM), Colección Antigua

Miami, Florida
University of Miami Libraries, Cuban Heritage Collection (CHC)

New Orleans, Louisiana
Tulane University, Latin American Library (LAL), Cortés, Hernando (1485–
  1547) Collection
Tulane University, Southeastern Architectural Archives

Washington, DC
  Library of Congress
Geography and Map Division
Hispanic Reading Room

NEWSPAPERS AND SERIALS
Bohemia (Havana)
New York Times (New York)

MANUSCRIPT COLLECTIONS (PRINT AND DIGITIZED)
Actas capitulares del Ayuntamiento de La Habana. Edited by Emilio Roig de
  Leuchsenring. 3 vols. Havana: Municipio de La Habana, 1937–46. (ACAH)

Cien planos de La Habana en los archivos españoles. Madrid: Servicio de Publicaciones del MOPU, Secretaría General Técnica, 1985.

Colección de documentos inéditos relativos al descubrimiento, conquista, y colonización de las posesiones españolas en América y Oceanía. 42 vols. Madrid, 1864–84. (CODOI)

Duque, Francisco M., and Julio G. Bellver, eds. *Jurisprudencia en material de policía urbana: Decretos, acuerdos, y otras resoluciones sobre dicha materia, dictados para el municipio de La Habana.* Havana: Imprenta y Librería La Moderna Poesía, 1924.

Índices y extractos del Archivo de Protocolos de La Habana, 1578–1585. Vol. 1. Edited by María Teresa de Rojas. Havana, 1947.

Papeles sobre la toma de La Habana por los ingleses en 1762. Havana: Archivo Nacional de Cuba, 1948.

BOOKS, PRINTED SOURCES, AND ARTICLES

Aiton, Arthur Scott. "Real Hacienda in New Spain under the First Viceroy." *Hispanic American Historical Review* 6, no. 4 (1926): 232–45.

Amores, Juan B. *Cuba y España, 1868–1898: El final de un sueño.* Pamplona: Eunsa, 1998.

Andreas, Peter. *Border Games: Policing the U.S.-Mexico Divide.* 2nd ed. Ithaca, NY: Cornell University Press, 2009.

Anzaldúa, Gloria. *Borderlands / La Frontera: The New Mestiza.* 4th ed. San Francisco: Aunt Lute Books, 2012.

Armitage, David, and Michael J. Braddick, eds. *The British Atlantic World, 1500–1800.* New York: Palgrave Macmillan, 2002.

Asociación de Propietarios, Industriales y Vecinos del Vedado y Príncipe. *Discusión pronunciado en al acto de descubrir el retrato del Dr. Manuel Varela Suárez.* Havana: Imprenta Seone y Fernández, 1928.

Bando de gobernación y policía de la Isla de Cuba, espedido por el escmo. Sr. Don Gerónimo Valdés, gobernador y capitán general; y Apéndice al bando de gobernación y policía de la Isla de Cuba. Havana: Imprenta del Gobierno y Capitanía General por S. M., 1842.

Barcia, Manuel. *The Great African Slave Revolt of 1825: Cuba and the Fight for Freedom in Matanzas.* Baton Rouge: Louisiana State University Press, 2012.

Barcia, María del Carmen. *Una sociedad en crisis: La Habana a finales del siglo XIX.* Havana: Editorial de Ciencias Sociales, 2000.

Barnet, Miguel. *Biography of a Runaway Slave.* Translated by W. Nick Hill. Rev. ed. Willimantic, CT: Curbstone Press, 1995.

Barton, Clara. *The Red Cross: A History of This Remarkable International Movement in the Interest of Humanity.* Washington, DC: American National Red Cross, 1898.

Barton, William E. *The Life of Clara Barton, Founder of the American Red Cross.* Vol. 2. New York: Houghton Mifflin, 1922.

Bedoya Pereda, Francisco. *La Habana desaparecida.* Havana: Ediciones Boloña, 2008.

Belot, Charles. *The Yellow Fever at Havana: Its Nature and Its Treatment.* Savannah, GA: Morning News Steam Printing House, 1878.

Benjamin, Jules R. *The United States and the Origins of the Cuban Revolution: An Empire of Liberty in an Age of National Liberation.* Princeton, NJ: Princeton University Press, 1990.

Bens Arrarte, José M. "Apuntes sobre La Habana del siglo XVIII: La urbanización del extramuro." In *Cuba: Arquitectura y urbanismo*, edited by Felipe J. Préstamo y Hernández, 159–62. Miami: Ediciones Universal, 1995.

Biehl, João. *Vita: Life in a Zone of Social Abandonment.* Rev. ed. Berkeley: University of California Press, 2013.

Bleichmar, Daniela, Paula De Vos, Kristin Huffine, and Kevin Sheehan, eds. *Science in the Spanish and Portuguese Empires, 1500–1800.* Stanford, CA: Stanford University Press, 2009.

Bonsal, Stephen. *The Real Condition of Cuba To-day.* New York: Harper and Brothers, 1897.

Broeze, Frank. "Introduction." In *Brides of the Sea: Port Cities of Asia from the 16th—20th Centuries*, edited by Frank Broeze, 1–9. Honolulu: University of Hawaii Press, 1989.

———, ed. *Brides of the Sea: Port Cities of Asia from the 16th—20th Centuries.* Honolulu: University of Hawaii Press, 1989.

Brown, Wendy. *Walled States, Waning Sovereignty.* Brooklyn: Zone Books, 2010.

Burns, Kathryn. *Into the Archive: Writing and Power in Colonial Peru.* Durham: Duke University Press, 2010.

———. *Colonial Habits: Convents and the Spiritual Economy of Cuzco, Peru.* Durham: Duke University Press, 1999.

Bryant, Sherwin K. *Rivers of Gold, Lives of Bondage: Governing through Slavery in Colonial Quito.* Chapel Hill: University of North Carolina Press, 2014.

Bryant, Sherwin K., Rachel Sarah O'Toole, and Ben Vinson III, eds. *Africans to Spanish America: Expanding the Diaspora.* Urbana: University of Illinois Press, 2014.

Butzer, Karl W. "From Columbus to Acosta: Science, Geography, and the New World." *Annals of the Association of American Geographers* 82, no. 3 (1992): 543–65.

Caldeira, Teresa P.R. *City of Walls: Crime, Segregation, and Citizenship in São Paulo.* Berkeley: University of California Press, 2001.

Calleja Leal, Guillermo. *1762, La Habana Inglesa: La toma de La Habana por los ingleses.* Madrid: Agencia Española de Cooperación Internacional, 1999.

Calvente, Lisa B.Y. "Keep on Keepin' on: Performing and Imag(in)ing Leadership and Homespace within the Black Diaspora." PhD diss., University of North Carolina at Chapel Hill, 2008.

———. "'This Is One Line You Won't Have to Worry about Crossing': Crossing Borders/Becoming Abject." In *Latina/o Discourse in Vernacular Spaces: Somos de Una Voz?*, edited by Michelle A. Holling and Bernadette M. Calafell. Lanham, MD: Lexington Books, 2010.

Calvente, Lisa B. Y., and Guadalupe García. "The City Speaks: Dis/articulating Revolutionary Havana, Cuba, and Global Belonging." *Cultural Studies* 28, no. 3 (2014): 438–62.

Cañeque, Alejandro. *The King's Living Image: The Culture and Politics of Viceregal Power in Colonial Mexico*. New York: Routledge, 2004.

Cañizares-Esguerra, Jorge, Matt D. Childs, and James Sidbury, eds. *The Black Urban Atlantic in the Age of the Slave Trade*. Philadelphia: University of Pennsylvania Press, 2013.

Casanovas, Joan. *Bread, or Bullets! Urban Labor and Spanish Colonialism in Cuba, 1850–1898*. Pittsburgh: University of Pittsburgh Press, 1998.

Castellanos, Jorge, and Isabel Castellanos. "The Geographic, Ethnologic, and Linguistic Roots of Cuban Blacks." *Cuban Studies* 17 (1987): 95–110.

———. *Cultura afrocubana*. Vol. 1, *El negro en Cuba, 1492–1844*. Miami: Ediciones Universal, 1988.

Castells, Manuel. *Imperialismo y urbanización en América Latina*. Barcelona: G. Gili, 1973.

Cerezo Martínez, Ricardo. *La cartografía náutica española en los siglos XIV, XV y XVI*. Madrid: Consejo Superior de Investigaciones Científicas, 1994.

Chailloux Cardona, Juan M. *Los horrores del solar habanero: Síntesis histórica de la vivienda popular*. 2nd ed. Havana: Editorial de Ciencias Sociales, 2008.

———. "Síntesis histórica de la vivienda popular: Los horrores del solar habanero." PhD diss., Universidad de La Habana, 1945.

Childers, William. "'Granada': Race and Place in Early Modern Spain." In *Spectacle and Topophilia: Reading Early Modern and Postmodern Hispanic Cultures*, edited by David R. Castillo and Bradley J. Nelson, 19–42. Nashville: Vanderbilt University Press, 2011.

Childs, Matt D. *The 1812 Aponte Rebellion in Cuba and the Struggle against Atlantic Slavery*. Chapel Hill: University of North Carolina Press, 2006.

Coclanis, Peter A., ed. *The Atlantic Economy during the Seventeenth and Eighteenth Centuries: Organization, Operation, Practice, and Personnel*. Columbia: University of South Carolina Press, 2005.

Colectivo de Autores de Plan Maestro para la Revitalización Integral de La Habana Vieja y Dirección Provincial de Planificación Física Ciudad de La Habana. *Regulaciones urbanísticas: Ciudad de La Habana: La Habana Vieja: Centro histórico*. Havana: Ediciones Boloña, 2008.

Collins, John F. "Culture, Content, and the Enclosure of Human Being: UNESCO's 'Intangible' Heritage in the New Millennium." *Radical History Review*, no. 109 (2011): 121–35.

Cosner, Charlotte. *The Golden Leaf: How Tobacco Shaped Cuba and the Atlantic World*. Nashville: Vanderbilt University Press, 2015.

Columbus, Christopher. *The Diario of Christopher Columbus's First Voyage to America, 1492–1493*. Abstracted by Bartolomé de las Casas. Translated by Oliver Dunn and James E. Kelley Jr. Norman: University of Oklahoma Press, 1991.

Concha, José de la. *Memoria dirigida al Excmo. Sr. Don Francisco Serrano y Domínguez, capitan general de la isla de Cuba*. Madrid: Imprenta de La Reforma, 1867.

Cope, R. Douglas. *The Limits of Racial Domination: Plebeian Society in Colonial Mexico City, 1660–1720*. Madison: University of Wisconsin Press, 1994.

Corbitt, Duvon C. "Mercedes and Realengos: A Survey of the Public Land System in Cuba." *Hispanic American Historical Review* 19, no. 3 (1939): 262–85.

Cowley, Luis M. "Recogida de basuras en las calles: Depósitos destinados a contener esos residuos domésticos." *Revista de Medicina y Cirugía de La Habana* 14 (1909): 631–39.

Cowling, Camillia. *Conceiving Freedom: Women of Color, Gender, and the Abolition of Slavery in Havana and Rio de Janeiro*. Chapel Hill: University of North Carolina Press, 2013.

Coyula, Mario. "La arquitectura del movimiento moderno en Cuba: Luces y sombras." Paper presented at "Relaciones entre la arquitectura moderna del Caribe y América Latina," Centro Cultural León, Santiago de los Caballeros, Dominican Republic, September 18, 2009.

———. "La lección de Alamar." *Espacio Laical* 4 (2011): 54–61.

Cruz, Mary. *Creto Gangá*. Havana: Contemporáneos, 1974.

Cuevas Toraya, Juan de las. *500 años de construcciones en Cuba*. Havana: Chavin, Servicios Gráficos y Editoriales, 2001.

Curet, L. Antonio, and Mark W. Hauser, eds. *Islands at the Crossroads: Migration, Seafaring, and Interaction in the Caribbean*. Tuscaloosa: University of Alabama Press, 2011.

De la Fuente, Alejandro. *Havana and the Atlantic in the Sixteenth Century*. Chapel Hill: University of North Carolina Press, 2008.

———. "Myths of Racial Democracy: Cuba, 1900–1912." *Latin American Research Review* 34, no. 3 (1999): 39–73.

———. *A Nation for All: Race, Inequality, and Politics in Twentieth-Century Cuba*. Chapel Hill: University of North Carolina Press, 2001.

———. "Su 'único derecho': Los esclavos y la ley." *Debate y Perspectivas: Cuadernos de Historia y Ciencias Sociales*, no. 4 (2004): 7–22.

Deegan, Mary Jo. *Jane Addams and the Men of the Chicago School, 1892–1918*. New Brunswick, NJ: Transaction, 1988.

de Vries, Jan. *The Economy of Europe in an Age of Crisis, 1600–1750*. Cambridge: Cambridge University Press, 1976.

———. *European Urbanization, 1500–1800*. Cambridge, MA: Harvard University Press, 1984.

Díaz, María Elena. *The Virgin, the King, and the Royal Slaves of El Cobre: Negotiating Freedom in Colonial Cuba, 1670–1780*. Stanford, CA: Stanford University Press, 2000.

Díaz Martínez, Yolanda. "Sociedad, violencia y criminalidad masculina en La Habana de finales del siglo XIX: Aproximaciones a una realidad." In *La sociedad cubana en los albores de la República*, edited by Mildred de la Torre Molina et al., 49–89. Havana: Editorial de Ciencias Sociales, 2002.

Director General, República de Cuba. *Censo de la República de Cuba, año de 1899*. Havana: Maza, Arroyo y Caso, S. and C., 1901.

Domínguez Compañy, Francisco. "Ordenanzas municipales hispanoamericanas." *Revista de Historia de América*, no. 86 (1978): 9–60.

Duharte Jiménez, Rafael. *El negro en la sociedad colonial.* Santiago de Cuba: Editorial Oriente, 1988.

Duplessis, Robert S. *Transitions to Capitalism in Early Modern Europe.* Cambridge: Cambridge University Press, 1997.

Earle, Rebecca. *The Body of the Conquistador: Food, Race, and the Colonial Experience in Spanish America, 1492–1700.* Cambridge: Cambridge University Press, 2012.

———. "'Temples diversos o contrarios a su salud, complexión y naturaleza': Spanish Health and the Colonial City in Early Modern Spanish America." Paper presented at "Urban Empire: A Symposium on Cities of the Early Modern Hispanic World," Tulane University, New Orleans, LA, March 20, 2010.

Echauz y Guinart, Félix de. *Lo que se ha hecho y lo que hay que hacer en Cuba: Breves indicaciones sobre la campaña.* Barcelona: Imprenta del Diario de Barcelona, 1872.

Edge, K., J. Scarpaci, and H. Woofter, "Mapping and Designing Havana: Republican, Socialist, and Global Spaces." *Cities* 23, no. 2 (2006): 85–98.

Eghigian, Greg. "Homo Munitus: The East German Observed." In *Socialist Modern: East German Everyday Culture and Politics.* Edited by Katherine Pence and Paul Betts, 37–70. Ann Arbor: University of Michigan Press, 2008.

Eldem, Edhem, Daniel Goffman, and Bruce Masters. *The Ottoman City between East and West: Aleppo, Izmir, and Istanbul.* Cambridge: Cambridge University Press, 2005.

Elliott, J.H. *Empires of the Atlantic World: Britain and Spain in America, 1492–1830.* New Haven, CT: Yale University Press, 2006.

Espinosa, Mariola. "A Fever for Empire: U.S. Disease Eradication in Cuba as Colonial Public Health." In *Colonial Crucible: Empire in the Making of the Modern American State,* edited by Alfred W. McCoy and Francisco A. Scarano, 288–96. Madison: University of Wisconsin Press, 2009.

———. "The Threat from Havana: Southern Public Health, Yellow Fever, and the U.S. Intervention in the Cuban Struggle for Independence, 1878–1898." *Journal of Southern History* 72, no. 3 (2006): 541–68.

Fernandez Nuñez, José Manuel. *Colonial Havana: A Fortress of the Americas.* Translated by Fernando Nápoles Tapia. Havana: Editorial José Martí, 1998.

Fernández Santalices, Manuel. *Las calles de La Habana intramuros: Arte, historia y tradiciones en las calles y plazas de La Habana vieja.* Miami: Saeta Ediciones, 1989.

Fernández y Simón, Abel. *Plano de la ciudad de la Habana, 1955.* In *Habana: Desarrollo urbano.* Havana: Ediciones GEO, 2002.

Ferrer, Ada. *Freedom's Mirror: Cuba and Haiti in the Age of Revolution.* Cambridge: Cambridge University Press, 2014.

———. *Insurgent Cuba: Race, Nation, and Revolution, 1868–1898.* Chapel Hill: University of North Carolina Press, 1999.

———. "Rustic Men, Civilized Nation: Race, Culture, and Contention on the Eve of Cuban Independence." *Hispanic American Historical Review* 78, no. 4 (1998): 663–86.

Fischer, Brodwyn. *A Poverty of Rights: Citizenship and Inequality in Twentieth-Century Rio de Janeiro.* Stanford, CA: Stanford University Press, 2010.

————. "A Century in the Present Tense: Crisis, Politics and the Intellectual History of Brazil's Informal Cities." In *Cities from Scratch: Poverty and Informality in Urban Latin America*. Durham: Duke University Press, 2014.

Fischer, Brodwyn, Bryan M. Cann, and Javier Auyero, eds. *Cities from Scratch: Poverty and Informality in Urban Latin America*. Durham: Duke University Press, 2014.

Florencio García, Juan. *Pepe Antonio: Biografía del héroe popular cubano Don José Antonio Gómez de Bullones*. Havana: Cultural, 1928.

Foner, Philip S. *A History of Cuba and Its Relations with the United States*. Vol. 1, *1492–1845: From the Conquest of Cuba to La Escalera*. New York: International Publishers, 1962.

Foucault, Michel. *Security, Territory, Population: Lectures at the Collège de France, 1977–1978*. Edited by Michel Senellart. Translated by Graham Burchell. London: Picador, 2009.

Fraser, Valerie. *The Architecture of Conquest: Building in the Viceroyalty of Peru, 1535–1635*. 2nd ed. Cambridge: Cambridge University Press, 2009.

Freitag, Ulrike, Malte Fuhrmann, Nora Lafi, and Florian Riedler, eds. *The City in the Ottoman Empire: Migration and the Making of Urban Modernity*. New York: Routledge, 2011.

Funes Monzote, Reinaldo. *From Rainforest to Cane Field: An Environmental History since 1492*. Translated by Alex Martin. Chapel Hill: University of North Carolina Press, 2008.

Games, Alison. "Atlantic History: Definitions, Challenges, and Opportunities." *American Historical Review* 111, no. 3 (2006): 741–57.

García Canclini, Nestor. *Consumers and Citizens: Globalization and Multicultural Conflicts*. Translated by George Yúdice. Minneapolis: University of Minnesota Press, 2001.

————. *Hybrid Cultures: Strategies for Entering and Leaving Modernity*. Rev. ed. Translated by Christopher L. Chiappari and Silvia L. López. Minneapolis: University of Minnesota Press, 2005.

García del Pino, César. *La Habana bajo el reinado de los Austria*. Havana: Ediciones Boloña, 2008.

García, Guadalupe. "'Nuestra patria La Habana': Reading the 1762 British Occupation of the City." *Nuevo Mundo / Mundos Nuevos*, Debáts (March 31, 2011). doi: 10.4000/nuevomundo.61119.

————. "Urban *Guajiros*: Colonial *Reconcentración*, Rural Displacement, and Criminalisation in Western Cuba, 1895–1902." *Journal of Latin American Studies* 43, no. 2 (2011): 209–35.

García Morales, Francisco. *Guía de gobierno y policía de la Isla de Cuba, compendio de las atribuciones gubernativas de los alcaldes, tenientes de alcalde y alcaldes de barrio, con un prontuario alfabético de la legislación vigente sobre policía y orden público*. Havana: La Propaganda Literaria, 1881.

García Pérez, María Sandra. "El padrón municipal de habitantes: Origen, evolución y significado." *Hispania Nova: Revista de Historia Contemporánea*, no. 7 (2007): http://hispanianoa.rediris.es/7/articulos/7a005.pdf.

Garofalo, Leo J. "The Shape of a Diaspora: The Movement of Afro-Iberians to Colonial Spanish America." In *Africans to Spanish America: Expanding the*

Diaspora, edited by Sherwin K. Bryant, Rachel Sarah O'Toole, and Ben Vinson III, 27–49. Urbana: University of Illinois Press, 2014.

Gelabert, Francisco de Paula. *Cuadros de costumbres cubanas*. Havana: Imprenta de la Botica de Santo Domingo, 1875.

G. G. Y. F. *Los criminales de Cuba y el inspector Trujillo*. Havana: La Propaganda Literaria, 1881.

Gómez Díaz, Francisco. *De Forestier a Sert: Ciudad y arquitectura en La Habana, 1925–1969*. Madrid: Abada Editores, 2008.

González, Mario. *Sobre planos, esquemas y planes directores de la ciudad de La Habana*. Havana: Grupo para el Desarrollo Integral de la Capital, 1993.

González Dávila, Gil. *Monarquía de España: Historia de la vida y hechos del inclito monarca, amado y santo D. Felipe Tercero*. Vol. 3. Madrid: D. Joachin de Ibarra, 1771.

Guerra, Ramiro. *Manual de historia de Cuba desde su descubrimiento hasta 1868*. Havana: Editorial de Ciencias Sociales, 1971.

Gutiérrez, Nicolás José. "Moción sobre los mercados habaneros, 25 March 1860." *Cuadernos de Historia de la Salud Pública* 67 (1984): 68.

Hall, Gwendolyn Midlo. *Social Control in Slave Plantation Societies: A Comparison of St. Domingue and Cuba*. Baltimore: Johns Hopkins University Press, 1971.

Hardoy, Jorge E. "Theory and Practice of Urban Planning in Europe, 1850–1930: Its Transfer to Latin America." In *Rethinking the Latin American City*, edited by Jorge E. Hardoy and Richard M. Morse, 20–49. Baltimore: Johns Hopkins University Press, 1992.

———. "Two Thousand Years of Latin American Urbanization." In *Urbanization in Latin America: Approaches and Issues*, edited by Jorge E. Hardoy, 3–55. Garden City, NY: Anchor Books, 1975.

Haring, C. H. "The Genesis of Royal Government in the Spanish Indies." *Hispanic American Historical Review* 7, no. 2 (1927): 141–91.

Harley, J. B. *The New Nature of Maps: Essays in the History of Cartography*. Edited by Paul Laxton. Baltimore: Johns Hopkins University Press, 2002.

Havana, Diputación de Policía. *Informe de la diputación de policía al excelentísimo señor presidente, gobernador y capitán general del estado de sus tareas y providencias que deben adoptarse para conserver la pública tranquilidad*. Havana: Oficina de Arazoza y Soler, 1816.

Hazard, Samuel. *Cuba with Pen and Pencil*. Hartford, CT: Hartford Publishing, 1871.

Hernández, Kelly Lytle. *Migra! A History of the U.S. Border Patrol*. Berkeley: University of California Press, 2010.

Hernández Suárez, Roberto A. *Cuba en la estrategia político militar del imperio español: 1561–1725*. Havana: Editoria Historia, 2007.

Herrera López, Pedro A. *Tres personajes de la noble Habana*. Havana: Editorial Letras Cubanas, 2005.

Herzog, Tamar. *Defining Nations: Immigrants and Citizens in Early Modern Spain and Spanish America*. New Haven, CT: Yale University Press, 2003.

Hiltpold, Paul. "Noble Status and Urban Privilege: Burgos, 1572." *Sixteenth Century Journal* 12, no. 4 (1981): 21–44.

Hippocrates. *On Air, Waters, and Places.* Translated by Francis Adams. http:// classics.mit.edu/Hippocrates/airwatpl.mb.txt.

Hitchman, James H. "Unfinished Business: Public Works in Cuba, 1898–1902." *The Americas* 31, no. 3 (1975): 335–59.

Hoffman, Paul E. *The Spanish Crown and the Defense of the Caribbean, 1535–1585: Precedent, Patrimonialism, and Royal Parsimony.* Baton Rouge: Louisiana State University Press, 1980.

Howard, Phillip A. *Changing History: Afro-Cuban Cabildos and Societies of Color in the Nineteenth Century.* Baton Rouge: Louisiana State University Press, 1998.

Humboldt, Alexander von. *Ensayo político sobre la isla de Cuba.* Translated by D. J. B. de V. Y. M. 2nd ed. Paris: Librería de Lecointe, 1836.

———. *The Island of Cuba.* Translated by J. S. Thrasher. New York: Derby and Jackson, 1856.

Hyde, Timothy. *Constitutional Modernism: Architecture and Civil Society in Cuba, 1933–1959.* Minneapolis: University of Minnesota Press, 2012.

Iglesia, Alvaro de la. *Pepe Antonio.* Havana: Editorial Letras Cubanas, 1979.

Incendio acaecido en el barrio de Jesús María el día 11 de febrero de este año. Havana: Oficina del Gobierno y Capitanía General por S. M., 1828.

Inclán Lavastida, Fernando. *Historia de Marianao de la época indígena a los tiempos actuales.* Marianao: Editorial "El Sol," 1943.

Informe sobre el censo de Cuba, 1899. Washington, DC: Imprenta del Gobierno, 1900.

Inglis, G. Douglas. "Historical Demography of Colonial Cuba, 1492–1780." PhD diss., Texas Christian University, 1979.

Johnson, Lyman L., and Sonya Lipsett-Rivera, eds. *The Faces of Honor: Sex, Shame and Violence in Colonial Latin America.* Albuquerque: University of New Mexico Press, 1998.

Johnson, Sherry. "'La guerra contra los habitantes de los Arrabales': Changing Patterns of Land Use and Land Tenancy in and around Havana, 1763–1800." *Hispanic American Historical Review* 77, no. 2 (1997): 181–209.

———. "'Honor Is Life': Military Reform and the Transformation of Cuban Society: 1753–1796." PhD diss., University of Florida, 1995.

———. "'Señoras en sus clases no ordinarias': Enemy Collaborators or Courageous Defenders of the Family?" *Cuban Studies* 34 (2003): 11–37.

———. *The Social Transformation of Eighteenth-Century Cuba.* Gainesville: University Press of Florida, 2001.

Kagan, Richard L. "A World without Walls: City and Town in Colonial Spanish America." In *City Walls: The Urban Enceinte in Global Perspective,* edited by James D. Tracy, 117–52. Cambridge: Cambridge University Press, 2000.

———. *Urban Images of the Hispanic World, 1493–1793.* New Haven, CT: Yale University Press, 2000.

Kagan, Richard L., and Geoffrey Parker, eds. *Spain, Europe, and the Atlantic World: Essays in Honour of John H. Elliott.* Cambridge: Cambridge University Press, 1995.

Kapcia, Antoni. *Cuba in Revolution: A History since the Fifties.* London: Reaktion Books, 2008.

———. *Havana: The Making of Cuban Culture.* Oxford: Berg, 2005.

Kiple, Kenneth F. *Blacks in Colonial Cuba, 1774–1899.* Gainesville: University Press of Florida, 1976.

Kirk Blackwelder, Julia, and Lyman L. Johnson. "Changing Criminal Patterns in Buenos Aires, 1890 to 1914." *Journal of Latin American Studies* 14, no. 2 (1982): 359–80.

Knight, Franklin W. *The Caribbean: The Genesis of a Fragmented Nationalism.* 2nd ed. New York: Oxford University Press, 1990.

Knight, Franklin W., and Peggy K. Liss, eds. *Atlantic Port Cities: Economy, Culture, and Society in the Atlantic World, 1650–1850.* Knoxville: University of Tennessee Press, 1991.

Kolluoğlu, Biray, and Meltem Toksöz, eds. *Cities of the Mediterranean: From the Ottomans to the Present Day.* New York: I. B. Tauris, 2010.

Kuethe, Allan J. *Cuba, 1753–1815: Crown, Military, and Society.* Knoxville: University of Tennessee Press, 1986.

———. "The Development of the Cuban Military as a Sociopolitical Elite, 1763–83." *Hispanic American Historical Review* 61, no. 4 (1981): 695–704.

Kutzinski, Vera M. *Sugar's Secrets: Race and the Erotics of Cuban Nationalism.* Charlottesville: University Press of Virginia, 1993.

Landers, Jane. *Atlantic Creoles in the Age of Revolution.* Cambridge: Cambridge University Press, 2011.

Lane, Jill. *Blackface Cuba, 1840–1895.* Philadelphia: University of Pennsylvania Press, 2005.

Lane, Kris E. *Pillaging the Empire: Piracy in the Americas, 1500–1750.* New York: Routledge, 1998.

Lauderdale Graham, Sandra. *House and Street: The Domestic World of Servants and Masters in Nineteenth-Century Rio de Janeiro.* Austin: University of Texas Press, 1992.

Leal, Rine, ed. *Teatro bufo, siglo XIX: Antología.* Havana: Editorial Arte y Literatura, 1975.

Lefebvre, Henri. *The Production of Space.* Translated by Donald Nicholson-Smith. Oxford: Blackwell, 1992.

Le Riverend, Julio. *La Habana, espacio y vida.* Havana: Editorial MAPFRE, 1992.

———. *Síntesis histórico de la cubanidad del siglo XVIII.* Havana: Molina, 1940.

Le-Roy y Cassá, Jorge. *Estudios sobre la mortalidad de La Habana durante el siglo XIX y los comienzos del actual.* Havana: Imprenta Lloredo y Cia., 1913.

Leuchsenring, Emilio Roig de. *Historia de La Habana.* Vol. 1. *Desde sus primeros días hasta 1565.* Havana: Municipio de La Habana, 1938.

Lewis, Oscar. *The Children of Sánchez: Autobiography of a Mexican Family.* Rev. ed. New York: Vintage Books, 2011.

Li, Tania Murray. *The Will to Improve: Governmentality, Development, and the Practice of Politics.* Durham, NC: Duke University Press, 2007.

Lobo Montalvo, Maria Luisa. *Havana: History and Architecture of a Romantic City.* Translated by Lorna Scott Fox. New York: Monacelli Press, 2000.

Lott, Eric. *Love and Theft: Blackface Minstrelsy and the American Working Class.* New York: Oxford University Press, 1993.

Ludlow, William. *Annual Report for Fiscal Year Ended June 30, 1899, from Dec. 22, 1898.* Havana: U.S. Army, Department of Havana, 1899.

Mackellar, Patrick. *A Correct Journal of the Landing His Majesty's Forces on the Island of Cuba; and of the Siege and Surrender of Havannah, August 13, 1762.* 2nd ed. London: Green and Russell, 1762. Early American Imprints, Series 1: Evans 1639–1800, no. 9165.

Martínez-Fernández, Luis. *Fighting Slavery in the Caribbean: The Life and Times of a British Family in Nineteenth-Century Havana.* Armonk, NY: M.E. Sharpe, 1998.

Marrero, Levi. *Cuba: Economía y sociedad.* Vols. 1–15. Madrid: Editorial Playor, 1972–1992.

Masashi, Haneda, ed. *Asian Port Cities, 1600–1800: Local and Foreign Cultural Interactions.* Singapore: National University of Singapore Press, 2009.

Mauri, Omar Felipe. *La primera de Cuba: La estación ferroviaria de Bejucal.* Havana: Editorial Unicornio, 2002.

McCoy, Alfred W., and Ed C. de Jesus, eds. *Philippine Social History: Global Trade and Local Transformations.* Honolulu: University of Hawaii Press, 1982.

McGee, Terence G. *The Urbanization Process in the Third World: Explorations in Search of a Theory.* London: G. Bell and Sons, 1975.

McNeill, John Robert. *Atlantic Empires of France and Spain: Louisbourg and Havana, 1700–1763.* Chapel Hill: University of North Carolina Press, 1985.

Mena, Luz M. "Raza, género y espacio: Las mujeres negras y mulatas negocian su lugar en la Habana durante la década de 1830." *Revista de Estudios Sociales* 26 (April 2007): 73–85.

Metcalf, Alida C. "Amerigo Vespucci and the Four Finger (Kunstmann II) World Map." *e-Perimetron* 7, no. 1 (2012): 36–44.

Miranda, Manuel M. *Memorias de un deportado.* Havana: Imprenta La Luz, 1903.

Montes Huidobro, Matías. "La reacción antijerárquica en el teatro cubano colonial." *Cuadernos Hispanoamericanos,* no. 334 (1978): 5–19.

Moore, John Preston. *The Cabildo in Peru under the Hapsburgs: A Study in the Origins and Powers of the Town Council in the Viceroyalty of Peru, 1530–1700.* Durham, NC: Duke University Press, 1954.

Moraga, Cherríe, and Gloria Anzaldúa, eds. *This Bridge Called My Back: Writings by Radical Women of Color.* 2nd ed. New York: Persephone Press, 1983.

Morales, Jorge Luis, ed. *Poesía afroantillana y negrista (Puerto Rico, República Dominicana, Cuba).* 2nd ed. Río Piedras: Editorial Universitaria, Universidad de Puerto Rico, 1981.

Moreno Fraginals, Manuel. *El ingenio: Complejo económico social cubano del azúcar.* Havana: Editorial de Ciencias Sociales, 1978.

Morris, Christopher. *The Big Muddy: An Environmental History of the Mississippi and Its Peoples from Hernando de Soto to Hurricane Katrina.* Oxford: Oxford University Press, 2012.

Morse, Richard M. "Cities as People." In *Rethinking the Latin American City,* edited by Jorge E. Hardoy and Richard M. Morse, 3–19. Baltimore: John Hopkins University Press, 1992.

Offen, Karl, and Jordana Dym. "Introduction." In *Mapping Latin America: A Cartographic Reader*, edited by Jordana Dym and Karl Offen, 1–18. Chicago: University of Chicago Press, 2011.

O'Flanagan, Patrick. *Port Cities of Atlantic Iberia, c. 1500–1900*. Burlington, VT: Ashgate, 2008.

Olmsted, Victor H., and Henry Gannett, eds. *Cuba: Population, History, and Resources, 1907*. Washington, DC: United States Bureau of the Census, 1909.

Ordenanzas de construcción para la ciudad de La Habana, y pueblos de su termino municipal. Havana: Imprenta del Gobierno y Capitanía General por S. M., 1866.

Ordenanzas municipales de la ciudad de La Habana. Havana: Imprenta del Gobierno y Capitanía General, 1855.

Ortiz, Fernando. *Contrapunteo cubano del tabaco y el azúcar*. Caracas, Venezuela: Biblioteca Ayacucho, 1987.

———. *Ensayos etnográficos*. Edited by Miguel Barnet and Angel L. Fernández. Havana: Editorial de Ciencias Sociales, 1984.

———. *Los negros brujos*. Miami: Ediciones Universal, 1973.

———. *Los negros curros*. Havana: Editorial de Ciencias Sociales, 1995.

Pagden, Anthony. *Lords of All the World: Ideologies of Empire in Spain, Britain, and France, c. 1500–c. 1800*. New Haven, CT: Yale University Press, 1995.

Parcero Torre, Celia María. *La pérdida de La Habana y las reformas borbónicas en Cuba, 1760–1773*. Valladolid, Spain: Junta de Castilla y León, 1998.

Parreño, Alberto. *Guía del comercio de La Habana para el año de 1823*. Havana: Oficina de D. Pedro Nolasco Palmer é Hijo, 1822.

Pérez Beato, Manuel. *Habana antigua*. Havana: Imprenta Seoane, Fernández y ca., 1936.

Pérez Guzmán, Francisco. *La Habana: Clave de un imperio*. Havana: Editorial de Ciencias Sociales, 1997.

Pérez, Louis A., Jr. *Cuba: Between Reform and Revolution*. 2nd ed. New York: Oxford University Press, 1995.

———. *Cuba in the American Imagination: Metaphor and the Imperial Ethos*. Chapel Hill: University of North Carolina Press, 2011.

———. *The War of 1898: The United States and Cuba in History and Historiography*. Chapel Hill: University of North Carolina Press, 1999.

———. *On Becoming Cuban: Identity, Nationality, and Culture*. Chapel Hill: University of North Carolina Press, 1999.

———. "The Pursuit of Pacification: Banditry and the United States' Occupation of Cuba, 1899–1902." *Journal of Latin American Studies* 18, no. 2 (1986), 313–32.

———, ed. *Impressions of Cuba in the Nineteenth Century: The Travel Diary of Joseph J. Dimock*. Wilmington, DE: Scholarly Resources, 1998.

Perl, Matthias. "Cultura y lengua gallegas en Cuba: Acerca de la caracterización lingüística del gallego en el teatro bufo del siglo XIX." *Santiago: Revista de la Universidad de Oriente* 70 (1988): 189–96.

Peset, Mariano, and Margarita Menegus. "Rey propietario o rey soberano." *Historia Mexicana* 43, no. 4 (1994): 563–99.

Pichardo Viñals, Hortensia. *Documentos para la historia de Cuba*. Vols. 1–2. 5th ed. Havana: Editorial de Ciencias Sociales, 1976–2000.

Pichardo y Tapia, Esteban. *Diccionario provincial casi razonado de vozes y frases cubanas*. Edited by Gladys Alonso González and Ángel L. Fernández Guerra. Havana: Editorial de Ciencias Sociales, 1985.

Pickles, John. *A History of Spaces: Cartographic Reason, Mapping, and the Geo-Coded World*. New York: Routledge, 2004.

Poumier, María. *Apuntes sobre la vida cotidiana en Cuba en 1898*. Havana: Editorial de Ciencias Sociales, 1975.

Pratt, Mary Louise. *Imperial Eyes: Travel Writing and Transculturation*. 1992. Reprint. New York: Routledge, 2003.

Price, Patricia L. "At the Crossroads: Critical Race Theory and Critical Geographies of Race." *Progress in Human Geography* 34, no. 2 (2010): 147–74.

Quesada, Gonzalo de, and Henry Davenport Northrop. *Cuba's Great Struggle for Freedom*. Washington, DC, 1898.

Rama, Angel. *The Lettered City*. Translated by John Charles Chasteen. Durham, NC: Duke University Press, 1996.

Rappaport, Joanne, and Tom Cummins. *Beyond the Lettered City: Indigenous Literacies in the Andes*. Durham, NC: Duke University Press, 2012.

Reeves, Peter, Frank Broeze, and Kenneth McPherson. "Studying the Asian Port City." In *Brides of the Sea: Port Cities of Asia from the 16th–20th Centuries*, edited by Frank Broeze, 29–53. Honolulu: University of Hawaii Press, 1989.

Reglamento para el régimen interior del Ayuntamiento de La Habana. Havana: Imprenta P. Fernández y Cía., 1900.

Reglamento para los arquitectos municipales de La Habana. Havana: Imprenta del Gobierno y Capitanía General por S. M., 1861.

Reid-Vazquez, Michele. *The Year of the Lash: Free People of Color in Cuba and the Nineteenth-Century Atlantic World*. Athens: University of Georgia Press, 2011.

Remington, Frederic. *The Collected Writings of Frederic Remington*. Edited by Peggy Samuels and Harold Samuels. Garden City, NY: Doubleday, 1979.

Romero León, Jorge. *Retórica de imaginación urbana: La ciudad y sus sujetos en Cecilia Valdés y Quincas Borba*. Caracas, Venezuela: Fundación Centro de Estudios Latinoamericanos Rómulo Gallegos, 1997.

Saco, José Antonio. *La vagancia en Cuba*. Havana: Ministerio de Educación, Dirección de Cultura, 1946.

Sanders, William T., and David Webster. "The Mesoamerican Urban Tradition." *American Anthropologist*, n.s., 90, no. 3 (1988): 521–46.

Sanz Camañes, Porfirio. *La ciudades en la América Hispana: Siglos XV al XVIII*. Madrid: Sílex Ediciones, 2004.

Santa Cruz y Montalvo, María de las Mercedes. *La Havane par madame la Comtesse Merlin*. Vol. 1. Paris: Librairie d'Amyot, 1844.

Sartorius, David. *Ever Faithful: Race, Loyalty, and the Ends of Empire in Spanish Cuba*. Durham, NC: Duke University Press, 2014.

———. "My Vassals: Free-Colored Militias in Cuba and the Ends of Spanish Empire." *Journal of Colonialism and Colonial History* 5, no. 2 (2004): 1–25.

Scarpaci, Joseph L., Roberto Segre, and Mario Coyula. *Havana: Two Faces of the Antillean Metropolis*. Rev. ed. Chapel Hill: University of North Carolina Press, 2002.

Schmitt, Carl. *The Nomos of the Earth in the International Law of Jus Publicum Europaeum*. Candor, NY: Telos Press, 2003.

Schoultz, Lars. *Beneath the United States: A History of U.S. Policy toward Latin America*. Cambridge, MA: Harvard University Press, 1998.

Schwartz, Rosalie. *Pleasure Island: Tourism and Temptation in Cuba*. Lincoln: University of Nebraska Press, 1999.

Scott, Rebecca J. *Slave Emancipation in Cuba: The Transition to Free Labor, 1860–1899*. Princeton, NJ: Princeton University Press, 1985.

Segre, Roberto. "Havana, from Tacón to Forestier." In *Planning Latin America's Capital Cities, 1850–1950*, edited by Arturo Almandoz, 193–213. London: Routledge, 2002.

Simmel, Georg. "The Metropolis and Mental Life." In *The Nineteenth-Century Visual Culture Reader*, edited by Vanessa R. Schwartz and Jeannene M. Przyblyski, 51–55. New York: Routledge, 2004.

Sippial, Tiffany A. *Prostitution, Modernity, and the Making of the Cuban Republic, 1840–1920*. Chapel Hill: University of North Carolina Press, 2013.

Smallman-Raynor, Matthew, and Andrew D. Cliff. "The Spatial Dynamics of Epidemic Diseases in War and Peace: Cuba and the Insurrection against Spain, 1895–98." *Transactions of the Institute of British Geographers*, n.s., 24, no. 3 (1999): 331–52.

Smith, Dennis. *The Chicago School: A Liberal Critique of Capitalism*. London: Palgrave Macmillan, 1988.

Smith, Peter H. *Talons of the Eagle: Latin America, the United States, and the World*. 3rd ed. New York: Oxford University Press, 2007.

Socolow, Susan Migden. *The Women of Colonial Latin America*. Cambridge: Cambridge University Press, 2000.

Socolow, Susan Migden, and Lyman L. Johnson. "Urbanization in Colonial Latin America." *Journal of Urban History* 8, no. 1 (1981): 27–59.

Soyer, François. "Faith, Culture, and Fear: Comparing Islamophobia in Early Modern Spain and Twenty-First-Century Europe." *Ethnic and Racial Studies* 36, no. 3 (2013): 399–416.

Tacón, Miguel. *Correspondencia reservada del Capitán General don Miguel Tacón, con el gobierno de Madrid, 1834–1836: El General Tacón y su época, 1834–1838*. Havana: Consejo Nacional de Cultura, Biblioteca Nacional José Martí, Dept. de Colección Cubana, 1963.

———. *Relación del gobierno superior y capitanía general de la Isla de Cuba, estendida por el teniente general D. Miguel Tacón . . .* Havana: Imprenta del Gobierno y Capitanía General, 1838.

TePaske, John Jay. "Integral to Empire: The Vital Peripheries of Colonial Spanish America." In *Negotiated Empires: Center and Peripheries in the Americas, 1500–1820*. Edited by Christine Daniels and Michael V. Kennedy, 29–41. New York: Routledge, 2002.

———. "La política española en el Caribe durante los siglos XVII y XVIII." In *La influencia de España en el Caribe, la Florida, y la Luisiana, 1500–1800*, edited by Antonio Acosta and Juan Marchena, 61–87. Madrid: Instituto de Cooperación Iberoamericana, 1983.

Tone, John Lawrence. *War and Genocide in Cuba, 1895–1898.* Chapel Hill: University of North Carolina Press, 2006.

Torre Molina, Mildred de la, et al., eds. *La sociedad cubana en los albores de la República.* Havana: Editorial de Ciencias Sociales, 2002.

Torres Ramírez, Bibiano. *La Armada de Barlovento.* Seville: Escuela de Estudios Hispano-Americanos, 1981.

Torriente, Loló de la. *La Habana de Cecilia Valdés.* Havana: J. Montero, 1946.

Translation of the General Law of Public Works of the Island of Cuba, and Regulations for Its Execution: with the Addition of All Subsequent Provisions Published to Date (1891). Washington, DC: War Department, 1899.

Tuan, Yi-Fu. *Space and Place: The Perspective of Experience.* Minneapolis: University of Minnesota Press, 2003.

Twinam, Ann. *Public Lives, Private Secrets: Gender, Honor, Sexuality, and Illegitimacy in Colonial Spanish America.* Stanford, CA: Stanford University Press, 1999.

Valdés Bernal, Sergio. *Lengua nacional e identidad cultural del cubano.* Havana: Editorial de Ciencias Sociales, 1998.

Vallín, Benjamín. *Las reformas en la isla de Cuba.* Madrid: Imprenta de M. Minuesa, 1862.

Van Norman, William C., Jr. "The Process of Cultural Change among Cuban Bozales during the Nineteenth Century." *The Americas* 62, no. 2 (October 2005): 177–207.

———. *Shade-Grown Slavery: The Lives of Slaves on Coffee Plantations in Cuba.* Nashville: Vanderbilt University Press, 2013.

Varela Zequeira, Eduardo. *La policía de La Habana (Cuebas y Sabaté).* Havana: Imprenta y Papelería "La Universal," 1894.

Venegas Fornias, Carlos. *Cuba y sus pueblos: Censos y mapas de los siglos XVIII y XIX.* Havana: Centro de Investigación y Desarrollo de la Cultura Cubana Juan Marinello, 2002.

———. "La Habana entre dos siglos." In *Arquitectura cubana: Metamorfosis, pensamiento y crítica: Selección de textos,* edited by Elvia Rosa Castro and Concepción Otero, 22–35. Havana: Artecubano Ediciones, 2002.

———. *La urbanización de las murallas: Dependencia y modernidad.* Havana: Editorial Letras Cubanas, 1990.

Villaverde, Cirilo. *Cecilia Valdés, o, La loma del angel: Novela de costumbres cubanas publicada en New York en 1882.* Edited by Esteban Rodríguez Herrera. Havana: Editorial Lex, 1953.

Vinson, Ben, III. *Bearing Arms for His Majesty: The Free-Colored Militia in Colonial Mexico.* Stanford: Stanford University Press, 2001.

———. "Free Colored Voices: Issues of Representation and Racial Identity in the Colonial Mexican Militia." *Journal of Negro History* 80, no. 4 (1995): 170–82.

Weber, Max. *The City.* Edited and translated by Don Martindale and Gertrud Neuwirth. Glencoe, IL: Free Press, 1958.

Weiss, Joaquín E. *La arquitectura colonial cubana.* Havana: Letras Cubanas, 1979.

Wey Gómez, Nicolás. *The Tropics of Empire: Why Columbus Sailed South to the Indies.* Cambridge, MA: MIT Press, 2008.

Weyler, Valeriano. *Mi mando en Cuba.* Havana: Imprenta, Litografía y Casa Editorial de Felipe González Rojas, 1910.

Wilson Moore, Rachel, John Wilson Moore, and George Truman. *Journal of Rachel Wilson Moore, Kept during a Tour to the West Indies and South America, in 1863–64.* Philadelphia: T. E. Zell, 1867.

Wirth, Louis. "Urbanism as a Way of Life." *American Journal of Sociology* 44, no. 1 (1938): 1–24.

Wood, Denis. *Rethinking the Power of Maps.* New York: Guilford Press, 2010.

Wright, Irene A. *The Early History of Cuba, 1492–1586: Written from Original Sources.* New York: Macmillan, 1916.

———. *Historia documentada de San Cristobal de la Habana en el siglo XVI.* Vol. 1. Havana: Imprenta "El Siglo XX," 1927.

———. "Rescates with Special Attention to Cuba, 1599–1610." *Hispanic American Historical Review* 3, no. 3 (1920): 358.

Wurdemann, John G. *Notes on Cuba, Containing an Account of Its Discovery and Early History* . . . Boston: J. Munroe, 1844.

Zilberg, Elana. *Space of Detention: The Making of a Transnational Gang Crisis between Los Angeles and San Salvador.* Durham, NC: Duke University Press, 2011.

Index